CW00498625

THE ASSOCIATION FOR SCOTTISH LITERARY STUDIES

SOMHAIRLE MACGILL-EAIN/
SORLEY MACLEAN

AN CUILITHIONN 1939
and UNPUBLISHED POEMS

*

THE ASSOCIATION FOR SCOTTISH LITERARY STUDIES

The Association for Scottish Literary Studies aims to promote the study, teaching and writing of Scottish literature, and to further the study of the languages of Scotland.

To these ends, the ASLS publishes works of Scottish literature (of which this volume is an example); literary criticism and in-depth reviews of Scottish books in *Scottish Literary Review*; short articles, features and news in *ScotLit*; and scholarly studies of language in *Scottish Language*. It also publishes *New Writing Scotland*, an annual anthology of new poetry, drama and short fiction, in Scots, English and Gaelic. ASLS has also prepared a range of teaching materials covering Scottish language and literature for use in schools.

All the above publications are available as a single 'package', in return for an annual subscription. Enquiries should be sent to:

ASLS, Department of Scottish Literature, 7 University Gardens, University of Glasgow, Glasgow G12 8QH. Telephone/fax +44 (0)141 330 5309 or visit our website at **www.asls.org.uk**

THE ASSOCIATION FOR SCOTTISH LITERARY STUDIES

SOMHAIRLE MACGILL-EAIN/ SORLEY MACLEAN

AN CUILITHIONN 1939 and UNPUBLISHED POEMS

Edited by

Christopher Whyte

GLASGOW

2011

Published in Great Britain 2011
by The Association for Scottish Literary Studies
Scottish Literature
University of Glasgow
7 University Gardens
Glasgow G12 8QH

ASLS is a registered charity no. SC006535

www.asls.org.uk

ISBN: 978-1-906841-03-4

All rights reserved. No part of this book may be reproduced, stored
in a retrieval system, or transmitted in any form or means, electronic,
mechanical, photocopying, recording or otherwise, without the prior
permission of the Association for Scottish Literary Studies.

Poetry text © The Estate of Sorley MacLean
Introduction and editorial notes © Christopher Whyte 2011

A catalogue record for this book
is available from the British Library.

The Association for Scottish Literary Studies acknowledges
support from Creative Scotland and the Gaelic Books Council
towards the publication of this book.

Typeset by AFS Image Setters Ltd, Glasgow
Printed and bound by Bell & Bain Ltd, Glasgow

CONTENTS

FOREWORD

As was the case with an earlier edition of MacLean's love sequence *Dàin do Eimhir*, published in 2002, it was Ronald Renton's successful mediation which persuaded the Association for Scottish Literary Studies to take on publication of the original, 1939 manuscript version of *An Cuilithionn*. Prodigal with encouragement and support, the poet's daughter Ishbel followed each stage of the project with lively interest. The decision to include all those unpublished poems by MacLean to have so far come to light was taken in consultation with her. The assistance of Ian MacDonald, until recently with the Gaelic Books Council, was crucial at many points in work on this volume, not least in deciding on a definitive printed form for the hitherto unpublished material. I am grateful to the Trustees of the National Library of Scotland and to Library and Historic Collections at Aberdeen University for permission to reproduce material in their possession. Staff at both institutions offered a high level of assistance and support. Glasgow University Library's printed and online resources were of great help in the preparation of the Commentary. An initial six-month period of work on *An Cuilithionn*, during the winter of 2003 to 2004, was made possible by sabbatical leave from Glasgow University's Department of Scottish Literature, plus funding for an extension from the Advanced Humanities Research Board. John MacInnes offered invaluable advice and information at several stages. Three study visits to Scotland in May and September 2010 and January 2011 could not have been made without the generous hospitality provided by Simon Taylor and Leslie Alan Reid in Aberdour, Kevin Anderson and Katy Logotheti in Edinburgh, and Jessica Burns in Glasgow. The expertise of Duncan Jones of the Association for Scottish Literary Studies was fundamental in giving the book its final form.

View from Druim Hain, Cuillin Hills, Skye

© British Geological Survey / NERC. All rights reserved. Licensor www.scran.ac.uk

Sgùrr Alasdair, the highest peak on Skye and part of the Cuillin Ridge

© Newsquest (Herald & Times). Licensor www.scran.ac.uk

View of the Cuillin Ridge from Bruaich na Frithe, looking south-south-west

© *Abrahams of Keswick. Licensor www.scran.ac.uk*

Sgùrr nan Gillean, from Coire a' Bhasteir

© *Abrahams of Keswick. Licensor www.scran.ac.uk*

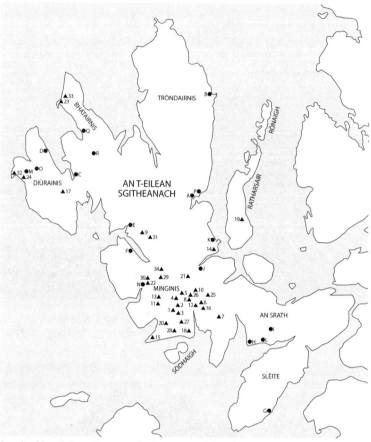

Reproduced from Ordnance Survey map data by permission of the Ordnance Survey © Crown copyright 2010.

A. Port Rìgh	1. Adharc an Sgùrr Dheirg	19. Dùn Cana
B. Bhaltos	2. Sgùrr Dearg	20. Coire Lagain
C. Dùn Bheagain	3. Sgùrr Alasdair	21. Coire 'n Uaigneis
D. Gleann Dail	4. Sgùrr na Banachdaich	22. Bràighe Aoineart
E. Bràcadal	5. Sgùrr a' Ghreadaidh	23. Àird Mhòr
F. Harport	6. Sgùrr nan Gillean	24. An t-Àigeach
G. Tòrr Mòr	7. Blàbheinn	25. Fiacail a' Bhàisteir
H. Suidhisnis	8. Coire a' Mhadaidh	26. Sgùrr an Fheadain
I. Srath Shuardail	9. Beinn Dubhagraich	27. Sgùrr Dubh an Dà Bheinn
J. Sligeachan	10. Bruach na Frithe	28. Sròin an Sgumain
K. Bràighe	11. Guala Bhreatail	29. Mararabhlainn
L. Boraraig	12. Bidean	30. Sgarral
M. Bhatairsteinn	13. Sgùrr nan Gobhar	31. Beinn Dubhagraich
N. Grùla	14. Beinn Lì	32. An Eist
O. Cille Chòmhghain	15. Rubha 'n Dùnain	33. Ùnais
P. Sgoirebreac	16. Sgùrr na h-Uamha	34. Coire an t-Seasgaich
Q. Geusto	17. Healghabhal Mhòr	
R. Beul Àtha nan Trì Allt	18. Gàrsbheinn	

INTRODUCTION

1.

Joy Hendry, editor of literary magazine *Chapman*, was jointly responsible, along with Raymond Ross, for the volume *Sorley MacLean: Critical Essays*. Its publication in 1986 marked the beginning of serious consideration of the entire range of MacLean's work, even though several significant items would still be added in the ten years before the poet's death. Having collaborated closely with MacLean on the biographical study 'Sorley MacLean: the Man and his Work' which opens the volume, Hendry felt able to ask his permission to publish a long poem written immediately before the Second World War, of which only extracts had so far appeared in print. Her request prompted MacLean to embark upon a process of reconsideration and redrafting no less drastic, in its way, than that which material from the original 'Dàin do Eimhir' sequence had undergone, in preparation for the 1977 publication of his selected poems, *Reothairt is Contraigh / Spring Tide and Neap Tide*. The result appeared in five successive issues of the magazine between summer 1987 and summer 1989 and subsequently formed part of MacLean's 1989 collected poems, *O Choille gu Bearradh / From Wood to Ridge*, of which improved, corrected editions appeared in 1990 and again in 1999.[1]

MacLean's prefatory remarks in that context offer an account of the genesis and writing of 'An Cuilithionn':

It was in the Spring or early Summer of 1939 that I started what was meant to be a very long poem radiating from Skye and the West Highlands to the whole of Europe. I was regretting my rash leaving of Skye in 1937 because Mull in 1938 had made me obsessed with the Clearances. I was obsessed also with the approach of war, or worse, with the idea of the conquest of the whole of Europe by Nazi-Fascism without a war in which Britain would not be immediately involved but which would ultimately make Britain a

Fascist state. Munich in September 1938 and the Nazi occupation of Czechoslovakia and Franco's victory in Spain in early 1939 convinced me that the only hope of Europe was the Red Army of Russia, and I believed that all the anti-Soviet propaganda, or most of it, came from Fascist or pro-Fascist sources. The first two parts of the poem were made by June 1939, when I was closest to Communism, although I never accepted the whole of Marxist philosophy, as I could never resolve the idealist-materialist argument. I regarded philosophical materialists as generally more idealistic morally than philosophical idealists.

The poem stopped abruptly with the conclusion of the second part in late May or June 1939 and was not resumed until late October or November 1939. It was abruptly stopped some time in December 1939, but the concluding lyric came to me in sleep in the last days of December 1939, or at least the 'Cò seo' verses did.

Having given this account, MacLean then clearly felt the need to distance himself energetically from what had been written then as well as, perhaps, from the material he was at last releasing for publication:

When I was invalided out of the army in 1943 there was talk of publishing it, but W. D. MacColl's objections to almost every line of my own translations of it delayed that until the behaviour of the Russian Government to the Polish insurrection in 1944 made me politically as well as aesthetically disgusted with most of it.

I reprint here what I think tolerable of it.[2]

This version of 'An Cuilithionn' is divided into seven parts or 'earrannan', preceded by an introductory dedication, and runs to a total of 1223 lines. In the present edition it is referred to as the C or 1989 version.

When, from 2002 onwards, the poet's papers became available for public consultation in the manuscripts room of the National Library of Scotland in Edinburgh, the nature of the cutting and pasting operation which resulted in the C version became fully apparent.[3] A quarter of the original text had been jettisoned. In actual fact, there had been no need to wait before drawing such conclusions. A copy of 'An

Cuilithionn' as first drafted had been lodged for more than half a century in the Special Collections department at King's College in the University of Aberdeen. According to a note by Derick Thomson, dated April 1964, these manuscripts were deposited by Douglas Young on June 11th 1941 and 'are to be regarded as an important original source'. It is possible that their existence subsequently escaped even the poet's own attention, for in spring 1968 MacLean would approach Young for copies of certain items from the 'Dàin do Eimhir' which are contained in the early, manuscript redaction of the sequence also deposited in Aberdeen, and would therefore have been available to him there.[4]

The handwritten copy of 'An Cuilithionn' in Aberdeen (on punched, lined pages inserted in a small format, black loose-leaf binder, from which they have only recently been removed) represents our earliest known source for the poem. Fourteen lines in Gaelic present in the Aberdeen manuscript are not to be found anywhere else. Of these, four (see VII: 285–288) were probably omitted due to an oversight on the part of whoever made a typed copy of MacLean's manuscript. A further ten, concerning Eliot, Pound and MacDiarmid constitute the first of many cuts MacLean would subsequently make, or consider making, in the body of 'An Cuilithionn'.

The present volume is an edition with commentary of the Aberdeen manuscript, which runs to 1638 lines and is here referred to as the A or 1939 version of the poem. 'An Cuilithionn', as originally conceived by MacLean, is now brought into the public domain for the first time.

2.

The breathtaking originality of MacLean's project in 'An Cuilithionn' deserves careful consideration. In retrospect, the 'Dàin do Eimhir' can be seen as a quintessentially Modernist production. Modes of earlier love poetry, in particular traditional Scottish Gaelic song and the sonnets of Shakespeare, are revisited, not without a pervasive element of pastiche and a notable degree of nostalgia. The sequence's intertextuality is probably beyond the grasp even of an exceptionally well-read public. The idiosyncratic canon it proposes brings together figures as diverse as the Russian Symbolist Alexander Blok and eighteenth-century Gaelic lyricist William Ross, Yeats and Baudelaire, Marvell and the Provençal poet Bertran de Born. The last-mentioned would have been familiar to MacLean in the versions prepared by Ezra Pound. Pound and Eliot, who overturned the hitherto prevailing hierarchies in the English literary tradition, championing the Metaphysical poets and the early Italian lyricists of the "dolce stil nuovo" while expressing open hostility towards Milton and the Victorians immediately preceding them, hover in the background of the love sequence. 'Dàin do Eimhir' is furthermore a strikingly Modernist text in its central focus on a speaker whom crisis has pushed to the verge of collapse. He is fissured by competing loyalties and by an incessant battle between his emotions and his rational faculty. Part of the sequence's charm derives from its sounding like so much that we already know, its orchestration of a rich selection of echoes culled from different languages and traditions.

By contrast, 'An Cuilithionn' is a subjectless poem: not in the sense of not being about anything, but because it is not built around a central figure in possession of a specific biography, however fictionalised. It is a dream poem about political commitment, visionary, even hallucinatory from beginning to end. Therein lies much of its paradoxical and disturbing fascination. In this regard, the haunting 'Cò seo' passage at the close represents the culmination of tendencies present throughout the remainder of the poem. MacLean chose to tackle what was the most hackneyed subject in Gaelic poetry, the eviction of the Gaelic-speaking peasantry from what had for centuries been their homelands in the north and west of Scotland. Barely a songmaker in the hundred years preceding, no matter how mediocre, had failed to try his or her hand at what must have appeared to be an obligatory theme. MacLean's boldness, even rashness, in choosing to deal with it yet again, but using modes which cast it in an entirely new light, in terms of both politics and literature, must not be underestimated.

It can therefore be argued that, though the composition of the love sequence neatly brackets that of 'An Cuilithionn', with its first four items preceding the start of the long poem, while twenty-five, possibly twenty-six were still to be written when 'An Cuilithionn' was finished, the latter constitutes a subsequent stage in MacLean's development.

Both works are profoundly bicultural in nature. Where the 'Dàin do Eimhir' are redolent of English-language High Modernism, 'An Cuilithionn' is the expression of a phase at which the concept of Scottish literature as a single entity, expressed through the medium of three different languages – Gaelic, Scots and English – exerted a power it would never again possess. One can perceive a twofold movement. MacDiarmid, one of the dedicatees of 'An Cuilithionn', had by the time it was written become more and more convinced of the at least potentially crucial role to be ascribed to Gaelic language and literature within the wider Scottish cultural panorama. It is not surprising that he should have seized upon MacLean, first as collaborator, then as a poet in his own right deserving of encouragement and support. Some forty years later, MacLean, for his part, would restate the importance to him of MacDiarmid's literary example in the early 1930s:

> the lyrics of Hugh MacDiarmid might very well have destroyed any chances I ever had of writing poetry had my reading of them not been immediately followed by my reading of the *Drunk Man, Cencrastus* and *Scots Unbound*. To me, the best of them were, and still are, the unattainable summit of the lyric and the lyric is the summit of all poetry, but they could not be followed even 'afar off' by me or anyone else. In them I saw a timeless and 'modern' sensibility and an almost implicit 'high seriousness' and an unselfconscious perfection of rhythm that could not be an exemplar because it was so rare. The *Drunk Man*, the greatest long poem of the century that I have read, is more accessible because, along with the subtlest and most daringly imaginative, the most organic and marvellously sustained use of symbolism, it has the variety that has something for most natures. It converted me to the belief that the long medley with lyric peaks was the great form for our age. I did not have the "vis comica" at all, but it made me want to write a long medley with as many lyric peaks as might grow out of it.[5]

In the same essay, MacLean asserts that 'the lyric is the

summit of all poetry'. Yet 'the great form of our age' must be a mixing of different modes – to this extent, a worthy heir to the "satura" of the ancients – in which the lyric would be included. This is what he attempted in 'An Cuilithionn', producing a poem more cogent, unified and consistent than anything MacDiarmid was ever to achieve.

The concern with politics, with the need for action and political commitment, also makes 'An Cuilithionn' very much a poem of the 1930s rather than a Modernist text. It is a fascinating document, more than of its time, of a specific moment, an instance of human and literary brinkmanship straddling, with the nine months over which it was created, the outbreak of the Second World War at the start of September 1939. It seems that everything can find a place there, from the poet's detestation of the first woman to become chief of Clan MacLeod, and (if Douglas Young is to be believed) of the man who took over as headmaster at Portree High School shortly after the poet joined the staff, to the funeral of Scottish socialist hero John Maclean in Glasgow, the dismal fate of German communist Ernst Thaelmann, shot on direct orders from Hitler in the camp at Buchenwald after spending eleven years in solitary confinement, and a speech given in Portree at an unspecified date by crofters' hero the Rev. Donald MacCallum.

At the close of the twelve-line dedication heading the poem, MacLean declares 'chumainn an Clàr-Sgìthe òirdheirc/ ceann-caol ri tuinn àr na h-Eòrpa' ('I would keep our noble Skye/ head-on to the waves of Europe's battle'). Both the 'Dàin do Eimhir' and 'An Cuilithionn' are resolute attempts to re-enfranchise Gaelic writing within the larger framework of European culture, winning back a centrality which it had been denied at least since the time of the Renaissance. Against a background where the survival of the language itself appeared to be threatened (as still continues to be the case), the boldness and even recklessness of MacLean's enterprise are remarkable. What makes 'An Cuilithionn' so distinctive is the bid being made in political as well as literary terms.

The topical nature of 'An Cuilithionn' may well have become, in MacLean's own eyes, an irredeemable weakness. Across a gap of seventy years this potential weakness is no longer so apparent. Readers today will find a guarantee of sincerity in the poem's implication with the day to day preoccupations and prejudices of a continent, indeed a world, precipitating into war, in its commitment to a perspective necessarily particularised, partial in the sense of being both incomplete and intrinsically biased. Few have, however, been willing to see that the value 'An Cuilithionn' possesses as the document of an unrepeatable historical moment coexists with literary merits which leave little to envy in MacLean's more highly valued cycle of love lyrics.

3.

The central imagery of MacLean's poem is provided by a range of hills in the south-eastern part of Skye, the Inner Hebridean island west of Raasay, where he was born, whose pre-eminence is so uncontested within the Gaelic world it can be referred to simply as 'an t-Eilean' ('the Island'). While taking a geological formation as its basis, the poem creates a pervasive impression of movement, specifically of dancing. One may therefore talk about a combination of "choreography" and "oreography", of carefully organised and orchestrated movement and detailed description of a mountain or mountains. The initial presentation of the Cuillins compares them explicitly to the sea:

> far am brist air ceann na spàirne
> muir mhòr, chiar nan tonn gàbro,
> roinn nan dromannan caola, àrda,
> an crios-onfhaidh dorcha stàilinn;
> cuan 's a luasgan teann an creagan,
> a chraosan maireann an caol-eagan,
> a spùtadh sìorraidh anns gach turraid,
> a bhàrcadh biothbhuan anns gach sgurra.[6] (I: 16–24)

The mountain resembles a series of waves which surge, yawn, spout and swell. If it is possible that this opening expresses the climber's direct, corporeal experience of the peak which he is climbing, then the sensation of his own movement upon the surface of the mountain becomes confused and impregnated with a perception of the latter as moving beneath his step. Part II similarly begins with a powerful evocation of the Cuillins, perceived as a body with which the speaker

brings his own into contact ('a' chiad là phòg mi do
ghruaidh... a' chiad là phòg mi do bhial... a' chiad là laigh mi
air t'uchd-sa'[7] II: 5, 7, 9) and, if the mountain is a living
body, one naturally expects it to move after its specific nature
and fashion.

MacLean then employs a deft Gaelic pun ('mòran *fhuaran*
's gainne *fhiùran*' (editor's italics), 'multitude of springs and
fewness of men', I: 35) to make the move from the landscape
perceptible by the naked eye to what it represents, that with
which the inner eye can people it. The gambit is Symbolist in
derivation and splendidly fruitful in poetic terms. It was also
essential (as in the later poem 'Hallaig') when writing about
an absence, about that which is no longer there. The land-
scape, or rather, specific items in the landscape act as stand-
in for the evicted population which had inhabited it through
the centuries.

A reference to a London ceilidh dance presided over by
the ignominious Dame Flora MacLeod, ('cabag phlamach,
bheag à Sasann', 'a little, yattering English female', I: 172)
announces the beginning of a visionary, diabolical ceilidh
which is the culmination of the poem's opening chapter: 'air
gach baideal den Chuilithionn/ bha riochd spùillear-sluaigh
a' tulgadh' ('on every pinnacle of the Cuillin/ the image of a
people's spoiler rocking', I: 205). MacLean proceeds to list,
drawing heavily on oral tradition, indifferent to the ab-
breviation and even distortion of historical fact which that
must inevitably represent, the notorious figures who super-
vised the expulsion of so much of the Skye peasantry:
'Thòisich na manaidhean air dannsa/ 's gum b' e siud an
iomairt sheannsail' ('The ghost band began a dance/ and that
was the auspicious exercise', I: 242–243). The 'caithream
diabhlaidh' ('devilish revelry', I: 263) of these detestable
festivities is powerful enough to drown out 'guth nan saoi is
glaodh nam piantan' ('the voice of the wise and the cry of the
tortured', I: 264), indicating that the poem will act out a
contest between opposing forces which demands eventual,
and definitive resolution – a further indication of the
changing, unstable nature of the poem's progress, despite it
taking the apparent fixity of a mountain range as its central
focus.

However deafening the ceilidh may prove to be, the
speaker insists that he cannot rid his ears of the cry of those

who are unjustly tortured, 'ged bhiodh Beul Àtha nan Trì Allt/ mar a' Bholga làn is mall' (though the Ford of the Three Burns were/ like the Volga, full and slow', I: 277–278). MacLean's poem resolutely connects a "microcosm" with a "macrocosm", the marginal, in geographical terms, and deceptively negligible, in historical terms, catastrophe affecting the Gaelic-speaking population of Scotland in the course of the nineteenth century, and the Marxist-inspired movement of revolutionary violence in and beyond Europe which looked set to transform human society as a whole. The Volga functions through synecdoche as an indication of the vast scale upon which Russian history develops. Beul Àtha nan Trì Allt is the Fairy Bridge of Dunvegan of modern tourist brochures. Rather than any supernatural associations, however, it interests MacLean as a major scenario of both the Evangelical Revival and mounting crofter militancy in the face of increasing encroachment by landlords on the livelihood and the rights of the peasant population. Even at this early stage, the close of its opening part, the poem envisages no resolution or redress for the tragedy of Gaelic Scotland 'gus am bi an t-Arm Dearg còmhla/ ri caismeachd tarsainn na Roinn Eòrpa' ('until the whole Red Army together/ comes battle-marching across Europe', I: 286).

In so far as the poem enacts a conflict between landowners and bourgeoisie, on the one hand, and the common people on the other, one would expect a compelling image which can balance the heroic qualities of the mountain range, temporarily usurped by the triumphing representatives of reactionary oppression. Part II issues in a series of verse paragraphs, each beginning 'Seo latha eile air na slèibhtean' ('Another day upon the mountains', II: 123, 156, 172, 182) where the extent of the current emergency is discussed in detail. The miners of Asturias in northern Spain, who rose up against the Republican government in October 1934, are an example of what has not yet happened, and may never happen, in Skye and in Scotland. Yet the Cuillin momentarily become a monument to that heroic struggle:

Nach èireadh Sgùrr dubh nan Gillean
's gach sgùrr eile agus binnean
mar chùirn-chuimhne air bhur cruaidh-chàs
agus air gaisgeachd mhòir an uabhais![8] (II: 134–137)

The image which opposes and balances, temporarily, the Cuillin in the world of the poem is 'aon shùil-chruthaich na Roinn-Eòrpa' ('the one quagmire of Europe', II: 193). This, in line with MacLean's fundamentally Symbolist approach throughout 'An Cuilithionn', and with his desire to connect "microcosm" and "macrocosm", is the bog of Mararaulin in Minginish, a short distance north and west of the mountain range.

Part III accordingly offers an evocation of the quagmire almost as detailed as the evocation of the Cuillin in the poem's first two chapters. Like the mountains, Mararaulin is depicted as an active entity in movement. It swallows, grows, spreads, streams, rises, drowns and shakes ('shluigeas', 'fàsaidh', 'sgaoilidh', 'sruthadh', 'èirigh', 'bàthadh', 'chrith-eanaich', II: 3, 5, 7, 8, 10). Much of Part III is an ironic and embittered paean of praise to the ceaseless activity and encroachment of the bog, credited with having defeated, and reduced to impotence, previous manifestations of the revolutionary spirit such as the French Revolution, or opposition to fascism in Spain at the time of the Civil War. Imagery of dancing from the diabolical ceilidh of Part I is recapitulated as the representatives of the triumphant bourgeoise are invited: 'thigibh a dhanns' a Mhararabhlainn... Thoiribh sgrìob a Chille Chòmhghain/ a dhannsa air uaigh an t-seòid ud... Dèanaibh dannsa chridheil aoibhneach' ('come to Mararaulin to dance... make a trip to St Congan's/ to dance on the hero's grave... dance heartily and joyfully' II: 74,77–78, 91). They, too, are doomed to be drowned in the morass in due course. But that is no reason for them not to enjoy a thoroughly good party in the meantime!

In Parts III and IV 'An Cuilithionn' sinks to its nadir, its dreariest, most depressed and blocked stage. Ever attentive to the topography and toponymy at his disposal, MacLean chooses a cliff formation near Neist Point in the west of Skye known as 'an t-Aigeach', literally 'the Stallion', as a more agile and concise embodiment of the heroic qualities which he attributes to the Cuillin.[9] The Stallion is caught in Mararaulin and castrated, deprived of its virility, by a combination of bourgeois and bailiffs. The crude imagery is paralleled by a practically farcical tone as MacLean parodies a well-known song of Tiree origin about how a dog named Pilot lost one eye ('Thug iad a' bhrìgh bhon ainmhidh bhochd', 'They have taken his virtue from the poor beast' III: 125ff.) The bog consequently rises, dances and overflows, threatening to encompass all that exists in its scum ('èirigh', 'dannsa', 'cur thairis', III: 105, 107). But we are dealing with a poem of carefully organised and orchestrated movement. However deep the morass of despair and discouragement into which the speaker may plunge (and supporters of Stalin's Russia were not alone in finding cause for despair in Europe's predicament at the onset of summer 1939), it cannot be allowed to come to a halt at one of its opposing poles. Earlier in Part III a passage had occurred which is striking for its doctrinaire championing of the potential of Bolshevik Russia:

> Cò idir a chartas a' bhàthaich
> mur tig an t-Arm Dearg nar càs-ne?
> Cò chuireas dhuinn a-mach am buachar
> mur teirinn Stàilin bho na cruachan?[10]

Part III concludes with a much more feeble, nonetheless determined, prophecy that the victory of the quagmire, and of everything it represents, cannot be permanent: 'èiridh latha air a' Chuilithionn' ('day will rise on the Cuillin', III: 218).

4.

A powerful argument against sporadic later assertions on the part of the poet himself that 'An Cuilithionn' was never effectively concluded lies in the poem's skilful, often understated architectonic properties. These are most powerful, and least noticeable, at the level of simple verbal repetitions. Among the dominant lexical items, in this respect, are 'èirigh', 'dannsa' and 'fada' ('rising', 'dancing', 'long'). The tactic can usefully be compared to what happens in symphonic music, as if a theme, or a new variant of a theme, were to be introduced in subdued tones so as to pass well nigh unnoticed in a larger tapestry of sounds. When blared forth by the whole orchestra at the symphony's close, it has a familiar ring for the listener, upon whose consciousness it has already subtly impinged. The conclusion is therefore endowed with rightness and a feeling of inevitability – an effect absolutely in line with the strain of historical determinism dominant in Marxist thinking.

Douglas Young, one of the poem's earliest readers, who responded to it with a sensitivity and acuteness rarely paralleled since, was aware of the distinctly musical properties of 'An Cuilithionn'. He wrote to MacLean on July 29th 1940 that

> When I said in my earlier letter that it was more like a piece of music than a piece of literature, I was exaggerating. It is still like a piece of music, with movements, "leitmotiv", etc ; but I am now more conscious of the aesthetic effects, such as the sensations of climbing and the descriptions of scenes, and of the dramatic effects, such as the evictors on their perches, the soirée of the bourgeois, the emigrant girl, and the 'Cò seo?' passage at the end. What makes it unlike literature is the curious structure, or lack of it; although it is like some of Blake's apocalyptic stuff. The 'Clio' passage especially so.[11]

Young was wrong about the lack of structure. The poem's concluding line, ''s e 'g èirigh air taobh eile duilghe' ('rising on the other side of sorrow' VII: 363), is prefigured at III: 109 with, two lines later, a repetition of 'coiseachd' ('walking') which prefigures the incantatory close at 328ff. This same line marks the beginning of the peroration at VII: 160, appearing again at 194, with the crucial word 'èirigh' at 347 and 355. 'Fada, cian fada, fada air fàire' ('Far, far distant, far on a horizon' VII: 324) recalls both the opening of Part IV (''S fhada cian bho àird nam beanntan', 'Long and distant it is from the heights of the mountains') and the plangent travail of its close, in turn taken up in the course of V (''S fhada, cian fada' 147ff.).

These effects need not have been fully conscious to the poet at the time of composition. A more obvious indication of plannedness is the way in which two successive quatrains, at I: 182 and 186, introduce the speakers, a girl from Gesto forced onto an emigrant ship and a man drowned off Vatersay in the *Annie Jane*, whose monologues (at VI: 1–40 and 75–89) are a high point in the latter part of 'An Cuilithionn'. It is an almost banal rule in extended verbal texts, whether written to be read or performed on stage, that new, enlivening elements need to be introduced as the conclusion approaches. The monologues fall into this category, as does the extended passage about Clio, the muse of history who, in her different personifications, bears witness to human society's current predicament and indicates some of the more encouraging responses evoked. The entry of other voices into the text offers relief and variety before the notional speaker returns to conclude the whole with an account of the vision vouchsafed him.

Relief is also provided by two extended and splendid lyrical passages, addressed to the Stallion (V: 35–146) and to the Cuillins themselves (VII: 212–323). They are cast in a pibroch metre whose energetic movement evokes 'port-à-beul' or 'mouth music', when a singer, usually unaccompanied, would stand in for an instrument to provide music for dancing. The pervasive choreographic element in 'An Cuilithionn' here becomes exultant, almost convulsive. If in 1989 MacLean severely curtailed the first, and cut the second entirely, this can perhaps only be explained through fundamental changes, at a distance of half a century, in his aesthetic views and perceptions. There can be no doubt that the second lyric in particular constitutes a high point of his work. Both are dominated by the vocative or address form, directed to a geological formation become symbol, almost an abstract entity. The second evokes unmistakably the high point of MacLean's sequence of love poems, 'Dàin do Eimhir' LVII. If much poetry can be accounted for in terms of a tension between the urge to musicality and comprehensibility, here MacLean weights the balance dizzyingly, dangerously in favour of the former. Where the larger scale architecture of this part and of the poem as a whole are concerned, it provides a much needed balance for, and transition towards, the leaden, weighted quality of the final paragraph.

In a poem inspired by movement, the equal balance of forces risks producing an immobility hostile to the text's essential nature. This happens in Part IV, the shortest of the seven making up the poem, a moment of profound crisis:

> Cas agam air Mararabhlainn
> agus cas air a' Chuilithionn,
> mo làmhan ceangailte san òtrach
> 's mo shùil ri torachd an iomaluais. (IV: 29–32)[12]

The turning hinted at the close of Part III actually happens at the start of Part V. MacLean introduces the first of two symbols he probably sourced directly from MacDiarmid's work which, lacking any connection to the topography of Skye, are not integrated into the poem's fabric with entire success. The rose which represents revolutionary activity in the shipyards of Clydeside may well have been inspired by MacDiarmid's image for the General Strike of 1926 in *A Drunk Man Looks at the Thistle*,[13] while the serpent hoisted out of the sea at VII: 78ff. is a homage to *To Circumjack Cencrastus*, which arguably had a more direct influence on MacLean's long poem.

Mention of the rose, which is also the flush of the breaking day of organised resistance directed towards unequivocal political ends, is followed by a miraculous reversal of the Stallion's gelding. Again "choreography" and "oreography" interact as the movement of what is, after all, a cliff is celebrated in its progress from one peak to another. The Stallion bounds, leaps, prances, jumps, takes a stride or 'gamag' and another bound, from Sgùrr a' Ghreadaidh to Sgùrr nan Gillean, from Sgùrr na h-Uamha to Blaven, then from Garsven to Sgùrr an Fheadain ('bocail', 'leum', 'prannsail' V 15ff.) till finally he transforms Mararulin into a 'rutting bog' ('poll-dàmhair', V: 28), a place of frenzied activity from which new life will emerge.

The positive turning cannot however be too easily achieved. Part VII opens with the image of a hero exposed for torment upon a mountain. In the last paragraph but one of Part III, the fact that Mararaulin proved unable to swallow the woman the poet loves was taken as an earnest of eventual victory. The speaker's attitude here is very far from the insoluble conflict between amorous involvement and political commitment which underpins the 'Dàin do Eimhir'. In the poem's final part, she becomes a vulture tearing gobbets out of the speaker's Prometheus, so that only gradually can a collectivity of heroes assemble along the ridge of the Cuillins as counterbalance to the diabolical ceilidh of Part I:

> Air na sgurrachan mun cuairt,
> bha na beò-mhairbh a thug buaidh:
> Toussaint, Marx, More, Lenin,   100
> Liebknecht, Connollaigh, MacGill-Eain
> agus iomadh spiorad àrdain
> a chuireadh às an càs na Spàinne.[14] (VII: 98–103)

The speaker has already gone so far as to assure Dimitrov, the Bulgarian communist whose self-defence against the charge of having set fire to the Reichstag in Berlin kindled solidarity on an international scale, that his features have been incised along the Cuillins themselves (VI: 261–263). It is significant that Dimitrov's impact on the range is to provoke movement:

> bha sgal aigeannach do chridhe
> toirt luasgain air Sgùrr nan Gillean;
> bha bàrcadh spèis a' chinne-daonna
> a' toirt a' chrathaidh air an aonach.[15] (VI: 263–266)

The dancing of the ceilidh in Part I is replaced by a more dignified and purposeful walking which, with a love of abstraction typical for MacLean, involves both men and events (the Paris Commune, Connolly and his fellow participants in the 1916 Dublin Easter Rising). Yet if 'An Cuilithionn' sings of the progress of history towards an inevitable goal deserving celebration, it is and nonetheless remains an oneiric vision, a dream poem. As the poem reaches its close, the mountains are inaccessible, themselves ghost-like and haunted by ghosts, while he who seeks them is irredeemably alone and spectre-like, a naked brain: 'Chan eil, chan eil ach am falbhan/ a' sireadh a' Chuilithinn thar fairge' ('It is only, it is only the journeying one,/ seeking the Cuillin over the ocean' VII: 350–351). The last line brings together the Cuillins and that over which victory is hoped for, but which nonetheless continues to separate us from them where they rise 'on the other side of sorrow' (' 'g èirigh air taobh eile duilghe', VII: 363).

5.

What would happen if, asked to quote a couple of lines from a major Gaelic poem of the twentieth century, one were to choose the following? 'Toussaint, Marx, More, Lenin,/ Liebknecht, Connollaigh, MacGill-Eain...' Can these lines be claimed as poetry at all? And if the answer is positive, what would make of them Gaelic poetry? The issue can usefully lead into discussion of those aspects of the poem which are likely to prove, at least on first impact, least

attractive to a contemporary reader. MacLean's deployment
of proper names throughout 'An Cuilithionn' is deserving of
careful consideration. When, for example, he forms a quartet
from James Connolly, John Maclean, Karl Liebknecht and
Lenin (at V: 180–187, recapitulated at VII: 99–100 and 205–
206), at least two things are happening. In line with the
linking of "macrocosm" and "microcosm", the speaker is
attempting to integrate Gaelic and Scottish history (Maclean
being a grandson of a Mull crofter) and thus to re-
enfranchise his community of origin within the larger
European context. But as a consequence his Gaelic verse
must expand, conceptually and linguistically, to include the
names of the people he is so determined to intrude upon.
MacLean's cultural and political project affects profoundly
(it does not matter how unintentionally) the very texture of
his verse. A thoroughly argued defence of what he does might
include reference to Milton's use of Biblical names and
toponyms throughout *Paradise Lost*, though the introduction
of foreign elements, in Milton's consistently Latinate syntax
and in Hebrew tradition mediated via the Authorised
Version, is far more uniform and, one might say, mono-
chrome than what happens in 'An Cuilithionn'.

The question of names brings one face to face with another
issue, which is the role of politics in the poem. Might 'An
Cuilithionn' have achieved publication, or found a sym-
pathetic audience, sooner if it had not so brashly, declaredly
been concerned with politics? The poem was written during
the months preceding and immediately following Britain's
declaration of war on Germany and could thus benefit from
none of the consoling myths which gradually coalesced after
Hitler's defeat. What is a totalitarian poem? A poem
produced within a society plagued with totalitarian rule? Or a
poem which advocates totalitarianism, the justified use of
violence to impose and maintain the transformation of
society in the name of a predetermined political ideology?
Almost certainly, the second. This suggests that, as with
MacDiarmid's 'Hymns to Lenin', or a splendid poem like
'The Seamless Garment',[16] we are dealing with a totalitarian
poem, no matter how radically the personal conduct of the
man who penned it may have diverged from the beliefs 'An
Cuilithionn' proclaims and the actions these would prompt.

In so far as it is an instance of discursive power, the

achievement of saying something successfully and in a sufficiently lapidary manner to assure it will be heard, all poetry is political, the love lyrics of 'Dàin do Eimhir' no less than 'An Cuilithionn', the delicate, early annotations of unhappy relationships, of sexual and emotional frustration of Anna Akhmatova no less than the proclamations verging on slogans of Mayakovsky or Yevtushenko. Dealing with this fact is particularly problematic in a Scottish context. Scotland throughout the twentieth century is too often envisaged as a place from which politics was excluded, political debate and decision-making being attributed to Westminster, almost as if power had not been exercised in specific ways and by specific agents within Scottish society during that time. In consequence, the antics of Hugh MacDiarmid, who rejoined the Communist party in 1956 in the wake of Soviet Russia's brutal repression of the uprising in Hungary, or consideration, in one of MacLean's letters to Young, of what it could mean were Hitler to set up a puppet government in Scotland, as he had done in Slovakia,[17] tend to be regarded with deprecation, as if these were the games, or speculations, of children, not to be taken seriously.

The political history of modern Scottish literature has yet to be written, and cannot be identified merely with the vicissitudes of the nationalist movement. If we dismiss the proclamations of poets and novelists as child's play, we sap their work of one of its most fundamental values, of its potential to both warn and teach us. To this extent, the publication of the original version of 'An Cuilithionn', in the centenary year of the poet's birth and at the start of the twenty-first century's second decade, is peculiarly timely, given the questions that it poses.

This could be the appropriate moment at which to offer an honest and sobre evaluation of the tradition of Scottish leftism – by which is meant, the espousal of revolutionary and totalitarian values by men and women living in western democracies, who would never have dreamed of residing in a society regulated according to such values. Few would deny that by the time MacLean wrote 'An Cuilithionn', events in Stalinist Russia posed serious problems for anyone who wished to offer that regime and its armies unreserved support.[18] But in his memoirs, art historian Dmitry Likhachev insists that the Bolshevik revolution was

disfigured from the very start by the means which it
deployed:

> One of the aims of these memoirs is to dispel the myth
> that the period of the hardest repression began in 1936–
> 37. I think that in the future the statistics of arrests
> and executions will show that waves of arrest,
> imprisonments and deportations had begun as early as
> 1918, even before the 'Red Terror' officially appeared in
> the autumn of that year. These waves continued to
> break in a constant crescendo right up to the death of
> Stalin, and it seems that the new wave of 1936–37 was
> merely the 'ninth wave'... When we opened our shutters
> at night in the flat in Lakhtinskaya Street even in
> 1918–19 we could hear spasmodic shots and short bursts
> of machine-gun fire from the direction of the Peter and
> Paul Fortress.
>
> It was not Stalin who started the 'Red Terror'. He
> merely increased it dramatically and took it to an
> incredible pitch on coming to power.
>
> The arrests of prominent activists in the all-powerful
> party began in 1935–37, and that, it would appear, has
> done more than anything else to inflame the imagination
> of my contemporaries. While officers, 'bourgeois',
> professors and, in particular, the clergy, together with
> Russian, Ukrainian and White Russian peasants were
> being shot by the thousand in the '20s and early '30s, it
> all seemed 'natural'. But then there began the 'self-
> devouring aspect of power', which left the country with
> only the most nondescript, those devoid of character
> and those who had gone into hiding or had reached an
> accommodation.[19]

A further, even more uncomfortable question concerns the
points in common, and the differences, between the two
major totalitarian systems which twentieth-century Europe
experienced, under Hitler and Stalin – who, it must be
remembered, during much of the time in which 'An
Cuilithionn' was being written, were military allies engaged
in the dismemberment of Poland.

The ideology celebrated so unequivocally in MacLean's
poem, which traces its origins to the French Revolution of
1789 through a series of uprisings characterised by frequently

indiscriminate violence, aimed to perform a surgical operation on society, to improve it through the physical annihilation of specific elements. There is a disquieting parallel between Bolshevism's persecution of, for example, the Ukrainian peasant farmer, the treatment of the former aristocracy under the French terror, and Nazism's horrendous crimes against the Jews. Is it so different to kill people on the basis of their social class, or of their perceived racial origin? As the twenty-first century takes its course, revolutionary ideology is falling a victim to the so-called failure of master narratives. This may therefore be a privileged moment at which to survey, evaluate and even enjoy MacLean's 'An Cuilithionn', a major poetic achievement so deeply and intrinsically implicated with that ideology. To this extent, the poem's commitment to revolutionary militancy, its absolute refusal to steer clear of politics, can be seen as an advantage rather than a drawback.

6.

Philosopher George Davie showed no inclination to shy away from the thornier issues raised by MacLean's poem. Having read an English version from which the conclusion – yet to be composed – was missing, he wrote in the following terms to MacLean on Christmas Day 1939:[20]

It has been a great honour and privilege, not to mention most exciting experience, to have a preview, so to speak, of 'The Cuillin'. [...] Obviously the only counterweapon against bourgeois journalese is found in good Socialist slogans; and who has a better right to express these than poets? Mayakovsky after all made a fine poem out of 'Hands off China'. So too, it is true that words like Dimitrov, Madrid etc. are more effective in a non-Imperialist language that doesn't suffer, like English, from spinelessness of rhythm and paucity of vocabulary etc. [...] I agree with Jessie [Scott] that the pibroch lyric on the Stallion has the deepest and widest content in the whole poem. It is really an exceedingly impressive poem and has stood up to many a reading from me without ceasing to give always fresh delight. It seems to me worthy to stand side by side with Grieve's stuff as a classic of our time... The revolutionary rhetoric is a bit like Buchanan's (I mean George, the Humanist, who's one of the best poets Scotland ever had), and as timely. As regards the political message, I can only say, what Grieve will say, that it expresses my sentiments in such a form that if asked 'What is your position?' I will refer to your poem. In this sense, the publication and circulation of the translation as well as original is a matter of great importance.

The ebb and flow of plans to get 'An Cuilithionn' into print, as well as the poet's gradual disillusionment with what he had produced, can be traced in MacLean's correspondence with Young. On March 15th 1942 he writes that he has 'wild hopes that the near future may see certain lines of "The Cuillin" fulfilled'. Considering the poetry he may yet write, he says of his work so far, in a letter dated October 6th 1942, that 'that whole manner is impossible for me now except the manner of "Ban-Ghàidheal" and some bits of "The Cuillin" and the Calvary thing'. Writing from Raigmore Hospital, Inverness, where he was still convalescing from wounds received when a land mine exploded near his battery command post at El Alamein on November 2nd 1942, MacLean proposes 'a cheap edition of the Gaelic' of 'An Cuilithionn' accompanied by the English version (Young called it a 'projection') Young had completed, in part while imprisoned for his refusal to be conscripted into war service by a Westminster administration (letter dated April 20th 1943). Young considered including his projection in the forthcoming volume *Auntrin Blads*, but MacLean did not approve:

I am not very keen on the appearance of any version of "The Cuillin" before the Gaelic appears. That is simply because I have the Gaelic readers first in mind and shouldn't like any version to precede the original by what would be now most likely a great length of time, as I don't foresee any publication of the Gaelic for ages, if ever. (May 2nd 1943)

In this same letter, MacLean announces (using Davie's playful misnomer for his poem) that he 'must take some care to get the "rant" out at a crofter's price', almost as if 'An

Cuilithionn' might operate as a sort of "agit prop", adding, on June 15th, that

> I consider, in the present state of affairs in Scotland, the practical political effect of all poetry to be nil. Politically poetry will influence only people who will be aesthetically influenced by it. Hence I am more than doubtful of any value at all in a bad translation, such as mine of 'The Cuillin', and feel very strongly tempted[21] to try to get the 'rant' out in the Gaelic alone...

When publication, along with an English translation, again seemed feasible, MacLean told Young, on July 17th 1944, that 'I am sick of certain parts of "The Cuillin" and will make one or two cuts which, going over it recently, I saw desirable. That would involve changes in your translation'. The process of cutting and pasting which would lead to the emergence of the C or 1989 version, the only form in which 'An Cuilithionn' has so far found a readership, was therefore adumbrated more than four decades earlier.

This lapse of time meant that the man who supervised the publication, or republication of much what had been written during the most fervid creative period in his life, running roughly from April 1939 to March 1940, was a somewhat different individual from the one who actually penned the poetry. MacLean got the opportunity to reinvent himself, imposing an angle on the way his work was perceived which reflected distinct aesthetic, political and cultural pre-occupations. The fact that publication now occurred almost exclusively with a facing English translation, and was aimed, at least in numerical terms, primarily at an English-speaking audience with no knowledge of Gaelic, made this process of reinvention all the easier. The task of recovering and publishing MacLean's work in its previous form, initiated with the edition of the nearly complete Eimhir sequence by the Association for Scottish Literary Studies in 2002 and continuing with the present edition, should not be interpreted as an attempt to undermine, or to invalidate, the specific cast the poet put upon his productions between 1978 and 1990. It will be more constructive, and more appropriate, to look upon the A and C versions of 'An Cuilithionn' as distinct entities, each possessing its own merits and coherence which, rather than cancelling one another out, complement one another.

The typescripts of 'An Cuilithionn' which remained among the poet's personal papers, and are now housed in the National Library of Scotland in Edinburgh,[22] detail a process of redrafting, in certain cases of rewording (as when the poet took exception to the Gaelic calque 'bùirdeasachd' of French 'bourgeoisie' and its derivatives) to which it is not possible to assign a precise date at the current stage of research. Pencilled comments on the English version of the poem in Robin Lorimer's neat and precise hand[23] date, in the opinion of the poet's daughter Ishbel, to a stage in the 1970s when publication of a version of 'An Cuilithionn' was again under consideration, a plan subsequently dropped. In the present edition the B version of the poem is taken to embrace all the possible redactions which might have resulted had the changes adumbrated in the Edinburgh typescripts ever reached a definitive form. B must therefore remain a fluid and somewhat impalpable entity.

A letter to Douglas Young dated September 25th 1940 from 10 Polwarth Crescent in Edinburgh, stored with the Aberdeen materials, vividly conveys the poet's state of mind at the time the materials were handed over:

> Could you keep this for me until this mess is over? Everything in it exists written elsewhere except 'Coilltean Ratharsair' of which herein is the only copy. I have not managed to finish it and may never...

MacLean goes on to express specific worries regarding 'An Cuilithionn':

> Beware, there is much Bolshevism in this book of mss. I am afraid the Nazis would not like it. I am sending the good typescript of 'The Cuillin' etc. home to be stored, a Skye schoolmaster has another copy, you have another one of your own and this manuscript but the typescript on the whole is better. I have a third typescript which I am sending off this afternoon to the West but I have not yet decided to whom.

MacLean left for training in the signals corps at Catterick Camp in Yorkshire at ten o'clock in the morning the day after writing this letter.

One further important source requires mention at this point. The Muniments at the University of St Andrews house a beautifully bound, palish green volume with 'An Cuilithionn' set in gold lettering on the front. The labour of binding was undertaken by Jackson of Back Wynd in Aberdeen in October 1940. A Gaelic inscription in green fountain pen states the copy to be the property of Douglas Young of Ardlogie in Fife, while below George Davie's assessment is quoted: 'a long opinionative rant, interspersed with lyrics'. A note added later in blue ballpoint pen, which should probably be attributed to Derick Thomson, indicates that this copy was typed by Young in May 1940 from materials supplied by the poet. The facing English text was typed from a partial copy made by Jessie Scott (later Kosmarova) of a literal translation by the poet. Additions were then made either in person by MacLean, when visiting Ardlogie in September 1940, or from correspondence with him. The St Andrews version cannot take precedence over the original Aberdeen manuscript which forms the basis of this edition. Perhaps its most valuable contribution to our understanding of the poem lies in the annotations made by Young, giving information presumably supplied by MacLean in person, and not available from any other source.

Also in the Muniments at St Andrews is a letter of MacLean's to the librarian, Dugald McArthur, dated from Peinnachorrain, Braes on December 16th 1980, evidently in response to an enquiry as to what ought to be done with Young's copy of the poem:

> I am very much in two minds about the Douglas Young manuscript. There are only a few pieces of the 'Cuilithionn' poem published. Actually the poem was never finished. It was stopped very abruptly in December 1939, before I had even met Douglas Young. When Robert Garioch published *17 Poems for Sixpence* in January or February 1940, Douglas came to see me and took away a typed or manuscript copy of what was finished, and translated it, but I had already taken a scunner of a great deal of it, and it was understood by Douglas and myself that it was not to be published with the other poems of mine that I gave him leave to get published. When I came back from Africa in 1943 there were a few proposals made to me to get it published (or some of it) with my own translation but by 1944 I

had such a strong revulsion against most of it that I
decided not to publish any but selected pieces of it, most
if not all of which have by now been published in
various magazines.

As was already proposed, MacLean's claim that 'An
Cuilithionn' never reached completion demands cautious
treatment, and is contradicted by the evidence of the text
itself. Nowhere in correspondence at the time of its writing,
or in the years immediately following, is 'An Cuilithionn'
spoken of as a project MacLean had been unable, or
unwilling, to complete, one which could therefore achieve
publication only in fragmentary form.

In a letter to Young dated September 11th 1941 MacLean,
discussing the background to his love poems, refers to the
period 'when I finished "The Cuillin" about New Year 1940'.
A letter of March 30th 1942 offers a chronology of its writing
slightly different from what MacLean would recall nearly
forty years afterwards:

'The Cuillin' was started in Edinburgh in April or
May 1939, was being rapidly written and had reached
the line before 'Seo latha eile' [II: 124] when a chance
meeting with Eimhir brought back the old passion and
it was completely interrupted until it was restarted in
Hawick in November 1939... I don't actually know
when in November 'The Cuillin' was restarted but there
was a short break between the end of Part II and the
beginning of Part III and then again after the end of
Part IV and again after the end of Part VI but it was
being written in November and early December 1939...
On the 20th December 'Eimhir' XXVIII to XXXVI were
all written. Meanwhile 'The Cuillin' was certainly all
finished except 'Cò seo' before the 23rd December.

7.

This edition of 'An Cuilithionn' is accompanied by an
English translation from the poet's own hand, sourced in the
Edinburgh typescripts, and reflecting an early stage of the
B version of the poem, at which relatively few changes had
been made with respect to A. The practice of publishing

Gaelic poetry almost exclusively with a facing English
version, increasingly dominant in Scotland from the 1970s
onwards, raises fascinating and compelling questions about
the politics of poetic translation, especially acute when one
of the two languages involved is threatened with obsolescence,
the target language being the very one set to oust it from use.
Translating Gaelic poetry into English, even when it is the
poet him or herself who does so, is simply not the same as
translating it into Italian or German or Russian.

It took some time for the practice to be contested, issuing in
one of the livelier debates on the Scottish cultural scene, of
which Corinna Krause's thesis offers eloquent testimony. The
presentation of MacLean's work, in a recent pamphlet about
Scottish literature, indicates how detrimental the hegemony
of the parallel text, in these specific circumstances, risks
becoming: 'MacLean translated his own poetry, first written
in Gaelic, into unforgettable English'.[24] It is surely not
unkind to detect here an implication that the Gaelic versions
constituted a species of preliminary, preparatory stage which
was then superseded when the poet produced translations of
his poems (or wrote them – better? – a second time) in
English. MacLean himself has stated unequivocally in print
that it is impossible to reach an adequate evaluation of Gaelic
poetry on the basis of an English translation.[25] Serious
consideration of his work can only be attempted on the basis
of a close examination of his original, Gaelic texts and, while
it is undeniable that interesting light may be shed on these
by those who comment on the poet's English versions, the
latter would do well to accept, and underline, the
insurmountable limitations on their understanding and
approach. Attempts to erect MacLean's English versions to a
status parallel to that of the Gaelic originals, when not
actually superseding them, are both tendentious and
irresponsible. Any translation, no matter who performs it,
can only explore certain possibilities implicit in the original.
Indeed, one way in which translations illuminate their
originals is by evoking, in informed readers' consciousness,
the many paths they were unable to pursue. Translation is an
enriching process but can never be one of substituting the
original, or rendering it obsolete.

The English version printed here formed the basis for the
one published in 1989 but is not identical with it. It can

therefore help to divest the latter of any pretensions to inevitability. Its imperfections are undeniable, as when MacLean calques the typically Gaelic syntactical pattern in which a finite verb precedes its subject (rather than following, as in English).[26] His version of the second 'pìobaireachd' passage, from Part VII, highlights the difficulties of even evoking (never mind reproducing or matching) in English what is one of the poem's most impressive achievements. Given that by 1989 it was obvious that the numerical majority of MacLean's readers would be English monoglots with no access to Gaelic, it is not beyond the bounds of possibility that the poet excised these wonderful quatrains due to the problems of rendering them into English with any pretence to adequacy. The present edition faces a similarly problematic predicament, being, as it is, emphatically a study of the original Gaelic text rather than of MacLean's version or versions of it, carried out in full awareness that the larger segment of its notional audience will be able to access the original only by means of the translation. It is nonetheless hoped the edition can at last prompt serious consideration of a major part of MacLean's overall achievement, along with the adjustments in our critical, literary and human perception of the poet which the publication of such significant new material renders possible.[27]

Endnotes

1. See MacLean 1999: 61–131.
2. MacLean 1999: 63.
3. For a detailed account of the relationship between the A and C versions of 'An Cuilithionn', see under (5) in the 'Textual Commentary' to the poem.
4. See letter from Young dated April 3rd 1968.
5. MacLean 1985: 11. The essay in question first appeared as 'My relationship with poetry' in *Chapman* 16 (Summer 1976).
6. 'where will break on the struggle's head/ the great grey sea of gabbro waves,/ knife-edge of slender high ridges,/ the dark steel surge-belt;/ an ocean whose welter is tight in rocks,/ its yawning mouths permanent in narrow chasms,/ its spouting everlasting in each turret,/ its swelling eternal in each sgurr.'
7. 'the first day I kissed your cheek... the first day I kissed your mouth... the first day I lay on your breast'.
8. 'Would that the black Sgurr nan Gillean/ and every other sgurr and pinnacle/ would rise as memorials to your hardship/ and great, awful valour' II: 134–137.

9. As argued in the 'Commentary' to the poem, MacLean comes close to blurring the distinction between 'an t-Àigeach' and Neist Point proper ('Eist Bhatarsteinn', 'the bridled Stallion of Waterstein'). The latter is in Gaelic 'an eist fhiadhaich', 'the wild stallion', with a possible implication of gelding that may have inspired MacLean's treatment of the image at this point in the poem (see note to I: 74). In the exultant 'pìobaireachd' which is the culmination of Part VII, the Stallion and the Cuillin are unequivocally identified with one another ('Àigich Cuilithinn', see VII: 296ff.)

10. 'Who at all will cleanse the byre/ unless the Red Army come in our extremity?/ Who will cast out the dung for us/ unless Stalin descends from the heights?' III: 23–26. The second couplet was cut from the 1989 version of the poem.

11. Letter preserved in NLS ms 29540 f65.

12. 'I have a foot in Mararaulin/ and a foot on the Cuillin,/ my hands bound beneath the dunghill/ and my eyes on the many-headed swiftness'. A similarly perilous equilibrium is evident at the start of Part IV: 'ach mar as àird' a thèid an dìreadh/ 's ann as doimhne 's fhaide chì neach/ tro an ruaimleach, tro a' chàthar/ tro chridhe boglach a' bhàthaidh' ('but the higher goes the ascent,/ deeper and longer one sees/ through the scum and through the bog,/ through the heart of the drowning morass' IV: 3–6).

13. 'I saw a rose come loupin oot/ frae a camsteerie plant', ll. 1118–1119, see MacDiarmid 1987: 90.

14. 'On the peaks around/ were the living dead and their triumph:/ Toussaint, More, Lenin, Marx,/ Liebknecht, Connolly, Maclean,/ and many a proud spirit/extinguished in the extremity of Spain.'

15. 'the spirited blast of your heart/ made Sgurr nan Gillean heave;/ the surging of the hopes of humanity/ made the mountain shake.'

16. See MacDiarmid 1978: I 297, 311, 321 & II 893.

17. See letter dated November 23rd 1940.

18. The nature of the illusions MacLean would appear to have nurtured emerges in the following passage from a letter to Young dated June 21st 1941: 'If it is true that in Russia there is no longer female prostitution and that the display of possessions is considered most "vulgar" of all things, then I consider that what happens to the rest of Europe matters little if that survives in Russia. Be Stalin anything at all, fool or blackguard, if he is the leader of a regime that has achieved such, then the continuance of his regime is priceless to humanity.'

19. Likhachev 2000: 62.

20. See NLS ms 29501 ff.7–9.

21. The original has 'attempted'.

22. The bulk of the relevant material can be found in ms 29558 (Gaelic) and ms 29559 (English). Ms 29561 contains Douglas Young's English 'projection'. A list of proposed cuts indicated in ms 29558 will be found in the 'Textual Commentary' to the present edition, where significant variants in the B typescripts with respect to A are also recorded.

23. The following comments, all concerning Part I, may be taken as indicative of Lorimer's general approach and tone: on ll. 43–64 'If you publish this passage... you will find yourself involved in heavy

controversy. I don't *think* there is anything defamatory, except perhaps in the passage sidelined'; on ll. 100–103 'This personal allusion should certainly be excised. (Better, I think, the whole passage in brackets than just the name)'; on ll. 143–146 'It sounds too much the result of a *personal* animosity. And a good many people know who's meant. Which being so, you should consider legal implications carefully before publishing', and on ll. 285–288 'Do you *believe* this now? If not, should you excise these lines? The test is do you *want* to say this now? And that is a point, – most of the poem is of enduring truth – or at least long-term truth – but points like this are very ephemeral. The other day you said it was all from a very transitory point of view. It doesn't strike me [like] that even on rereading it, not as regards *most* of the poem. P.S. You will certainly have to write a preface redefining your views on all these questions' (see NLS ms 29559 ff.2, 4, 5 & 8).

24. Riach [2010]: 20.

25. 'Gaelic poetry that is published with English translations cannot be assessed on its translation alone even by the most honest and perceptive of critics who do not know Gaelic.' MacLean 1985: 14.

26. See for example I: 174, 178, 182 &c.

27. Though consideration of the reception to date of 'An Cuilthionn', within the larger context of MacLean's work in poetry and prose, is beyond the scope of this introduction, it may be helpful to signal two recent contributions by younger scholars – Emma Dymock's thesis and Peter Mackay's treatment in his 2010 monograph. Both are listed in the bibliography at the close of this book.

Somhairle MacGill-Eain

AN CUILITHIONN (1939)

**from manuscript copy in Aberdeen University
Special Collections 2864**

Sorley MacLean

THE CUILLIN (1939)

**compiled from manuscript copies in National Library of
Scotland, Edinburgh ms 29559**

Dedication

Christopher Grieve 'MacDiarmid',
had I but the remnant
scraped from the dregs of a small third part
of your sharp profound great spirit,
I would put the awful Cuillin
in phosphorescence in the sky
and I would make the Island shout
with a cry of fate in the skies.
And, glorious MacDonald,
had I a third of your might,   10
I would keep our noble Skye
head-on to the waves of Europe's battle.

Part I

Sgurr Alasdair the highest sgurr
but Sgurr nan Gillean the best sgurr,
the black-blue gape-mouthed strong sgurr,
the sapling, slender, horned sgurr,
the forbidding, great, dangerous sgurr,
the sgurr of Skye above all other sgurrs.
It would become me above every place
to be on your high shoulder-blades,
striving with your rocky, grey of greys throat,
wrestling with your hard-peaked surging chest.   10

In the ascent from the corrie,
foot on shelf, finger on little edge,
chest to boulder, mouth to jutty,
on unbalanced step head undizzied,
tough arm strong, unturning,
till it grasps the skyline of your fifth pinnacle
where will break on the struggle's head
the great grey sea of gabbro waves,
knife-edge of slender high ridges,
the dark steel surge-belt;   20
an ocean whose welter is tight in rocks,
its yawning mouths permanent in narrow chasms,
its spouting everlasting in each turret,
its swelling eternal in each sgurr.

Coisrigeadh

A Chrìsdein MhicGhrèidhir, MhicDhiarmaid,
nam biodh agamsa an iarmad
à sgrùdadh bho bhàrrlach trian bheag
t' aigne ghèir, dhomhainn, mhiadmhoir
gun cuirinn-sa an Cuilithionn iargalt
'na theine-sionnachain san iarmailt,
's gun toirinn air an Eilean èigheach
a dhèanadh iolach dàin sna speuran
Agus, a Dhòmhnallaich ghlòrmhoir,
nam biodh agam trian do threòir-sa,   10
chumainn an Clàr-Sgìthe òirdheirc
ceann-caol ri tuinn àr na h-Eòrpa.

Earrann I

Sgùrr Alasdair an sgùrr as àirde
ach Sgùrr nan Gillean sgùrr an àigh dhiubh,
an sgùrr gorm-dhubh, craosach, làidir,
an sgùrr gallanach, caol, cràcach,
an sgùrr iargalta, mòr, gàbhaidh,
an sgùrr Sgitheanach thar chàich dhiubh:
gun tigeadh dhòmhsa thar gach àite
bhith air do shlinneanan àrda,
a' strì rid sgòrnan creagach, sàr-ghlas,
mo ghleac ri t' uchd cruaidh, sgorrach, bàrcach.   10

Anns an dìreadh bhon choire,
cas air sgeilpe, miar air oireig,
uchd ri ulbhaig, bial ri sgorraig,
air ceum corrach ceann gun bhoile;
righinn-ghàirdean treun gun tilleadh
gu ruig fàire do chòigeimh bidein
far am brist air ceann na spàirne
muir mhòr, chiar nan tonn gàbro,
roinn nan dromannan caola, àrda,
an crios-onfhaidh dorcha stàilinn;   20
cuan 's a luasgan teann an creagan,
a chraosan maireann an caol-eagan,
a spùtadh sìorraidh anns gach turraid,
a bhàrcadh biothbhuan anns gach sgurra.

I see the noble Island in its storm-showers
as Màiri Mhòr saw in her yearning,
and in the breaking of mist from Garsven's head
creeping over desolate summits
there rises before me the fate of my people,
the woeful history of the lovely Island.   30

Loch of lochs in Coire Lagain
were it not for the springs of Coire a' Mhadaidh,
the spring above all other springs
in the white green Fionn Corrie;
multitude of springs and fewness of men
today, yesterday and last night keeping me awake,
the miserable loss of our country's people,
clearing of peasants, exile, exploitation.
And I see the great Island in its folds
and a hoodie-crow 'couchant' on its every dun,   40
black, soft, crass hoodie-crows
who think themselves all eagles;
a flabby hoodie-crow on one dun
sitting on the slippery roosts of a castle,
a lying hoodie-crow in Portree
beak-fawning on the sleekit one.

It was the Devil himself who built this wall
to hide Rubha an Dunain
and the laird of Dunvegan shearing there,
MacLeod exploiting behind the holy ones,   50
clearing crofters and planting brutes.
The like thanks to the same One
that Loch Slapin is not to be seen
where MacDonald made the tingling shuddering cry,
where the Baron made the slavery:
he lifted crofters and planted sheep.
But Duirinish of the rocky girdles
where the disgust of the Isles was checked,
where the Dale men made a kicking
to split the castle of Dunvegan;   60
and my own country, the Braes of Clan Nicol
where the withered vigour was renewed,
where one onset was made
which brought Scotland to a turn of wakening.

Chì mi an sàr-eilean 'na shiantan
mar chunnaic Màiri Mhòr 'na h-iargain;
's an sgaoileadh ceò bho cheann na Gàrsbheinn
ag èaladh thar chreachainnean fàsa,
's ann dhiùchdas dhòmhsa càs mo chàirdean,
eachdraidh chianail an eilein àlainn. 30

Loch nan loch an Coire Lagain
mur b' e fuarain Coire a' Mhadaidh;
am fuaran os cionn gach fuarain
san Fhionn-Choire gheal, uaine:
mòran fhuaran 's gainne fhiùran
an-diugh 's an-dè 's a-raoir gam dhùsgadh,
call dòrainneach luchd ar dùthcha,
togail tuatha, fògairt, spùilleadh.
'S chì mi an t-Eilean mòr 'na lùban,
gurrach feannaig air gach dùn ann, 40
feannagan dubha, boga, claona,
ar leò gur h-iolaire gach aon dhiubh;
feannag phlamach air aon dùn,
'na suidhe air sparran sleamhna tùir,
feannag bhreugach am Port Rìgh
a' sodal-guib ris an tè shlìom.

'S e an Diabhal fhèin a thog am mùr seo
a chur air falach Rubha 'n Dùnain
is Fear Dhùn Bheagain ann a' rusgadh,
MacLeòid air cùl nan naomh a' spùilleadh, 50
a' togail tuatha 's a' cur bhrùidean;
am buidheachas eile don aon Fhear
a chionn nach fhaicear Loch Shlaopain
far an d' rinn MacDhòmhnaill gaoir ann,
far an d' rinn am Morair daorsa –
thog e tuath 's gun chuir e caoraich.
Ach Diùrainis nan criosan creige
far an do chaisgeadh sgreamh nan eilean,
far an tug na Dalaich breabadh
gu sgoltadh Caisteal Dhùn Bheagain. 60
'S mo thìr fhìn, Bràighe Chloinn MhicNeacail,
far an do dh'ùraich an treòir sheacte,
far an tugadh aon ionnsaigh
a thug Alba gu car dùsgaidh.

A croft that would please my kind,
a part of Minginish in heaven;
a bit of Trotternish in glory,
land that would suit my desire;
a piece of Waternish in blessedness
above the Green Isle in goodness;   70
Bracadale of the ever-rain-green swards
that would make lovely the causeways of hell;
and I would hear from the bottom of the pit of torment
the snorting of the bridled Stallion of Waterstein.
Brown-green Sleat of the beautiful women,
great, wide Strath of the noble pinnacles,
to them I'd give my love together
while the skull of Blaven stood bald over the straits.
But Brittle Shoulder to me myself
though it would reach in price   80
the sheep of Scorrybreck and thrice
what was there disbursed
for the sake of the patrician trafficking.
And then I would stand
above the top of Seasgach Corrie
contemplating the rocky Cuillin
from the Sguman promontory to the crevasse
that splits Sgurr an Fheadain;
and then I would tell Michael
or Gabriel, unashamed,   90
to take what they wanted
east, west, south and north,
and I would give their heart's fill
to them and to every pair
of angels or archangels,
of sheep cattle and sheep-pens
so that they would clear out of my neighbourhood
and leave Skyemen in their place.

Then everything would be in order
if only I were Seton Gordon   100
who will not mention an unclean history
that displeases our kind gentry.

And everything else would go smoothly
if only I were Kennedy-Fraser:

Croit a chòrdadh ri mo ghnè
roinn de Mhinginis air nèimh;
pìos de Thròndairnis an glòir
fearann thigeadh ri mo dheòin;
bloigh de Bhatairnis am Flaitheas
thar an Eilein Uaine am maitheas.　70
Bràcadal nam braon-ghorm suthainn
chuireadh loinn air cabhsair Iuthairn;
's gun cluinninn bho ghrunnd sloc a' phèin
seitrich Eist Bhatairsteinn air srèin.
Slèite dhonn-ghorm nam bàn bòidheach,
srath farsaing, mòr nam baideal òirdheirc,
dhaibhsan bheirinn mo ghaol còmhla
is claigeann Blàbheinn maol thar òban.
Ach Guala Bhreatail leam dhomh fhìn
ged a ruigidh i am prìs　80
caoraich Sgoirebreac is trì-
fillte 'na dhìoladh bhuapa
air sgàth fiachan an uasail.
Agus an uair sin 's ann sheasainn
os cionn mullach Coire an t-Seasgaich
ag amharc air a' Chuilithionn chreagach,
bho Sh ròin an Sgumain thun na h-eige
a tha a' sgoltadh Sgùrr an Fheadain;
's gun canainn fhìn an sin ri Mìcheal
no ri Gàbriel, gun mhì-ghean,　90
iad a ghabhail na bha bhuapa,
an ear 's an iar is deas is tuathail;
agus bheirinn làn an cridhe
dhaibhsan is do gach dithis
ainglean no àrd-ainglean,
de chaoraich, crodh agus faingean,
los gun seachnadh iad mo nàbachd
a chur Sgitheanach 'nan àite.

Gum biodh a h-uile ni an òrdan
nam bu mhise Seton Gòrdan,　100
gun cuirinn tuairisgeul air dòigh dhaibh
ri maithean bùirdeasach a chòrdadh.

Agus bhiodh gach eile rèidh ann
nam bu mhise Kennedy-Fraser:

for I would weave adulterated music
to make a crooning in their ears;
telling of you, doubtless
I would make silk of your rocks,
I would make fairy-music of the Terror,
I would drink of the Well of the Gentry.   110

But who at all would be pleased
although I were Neil MacLeod,
for he saw gloomy corries
with the travail of his country.

Some put the curse of waving bracken
on the glens they had to leave,
and if they did, heavy is their prophecy
on the towers highest today.

I see the castle of Dunvegan
one sheet-flame of bracken,   120
and I see the great Sleat residence
blossoming, towers and foundations.

I see villages that were in Brae Eynort
rivers in the pouring of bracken,
and I see the faint Twilight of the Gael
flare with its bracken-light to heaven.

But I saw Kennedy-Fraser
defiling music with the flowers of that shrub;
and I saw a little mouthy old woman
with froth of that green colour about her mouth.   130
Since all those have been seen –
Devil am I! – I'll ask no more.

But if there is a civil question,
where does the disgust of the worthy Island reach?
I say a creature, even if a Skyeman,
who fawns on a rump of chieftains,
a vain, black, slimy hoodie-crow,
a base, jealous creature,
cowardly, scheming, sneaking,
slippery, loquacious, weak, oily,   140

shnìomhainn ceòl air mhòr-thruailleadh
a dhèanadh cagarsaich 'nan cluasan.
An iomradh dhaibh ort, gun teagamh,
dhèanainn sìoda de do chreagan,
dhèanainn ceòl-sìthe den Fhuathas,
dh'òlainn à Tobar nan Uaislean.   110

Ach cò an neach a bhiodh air dòigh
ged bu mhise Niall MacLeòid,
oir chunnaic esan coireachan ùdlaidh
mar ri allaban a dhùthcha.

Dhùraich cuid fraineach fhàsmhor
do na glinn a b' fheudar fhàgail;
ma dhùraich, gur trom an fhàisneachd
air na tùir an-diugh as àirde.

Chì mi Caisteal Dhùn Bheagain
'na aon chaoir lasair frainich,   120
agus an aitreabh mhòr Shlèiteach
fo bhàrr-gùc, tùir is stèidhean.

Chì mi bailtean bha 'm Bràighe Aoineart
fo thaomadh frainich 'nan aibhnean;
's chì mi feasgar fann nan Gàidheal,
leus frainich bhuaithe ruigheachd nèimhe.

Ach chunnaic mi NicUalraig-Fhriseal
a' truailleadh ciùil le flùr a' phris ud;
's chì mi cailleach bheag, chabach,
cop ma beul 's an tuar glas air.   130
A chionn gum facas iadsan uile –
an Diabhal mi! – chan iarr mi tuilleadh.

Ach, ma dh'fheòraichear gun fhiatachd
dè ruigeas sgreamh san Eilean fhiachail,
their mi creutair nach e Sgitheanach
's e sliomaireachd ri fuidheall nan triathan.
Feannag fhaoin, dhubh, shlìomach,
creutair suarach 's e ri iadach,
gealtach, cuilbheartach, snèagach,
sleamhainn, labhar, lag, lèagach,   140

turning, twisting, vapid, chattering,
sleek, fawning, sweet, lying.

He said I would never never attain bourgeoisie
because my tongue's so brutal,
and I know I'll never reach the insidiousness
respectable in a demure tongue.

But, never mind, I'll let him be
though he goes through Inverness
sucking position like a stoat
feeding on the soft slavers of prematurely-laid eggs: 150
he sucked many from both sides.

One day and I on Sgurr a' Ghreadaidh,
standing on the high notched knife-edge,
looking down on the Corrie of Loneliness
through the surging mists around me,
in a breaking of the drift
there glittered a flash of gold on the wings
of an eagle passing below,
along the flanking walls:
above the glory of all bird-life to me   160
the gold gleam of the Skye bird.
I turned, and behind
Minginish was in the sweep of my eye
and green Bracadale
and Duirinish and Trotternish beyond.
There arose the glory of the excellent Island,
arose, but came another thought:
what to the Skyeman the significance of my desire
when he rises bourgeois-ward?

In a big hall of London   170
gathered the bourgeois of Clan Leod,
a little, yattering English female
arranging pomp.

And shouted every hill and mountain-meadow
from Sgurr Thuilm to Great Helval
in joy of the turn of events
from the days of the Great Ship.

curach, carach, baoth, bialach,
slìom, sodalach, milis, briagach.

Gun tubhairt e nach ruiginn bùirdeas
a chionn mo theanga bhith cho brùideil;
's tha fhios a'm fhìn nach ruig mi an liùigeadh
th' aigesan 'na theangaidh chiùigich.

Coma leam, cha bhi mi ris
ged shiubhail e feadh Inbhir Nis
a' deothal inbhe mar an nios
a' deothal sraimh bhoga mhaothag;   150
dheoc esan mòran bho gach taobh ann.

Latha dhomh air Sgùrr a' Ghreadaidh
'nam sheasamh air an roinn àird, eagaich,
ag amharc sìos air Coire 'n Uaigneis
tro bhàrcadh a' cheò mun cuairt orm,
ann am bristeadh an t-siabain
dheàlraich aiteal òir air sgiathan
iolaire dol seachad shìos ann
tarsainn nam ballachan cliathaich.
Is dhòmhsa thar glòir gach ianlaith   160
aiteal òir an eòin Sgitheanaich;
thionndaidh mi 's air mo chùlaibh
bha Minginis am beachd mo shùilean,
agus Bràcadal uaine,
Diùrainis is Tròndairnis bhuaipe;
dhiùchd dhomh glòir an t-sàr-Eilein,
dhiùchd, ach thàinig smuain eile:
dè don Sgitheanach fàth mo rùin –
an uair a dhìreas e gu bùirdeas?

Ann an talla mòr an Lunnainn   170
chruinnich bùirdeasaich Chloinn Leòid,
cabag phlamach, bheag à Sasann
a' cur fleadhachais air dòigh

agus ghlaodh gach cnoc is cluaineag
bho Sgùrr Thuilm gu Healghabhal Mhòir
an àbhachdas mar thachair nithean
bho làithean an t-Soithich Mhòir.

Cried many a mountain-bluff and spring
from Bruach na Frìthe to Ardmore;
came many a homesick spirit   180
from far land and the great ocean.

Was heard a faint eerie voice
on the gusts of the west:
"Ben Thota-Gormuil of the beautiful men
Ben Duagraich my love and darling."

Arose the bare, cold bones
from the welter of Kyle Vatersay;
their dryness and hardness
clanked laughter to that merriment.

Came the spirit of Neil the poet   190
lamenting the glen where he was young;
and came Màiri Mhòr
to tell of the deed of Macleod.

And every other who lamented
the speckled mountain and high creachann
and the hateful injustice of the people of the Dun
who put his back to their shores.

Came John, man of men,
from St Congan's down in the Glen;
his mirth did not increase   200
listening to that gabbling.

One evening and I on Sgurr na Banachdaich
ghosts rose in the lateness,
on every pinnacle of the Cuillin
the image of a people's spoiler rocking.
Straddle-legged on Sgurr a' Ghreadaidh
was a rabble of the lairds of Dunvegan,
and on the Tooth of Vaisteir
the barons, an ugly troop;
south-west on Garsven's head   210
was seen Doctor Martin
and MacAlister of Aird was
stalking about the top of Blaven;

Dh'èigh iomadh fireach agus fuaran
bho Bhruaich na Frìthe gu Àird Mhòir;
thàinig iomadh spiorad iargain 180
à fearann cian 's às a' chuan mhòr.

Chualas guth fann, tiamhaidh
air osagan na h-àird an iar:
"Beinn Thota-Gormail nam fear sgiamhach,
Beinn Dubhagraich, m' ionam 's mo chiall."

Dh'èirich na cnàmhan loma, fuara
à luasgadh Caolas Bhatarsaigh;
gun d' rinn an tiormachd-san 's an cruas
glag gàire ris an aiteas ud.

Thàinig spiorad Nèill, am bàrd, 190
a' caoidh a' ghlinne 'n robh e òg;
agus thàinig Màiri Mhòr
thoirt iomraidh air gnìomh MhicLeòid.

Agus gach eile a bha a' caoidh
na beinne brice is creachainn àird,
is fòirneart shanntach luchd an Dùin
a chuir an cùl-san ris an tràigh.

Dh'èirich Iain, an siad,
à Cille Chòmhghain shìos sa Ghleann;
cha deachaidh aoibhneas-san am miad 200
ag èisteachd a' ghoileim a bha ann.

Feasgar dhomh air Sgùrr na Banachdaich
dh'èirich samhlaidhean san anmoch;
air gach baideal den Chuilithionn
bha riochd spùillear-sluaigh a' tulgadh.
Gòbhlach air Sgùrr a' Ghreadaidh
bha gràisg de thriathan Dhùn Bheagain,
agus air Fiacail a' Bhàisteir
morairean, am prasgan grànda.
An iar-dheas air ceann na Gàrsbheinn 210
chunnacas an Dotair Màrtainn
's bha MacAlasdair na h-Àirde
ag èaladh mu mhullach Blàbheinn;

Big Ewen was on Sgurr an Sgumain
looking down on Rubha an Dunain
and Cameron near him,
contemplating the Minginish they had shorn;
east on the skyline of Sgurr nan Gillean
arose the likeness of Major Fraser;
and on their hunkers on the Bidean   220
were Ballingall and Mr Gibbon;
alone on the thigh of Bruaich
were Tormore and Alasdair Roy;
Mackay and Rainy on Dun Can,
no gentler shades.

And in every corrie under
every fawning liar who helped them,
who earned the cream of the big rewards,
every factor, lawyer and gent
who ate and licked around,   230
who stole and drove and plundered.
From every corrie and sgurr
surged the one hymn in unison:
"With wealth and rank
ever goes the devotion of the talented;
all they want will come and be given to them;
'noblesse oblige' and eternal law."
Burst on me the hard cry of their slogan:
"Lazy, inefficient peasants,
oppress them, clear them and sweep them,   240
break them, drive them and rout them."
The ghost band began a dance
and that was the auspicious exercise,
the coronach of the people leaving
mingled in the din of the gentlemen.
Over width of sea and march
answered Franco of Spain
and the grey Pope of Rome
and wily Chamberlain
and the revel-shout of Odin.   250
Appeared Vienna and Barcelona,
Shanghai, Hamburg and Harbin,
Calcutta, Boreraig and London,
Prague, Naples and Munich –

bha Eòghann mòr air Sgùrr an Sgumain
's e ag amharc sìos air Rubha 'n Dùnain,
agus an Camshronach dlùth ris,
a' coimhead Minginis a rùisg iad.
An ear, air fàire Sgùrr nan Gillean,
dh'èirich fiamh a' Mhàidseir Friseal,
agus 'nan gurraich air a' Bhidean   220
bha Ballingall is Maighstir Gibbon;
leotha fhèin air slios na Bruaich
bha Tòrr Mòr is Alasdair Ruadh;
MacÀidh is Rèanaidh air Dùn Cana,
's cha b' iadsan bu chaoine tannasg.

Agus anns gach coire fòdhpa
gach breugaire sodail chum riù còmhnadh,
a choisinn bàrr am mòr-dhuaisean,
gach bàillidh, fear-lagha is uasal,
a dh'ith 's a dh'imlich mun cuairt,   230
a shlaod 's a spùill agus a ruaig:
bho gach coire agus sgurra
bhàrc an aon laoidh cuideachd:
"An ceann beairteis agus uaisle
gheibhear a-chaoidh ùidh nam buadhmhor;
thig is bheirear dhaibh mar dh'iarrar;
siud an comain 's an lagh sìorraidh."
Bhrùchd orm gàir chruaidh an iolaich:
"Tuath na leisge 's na droch ghiullachd,
claoidh iad, tog iad agus sguab iad,   240
brist iad, iomain iad is ruaig iad."
Thòisich na manaidhean air dannsa
's gum b' e e siud an iomairt sheannsail,
corranach an t-sluaigh a' fàgail
an ceann gliongarsaich nan àrmann.
Thar farsaingeachd cuain agus àrainn
fhreagair Franco na Spàinne,
agus Pàp glas na Ròimhe
agus Chamberlain na seòltachd
agus caithream iolach Òdain.   250
Dhiùchd Bhinn is Barsalòna,
Seangaidh, Hamburg agus Hàirbinn,
Calcat, Boraraig is Lunnainn,
Pràtha is Napalais agus Muinich;

every poor room under the sun's eye
to which comes the cry and extremity of the humble,
like the wail throughout Strath
which Geikie heard and did not conceal.
And though another voice split the fog,
Lenin, Marx, Maclean,   260
Thaelmann, Dimitrov, MacPherson,
Mao Tse Tung and his men,
the devilish revelry would drown
the voice of the wise and cry of the tortured.
And though in the face of distress
I had the strength and courage of Stalin,
the screeching noise would oppress me
while the great Cuillin reeled dizzily.

On Sgurr Alasdair, in the glitter
and silver loveliness of the moon,   270
that cry clung to my hearing,
pierced and spoiled my strength's marrow.
And though our Ben Lee stood towering
above every sgurr and brae of them,
and though I saw the rocks of Valtos
excelling the birds' career,
and though the Ford of the Three Burns were
like the Volga, full and slow,
the hard screech of the Cuillin
would cleave to my hearing, a distress.   280
And though one night in the hall
of my beloved well-known Portree
I heard the old hero Donald MacCallum,
that cry alone will remain;
and until the whole Red Army together
comes battle-marching across Europe,
that song of wretchedness will seep
into my ears and my heart.

Thousands of poor men rotting,
mouldering carcasses in Spain,   290
and hundreds of thousands in China,
a sacrifice of most distant effect;
the many Thaelmanns in Germany
and the one or two John Macleans in Scotland,

gach seòmar truagh fo roisg na grèine
don tig gaoir nam bochd 's an èiginn,
mar a' ghaoir air feadh an t-Sratha
a chuala Geikie is a bhrath e.
'S gcd sgoilteadh guth eile an ceathach,
Lenin, Marx no MacGill-Eain,   260
Thaelmann, Dimitrov, MacMhuirich,
Mao Tse Tung no a chuideachd,
bhàthadh an caithream diabhlaidh
guth nan saoi is glaodh nam piantan.
'S ged bhiodh neart is misneachd Stàilin
agamsa ri uchd na h-àmhghair,
chlaoidhteadh le sgread na fuaim mi
's an Cuilithionn mòr a' dol 'na thuaineal.

Air Sgùrr Alasdair ri lainnir
's àilleachd airgid na gealaich,   270
lean an glaodh ud ri mo chlaistneachd
dhrùidh is mhill e smior mo neairt-sa.
'S ged sheasadh ar Beinn Lì an uachdar
thar gach sgùrr agus bruaich dhiubh,
's ged a chithinn creagan Bhaltois
a' toirt bàrr air rèis na h-ealtainn,
's ged bhiodh Beul Àtha nan Trì Allt
mar a' Bholga làn is mall,
leanadh sgread cruaidh a' Chuilithinn
ri mo chlaistneachd 'na dhuilghinn.   280
'S ged chuala mi oidhche an talla
Phort Rìgh mo ghaoil, m' eòil is m' aithne
an seann seud, Dòmhnall MacCaluim,
siud a' ghaoir a-mhàin a mhaireas;
is gus am bi an t-Arm Dearg còmhla
ri caismeachd tarsainn na Roinn Eòrpa,
drùidhidh iorram na truaighe
air mo chridhe 's air mo chluasan.

Mìltean de dhaoine bochd air cnàmh
'nan closaich lobhte anns an Spàinn,   290
's na ceudan mìle anns an t-Sìn,
ìobairt air am faide brìgh.
A liuthad Thaelmann anns a' Ghearmailt
is "John Maclean" no a dhà an Albainn,

MacPherson in the earth at St Congan's
and the Great Island languishing,
and I here on sporting rocks,
and Scotland rotting in sick slumber.   298

Part II

Rocky terrible Cuillin,
you are with me in spite of life's horror.
The first day I ascended your black wall,
I thought the Judgement was descending;
the first day I kissed your cheek,
its likeness was the face of the Great Flood;
the first day I kissed your mouth,
Hell opened its two jaws;
the first day I lay on your breast
I thought I saw the loading   10
of the heavy swift skies
for the destructive shaking of the earth.
Reaching the blade-back of Bruach na Frìthe
I came in sight of the savageness of the country –
a heavy black-red mantle of the clouds,
the storm winds in the[ir] mouths;
about the girdling summits of the awesome sgurrs,
a dun opening in the firmament,
under the low red-black compact pall
of brindled dark surly clouds,   20
congregation of the horrors of the elements,
gathering of the storms for exercise.
Hurricane clangour of every blast
about the grim, savage pinnacles;
shaking and quivering of the yelling blast
about the battlements of every grey bare-swept summit;
the sides and thighs of the Cuillin
stripped naked for the giant wrestling,
with no flesh on them but the scree
thrown headlong in cairns   30
from hip and knees
down to the depth of the gloomy abysses.
Compared with the giant Son of Cuillin
neither Goll nor Fionn nor monster

Mac a' Phearsain fo ùir Chille Chòmhghain
's an t-Eilean mòr glè rongach,
mise an seo air creagan spòrsa,
Alba a' lobhadh an suain bhreòite. 298

Earrann II

A Chuilithinn chreagaich an uabhais,
tha thusa mar rium dh'aindeoin fuathais.
A' chiad là dhìrich mi do mhùr dubh,
shaoil leam am Breitheanas bhith tùirling;
a' chiad là phòg mi do ghruaidh,
b' e choimeas fiamh an Tuile Ruaidh;
a' chiad là phòg mi do bhial,
dh'fhosgail Iutharn a dhà ghiall;
a' chiad là laigh mi air t' uchd-sa
ar leam gum faca mi an luchdadh 10
aig na speuran troma, falbhaidh
gu crith sgriosail na talmhainn.
'S mi ruigheachd roinn-dhruim Bruach na Frìthe,
nochd mi allaidheachd na tìre,
brat trom, dubh-dhearg air na neòil,
doineannachd nan gaoth 'nam beòil;
mu bhàrr cearcall nan sgùrr iargalt
fosgladh lachdann anns an iarmailt
fo bhrat ìosal, dearg-dhubh, dùmhail
nan sgòth riabhach, dorcha, mùgach, 20
coitheanal uabhais nan dùilean,
cruinneachadh nan sian gu lùth-chleas.
Srannaich ghailleanach gach sgala
mu na biodan gruamach, allaidh,
crathadh is crith na h-osaig-èighich
mu bhaidealan gach creachainn lèithe,
sliosan is slèistean a' Chuilithinn
lom, nochdta ri gleac an fhuirbhidh,
gun de dh'fheòil orra ach an sgàirneach
a thilgeadh comhair a cinn 'na càrnaich 30
bho do chruachann 's bho do ghlùinean
sìos gu grunnd nan glomhar ùdlaidh.
Ris an fhaobairne Mac Cuilithinn
cha robh Goll no Fionn no uilebheist

devised by man's imagination
was more than a louse on a worm's back
compared with Cuchulainn in his war gear.
What likeness knee or calf,
chest, thigh or mortal shoulder
to the ramparts of grim precipices   40
black with ice or with cold wet ooze –
to the heaving chest of the high mountain bluffs
surging in proud crags
like the mother-breasts of the world,
erect with the universe's concupiscence?
I saw the horn of Sgurr Dearg
rising in furious challenge
in the haste of the skies
and, throwing the stars in spindrift,
the trinity of the Sguman risen.   50

On Sgurr Dubh of the Two Hills
a voice came to my ear singing,
Patrick Mor and his music mourning
all the children of mankind.
And an evening on Garsven
there was another music that came,
'Maol Donn' and its theme of love-fullness
breaking the hearts of lovely tunes.
In the white lying-down of the sun,
the west gave to my sight   60
the gleam of seas behind Barra
going round the islands of our blood;
and the great Island in its storm-showers,
as seen by the homesick eye
that looked on America while it desired
Grula, Brunnal and the two hills of Scarral,
that surged in the pulsations of the blood;
Duirinish of the high headlands,
Minginish of the abundant breast,
soft Bracadale of the lovely pap hollows   70
washed by the hidden kiss of the sea,
and the great Aird of Strath Swordale,
the long smooth thigh of the cold mountains
on which heather and grass lie high in jewels
like the clustered gold-lit hair of my beloved.

a dheachdadh le mac-meanmna daonnda
ach mar mhìol air druim na daolaig
ri Cù Chulainn 'na arm-aodach.
Dè an coimeas glùn no calpa,
uchd, sliasaid no guala thalmhaidh
ri ballachan nan stalla gruamach,   40
dubh le deigh no snighe fuaraidh,
ri uchdaich nam fireach àrda
'nan creagan uamharra bàrcadh
mar chìochan-màthar an t-saoghail
stòite, 's an cruinne-cè ri gaoladh.
Chunnaic mi Adharc an Sgùrr Dheirg
ag èirigh ann an dùbhlan feirg
a thoirt deifir do na speuran,
's 'nan cathadh a thilgeil nan reultan
trianaid an Sgumain air èirigh.   50

Air Sgùrr Dubh an Dà Bheinn
thàinig guth gum chluais a' seinn,
Pàdraig Mòr 's a cheòl a' caoineadh
uile chlann a' chinne-daonna.
Agus feasgar air a' Ghàrsbheinn
bha ceòl eile ann a thàinig,
Maol Donn agus ùrlar sàth-ghaoil
a' bristeadh cridhe nam fonn àlainn.
Ann an laighe geal na grèine
bha an àird an iar a' toirt dom lèirsinn   60
lainnir a' chuain air cùl Bharraigh
's e 'g iathadh eileanan ar fala;
agus an t-Eilean mòr 'na shiantan
mar chunnacas le sùil an iargain
a nochd Ameireaga 's i ag iarraidh
Grùla, Brunnal, dà chnoc Sgarrail
a bhàrc am plosgartaich na fala,
Diùrainis nan rubhachan àrda,
Minginis a' bhroillich lànmhoir,
Bràcadal bhog nan cìoch-lag àlainn   70
gan nighe le falach-phòig an t-sàile;
agus Àird mhòr Shrath Shuardail,
sliasaid fhada, rèidh nam fuar-bheann,
fraoch is feur 'nan leugan shuas oirr'
mar chuachan òr-laist' ceann mo luaidhe.

Rising from the bog-myrtle of Rubha an Dunain
in sharp fragrant wafts,
the love and grief of the peasants of the land,
scattered for exploiters' wealth;
on the green hill-slopes   80
the mists of history wound,
the heart, blood and flesh of my people
in a nightmare on the fields;
Minginish gathering into a fold
Waternish and Sleat,
Trotternish, Raasay and Rona,
Duirinish and the Strath and Soay
in the soft drizzle.
And, heavy on the slumber of the moorland,
the hardship and poverty of the thousands   90
of the peasantry and lowly of the land,
my kin and my own people.
And though their fate did not make
the sore world-cry of Spain;
and though their dispensation did not make
a mantle of blood on the face of the firmament,
as Marlowe saw the blood of Christ
and Leonhard the blood of Liebknecht;
and though no news came
of their destruction's night   100
to rival the world agony of grief,
the fall of the Asturians in glory,
their lot was the lot of peasant and poor,
hardship, want and injury,
ever since the masses of the lands
were deceived by ruling-class, state and civil law,
by priests, ministers and prostitutes,
who sold their souls for the price
which the bitches of the world have earned
since the ruling-classes piled capital.   110
I'd see them in one drowning-sack,
ruling-class, lawyers and popes,
thrown over the Stallion
through the middle depth of the surging sea
down to the hell of gentry.
And, God, were I in Dunvegan
having a big gun on a crag,

'S ag èirigh bho roid Rubha 'n Dùnain
anns na tlàman geura cùbhraidh,
gaol is bròn tuath na dùthcha
a sgapadh le beairteas an spùillidh.
Air na leathadan uaine   80
ceò na h-eachdraidh ga shuaineadh,
cridhe, fuil is feòil mo dhaoine,
an trom-laighe air na raointean;
Minginis a' cròdhadh le chèile
Bhatairnis agus Slèite,
Tròndairnis, Ratharsair is Rònaigh,
Diùrainis, an Srath is Sòdhaigh
anns a' mhèath-chiuchar còmhla.
Agus trom air suain na frìthe
cruadh-chàs is bochdainn nam mìltean   90
de thuath is de mhith-shluagh na tìre,
mo chàirdean is mo chuideachd fhìn iad.
Agus ged nach d' rinn an càs-san
gaoir ghoirt saoghail na Spàinne,
agus ged nach d' rinn an dìol-san
brat fala air aodann na h-iarmailt
mar chunnaic Marlowe fuil Chrìosda
agus Leonhard fuil Liebknecht,
agus ged nach d' fhuaradh fios
air oidhche challa an sgrios   100
a ràinig gal saoghail a' bhròin,
tuiteam nan Asturaidheach le glòir,
b' e an càs-san càs na tuath 's nam bochd,
an cruadhchàs, a' ghainne is an lochd
bhon mhealladh mòr-shluagh nan tìrean
le uachdarain, le stàt 's lagh sìobhalt,
le sagart, ministear is strìopaich
a reic an anam air a' phrìs ud
a fhuair gallachan an t-saoghail
bhon chàrn uachdarain am maoineas.   110
Nach robh iad an aon phoca-bàthaidh,
uachdarain, fir-lagha is pàpan,
air an tilgeil thar an Àigich
tro ghrinneal meadhan a' chuain bhàrcaich
sìos gu Iutharna nan àrmann.
'S a Dhia, nach robh mi an Dùn Bheagain
is gunna mòr agam air creagan –

I'd pound the castle of the wretches
to a soft eggshell in the crannies;
and were I in Sleat   120
using the same armament,
I'd throw the towers of the foul battlements
whence they might not rise.

Another day upon the mountains
and the Asturians risen again,
oh, God, that I would see the steel of their challenge
descending on the masses of the Cuillin!
Oh best men on the face of the earth,
though your case and dispensation was chill with death,
you brought shame to the cheeks   130
who felt the majesty of your hardihood
and suffered to see your burden,
the cowardice and foul perfidy of others.
Would that the black Sgurr nan Gillean
and every other sgurr and pinnacle
would rise as memorials to your hardship
and great, awful valour.

Another day upon the mountains
and the Skyemen not yet risen;
another day this upon the moors   140
and the great Island losing its people;
another day this, dappling the firmament,
that will give no satisfaction to their yearning;
another day this, breaking the horizon
that will see neither their joy nor laughter;
another day this before my eyes
that will give no respite to the desires
that follow each year
as it creeps to its gloaming.
I am without my people   150
since the men of Braes have failed,
and there was neither a MacCrimmon nor MacPherson
wth us this year nor last;
and if I reach tomorrow,
my portion will be in the shame.

Another day this upon the mountains
and great Scotland under doom of beasts;

phronnainn caisteal nam fùidse
'na phlaosg maothaig anns na cùiltean.
Agus nach robh mi ann an Slèite,   120
a' cur an aoin airm gu èifeachd –
thilginn tùir nam baideal breuna
far nach rachadh aca air èirigh.

Seo latha eile air na slèibhtean
's na h-Asturaidhich a-rithist air èirigh:
a Dhia, nach fhaicinn cruas an dùbhlain
air meallan a' Chuilithinn a' tùirling!
O fheara 's fheàrr air clàr an t-saoghail,
ged a bha bhur càs-se 's bhur dìol aognaidh,
thug sibh nàire do na gruaidhean   130
a dh'fhairich mòralachd bhur cruadail,
's a dh'fhuiling faicinn bhur n-èire
fo ghealtachd is cealgaireachd na brèige.
Nach èireadh Sgùrr dubh nan Gillean
's gach sgùrr eile agus binnean
mar chùirn-chuimhne air bhur cruadhchàs
agus air gaisgeachd mhòir an uabhais.

Seo latha eile air na slèibhtean
's na Sgitheanaich fhathast gun èirigh;
seo latha eile air na raointean   140
's an t-Eilean Mòr a' call a dhaoine;
seo latha eile a' breacadh iarmailt
nach toir sàsachadh don iargain:
seo latha eile a' bristeadh fàire
nach fhaic an aoibhneas no an gàire;
seo latha eile ri mo shùilean
nach toir faochadh do na rùintean
a tha a' leantainn gach bliadhna
is i a' snàgadh gu a ciaradh.
Chan eil agamsa mo dhaoine   150
a chionn fir a' Bhràighe bhith air aomadh;
's cha robh MacCruimein no MacMhuirich
ann am-bliadhna no an-uiridh;
agus ma ruigeas mi a-màireach,
bidh mo chuibhreann anns an tàmailt.

Seo latha eile air na slèibhtean
is Alba mhòr fo bhinn bhèistean,

her thousands of poor exploited,
beguiled to a laughing-stock,
flattered, doctored,   160
cleansed with the unction
of the godly divines
who make a bourgeois of Christ;
and the press of Clyde's capitalism,
to which soul and talent are sold,
where poetry is assessed
according to Lithgow and his gents,
where MacDiarmid's name is unheard
because he would not pay them interest,
where the coxcomb and buffoon burst   170
with the food of the weak infant of the backlands.

Another day this upon the mountains
and white Scotland a porridge of filth,
England and France together
a dung-heap under bourgeois capitalism,
great Germany a delirium of falsehood
and Spain a cemetery where valour lies,
the slippery, oily pope of Rome
slickly defending bourgeoisdom
and the landlords of Poland   180
the laughing-stock of Europe.

Another day this upon the mountains
and the bourgeoisie striving
to cut every throat
on the bodies of the people of Europe;
another day this on the mountains
and God beating a retreat
in spite of the Creed's bishops
and its acute ministers;
another day this upon the uplands   190
and bourgeoisdom a bog of scum,
swallowing tens of thousands together,
the one quagmire of Europe.

I see the chained sons of men
floundering in Mararaulin,
Chamberlain, Hitler, Mussolini

a mìltean bhochdan air an spùilleadh,
air am mealladh 'nan cùis-bhùrta,
air am briagadh, air an cungadh,   160
air an glanadh leis an ungadh
aig na diadhairean diadhaidh
tha a' dèanamh bùirdeasach de Chrìosda.
Agus clò-bhualadh maoineas Chluaidh
don reicear anam agus buaidh,
far am faighear meas na Bàrdachd
a-rèir Litchù agus 'àrmann,
far nach cluinnear ainm MhicDhiarmaid
a chionn nach pàigheadh e an riadh dhaibh,
far an spreadh an sgeamaig 's an t-ùmpaidh   170
le biadh naoidhean lag nan cùiltean.

Seo latha eile air na slèibhtean,
is Alba gheal 'na brochan breunaid,
Sasann agus an Fhraing còmhla
fo mhaoineas bùirdeasach 'nan òtraich;
a' Ghearmailt mhòr 'na boile brèige
's an Spàinn 'na cladh san laigh an treuntas;
Pàp sleamhainn, slìomach na Ròimhe
a' dìon nam bùirdeasach gu seòlta,
agus uachdarain nam Pòlach   180
'nan culaidh-mhagaidh na Roinn-Eòrpa.

Seo latha eile air na slèibhtean
is bùirdeasachd a' dèanamh streupa
fiach an geàrr i gach sgòrnan
a tha air bodhaig clann na h-Eòrpa;
seo latha eile air na slèibhtean
is Dia a' gabhail an ratreuta
a dh'aindeoin easbaigean na crèide
agus mhinistearan geura.
Seo latha eile air na cruachan   190
's a' bhùirdeasachd 'na boglaich ruaimle
a' slugadh nan deich mìle còmhla,
aon shùil-chruthaich na Roinn-Eòrpa.

Chì mi clann nan daoine fo shlabhraidh
a' plubartaich am Mararabhlainn,
Chamberlain, Hitler 's Mussolini

and godly Franco
guiding every troop
to drowning in the morass.
Oh Mararaulin moss,   200
ghosts were not your wont,
though you heard the mountain clangour
the day the Desperate Battle was fought,
and though you heard the lamentation
the day Minginish lost its people.
What will avail our Island
another Festubert and Loos
when there are more names than enough
on the stone of Portree under the lion's arse?
It is devilish little that came to your enjoyment   210
though you took Beaumont-Hamel,
and if you survive, you will see
other rotters with the O.B.E.
and wealthy old women in pleasant Sligachan,
guzzling and viewing the Cuillin.   215

Part III

Oh morass of Mararaulin,
you are the fortunate bog;
you will swallow Europe's people,
America's and Asia's altogether,
your virtues will grow and spread,
you great red-scum quagmire.
You are streaming and rising,
drowning in your great flood of falsehood
all that is hospitable, generous and straight,
you shaking bog of every land.   10
You have grown great, soft, fat and rich
swallowing the land of the unfortunate,
mantle of fat on the red-scum
drowning thousands of wretches.
Many a peak and many mountains
have you put under with your filth,
you have drowned God in the heavens,
you will drown the Cuillin and Braes,
you have drowned Minginish before

is Franco diadhaidh a' strì riù
a' toirt seòladh do gach fòirne
a dh'ionnsaigh bàthaidh anns a' mhòintich.
Och, a mhòinteach Mararabhlainn,   200
cha bu dual dhutsa taibhsean
ged a chuala tu a' ghailbheinn
an là a chuireadh an Cath Gailbheach,
's ged a chuala tu an caoineadh
an là chaill Minginis a daoine.
Dè nì siud do ar n-eilean,
Festubert eile is Loos eile,
is barrachd ainmean na dh'fhòghnas
air cloich Phort Ruigh'dh fo thòin an leòmhainn?
'S e diabhlaidh beag a bha gur mealtainn   210
ged ghabh sibhse Beaumont-Hamel;
's ma bhios sibh beò a-rithist, chì
sibh garraich eile le O.B.E.
is cailleachan beairteach an Sligeachan suilbhir
ag ithe 's a' faicinn a' Chuilithinn.   215

Earrann III

Och, a mhòinteach Mararabhlainn,
's tusa fhèin a' bhoglach sheannsail,
's tu a shluigeas sluagh na h-Eòrpa,
Ameireaga 's na h-Àisia còmhla;
fàsaidh is sgaoilidh do bhuadhan,
a shùil-chruthaich mhòr ruaimlich:
tha thu sruthadh 's tha thu 'g èirigh,
a' bàthadh 'na do thuil mòr brèige
na tha fialaidh, còir is dìreach,
a chritheanaich gach uile thìre.   10
Dh'fhàs thu mòr, bog, reamhar, saidhbhir
a' slugadh fearann nan neo-aoibhneach,
brat an t-saille air an ruaimlich
a' bàthadh nam mìltean thruaghan.
'S iomadh sgùrr is mòran shlèibhtean
a chuir thu fodha le do bhrèinead;
bhàth thu Dia anns na nèamhan;
bàthaidh tu an Cuilithionn 's am Bràighe;
bhàth thu Minginis roimhe

and Bracadale too.   20
Och great, bloody morass,
who at all will stop your floods?
Who at all will cleanse the byre
unless the Red Army come in our extremity?
Who will cast out the dung for us
unless Stalin descends from the heights?

Many a rose and lovely lily
grows on the surface of the bog,
lovely in blood and flesh
though they grew on the dung-heap;   30
but the filth will penetrate the soul,
belying the flush of the blood.
Many a spreading, sappy tree
grows in the hostile bog;
many a beautiful, winged bird
has perched on it before being drowned;
but when it sprouts to seed
swallowed are flowers, birds and trees.

Here's to you, Mararaulin,
you swallowed the great Revolution of France,   40
you swallowed Germany and Italy,
long since you swallowed Scotland and Britain,
you swallowed America and India,
Africa and the great plain of China;
and, great God, that is the anguish
that you swallowed the heroism of Spain.

You are the bog of grace
for casting the lie in the throats of prophets.
Many a man has given you love
on the two sides of the ocean;   50
the press of France and Rome,
Germany and England together
always praise your streaming,
and it is not alone;
the slippery pens of many whoremongers
ever declare your worthiness,
and the shapely buttocks of harlots
give you strength anew;

agus Bràcadal cuideachd. 20
Och, a mhòinteach sgriosail, fhuilteach,
cò idir a stadas do thuiltean?
Cò idir a chartas a' bhàthaich
mur tig an t-Arm Dearg nar càs-ne?
Cò chuireas dhuinn a-mach am buachar
mur teirinn Stàilin bho na cruachan?

Tha iomadh ròs is lilidh bòidheach
a' cinntinn air uachdar na mòintich,
bòidheach o thaobh fala 's feòla
ged a dh'fhas iad air an òtrach. 30
Ach thig a' bhrèinead anns an anam
a' mealladh rudhadh na fala.
'S iomadh craobh dhosrach, snodhaich
tha fàs anns a' bhoglaich choimhich;
's iomadh eun sgiathach àlainn
a shuidh orra mun deach a bhàthadh.
Ach an uair a thig an laomadh,
sluigear flùr is eòin is craobhan.

Siud ort fhèin, a Mhararabhlainn,
shluig thu 'n t-Ar-a-mach mòr Frangach; 40
shluig thu a' Ghearmailt, shluig thu 'n Eadailt,
's fhad' on shluig thu Alba 's Breatainn:
shluig thu Ameireaga 's na h-Innsean,
Afraga 's mòr-roinn na Sìne;
's a Dhia mhòir, b' e siud an t-àmhghar,
gun shluig thu gaisgeachd na Spàinne.

'S tusa mòinteach an àigh
gu cur nam breug an amhaich fhàidh:
's iomadh fear a thug luaidh dhut
eadar dà thaobh a' chuain mhòir, 50
pàipearan na Frainge 's na Ròimhe,
na Gearmailte is Shasainn còmhla
a' moladh do shruthaidh daonnan,
's chan eil iadsan 'nan aonar.
Tha pinn shleamhna iomadh trùillich
a' sìor ràdh gu bheil thu ùiseil;
agus màsan cuimir shiùrsach
a' toirt nearta dhut gu h-ùrail;

the gentle doves of the B.B.C.
are not behind in the strife,   60
and the highly-placed godly
will proclaim your virtues.

Here's to you, Mararaulin,
you are great, exultant, lucky;
well you may be, for you have right
to the service of brain without heart;
you have gained the service of genius
for many a day despite regret:
you got Mozart and Patrick Mor;
you got Shakespeare and Yeats and the rest;   70
and it was not your fault but your hardship
that you did not get Shelley and Livingston.

Children of the authoritative bourgeois,
come to Mararaulin to dance,
come to disport on its braes,
not long will you yourselves be on top;
make a trip to St Congan's
to dance on the hero's grave,
and take a turn to Glasgow
where Maclean's grave is green;   80
dance heartily and joyfully
before you yourselves are drowned in the rivers;
great is the morass, great the plain,
though you are forbidden the Red Peak.

The palsy of all the many deceits
skims the cream of Mararaulin,
and many a consumptive philosophy
is there heaped on the midden.
A health to you, brutal bog,
the belching of the bourgeoisie;   90
fie, fie God, my opinion is
that is the great belching of the world.

Have you heard the shameful story
that the Stallion has been gelded?
He was caught in Mararaulin,
he was bound with many chains,

calmain chaoine a' Bh.B.C. –
chan iadsan as lugha strì –   60
agus easbaigean luachmhor,
bheir iad iomradh air do bhuadhan.

Siud ort fhèin, a Mhararabhlainn
tha thu mòr, moiteil, seannsail;
's tusa dh'fhaodas; tha thu dligheach
air seirbheis eanchainne gun chridhe;
fhuair thu seirbheis nan saoidhean
iomadh latha dh'aindeoin caoidhe:
fhuair thu Mozart 's Pàdraig Mòr;
fhuair thu Shakespeare 's Yeats 's gu leòr;   70
chan e do choire bh' ann ach t' èiginn
nach d' fhuair thu Shelley 's MacDhunlèibhe.

A chlanna nam bùirdeasach ceannsail,
thigibh a dhanns' a Mhararabhlainn;
thigibh gu spòrsa air na bruachan –
chan fhada bhios sibh fhèin an uachdar.
Thoiribh sgrìob a Chille Chòmhghain
a dhannsa air uaigh an t-seòid ud;
agus dèanaibh turas Ghlaschu,
uaigh MhicGhill-Eain ann a' glasadh.   80
Dèanaibh dannsa chridheil aoibhneach
mus bàthar sibh fhèin sna h-aibhnean;
mòr a' mhòinteach, mòr an learg
ged bhacar dhuibh an Sgùrr Dearg.

Tha critheanaich gach iomadh feallsachd
a' toirt a' bhàirr de Mhararabhlainn
is iomadh feallsanachd eitig
an siud a' càrnadh air an t-sitig.
Slàinte dhut, a mhòinteach bhrùideil,
a' bhùirdeasachd ri brùchd-rùdhain: 90
fuibh, fuibh, a Dhia, siud a shaoil mi –
's tu brùchd-rùdhain mòr an t-saoghail.

An cuala sibh an sgeul nàrach
gun do spothadh an t-Àigeach?
Rugadh air am Mararabhlainn,
cheangladh e le iomadh slabhraidh;

many a bourgeois and bailiff
was keeping him down in the bog:
his stones and brain were severed,
the animal was badly dealt with.   100
They made his snorting a bleating,
he was left on the midden.
Our renowned horse has been taken from us;
this morass will drown all.
It is rising and dancing,
it is being more greatly esteemed,
overflowing with its scum
and ever increasing in virtues.
It has reached the Peak of Goats
since it has been reinforced with manure.   110
If it puts the Cuillin under,
we must make our peace
with the great august morass,
we must prostrate ourselves before Mararaulin.

Have the Dale men been told
the fate of the virile, famous horse?
Has it been told in the Braes
what was done to the mettlesome strong animal?
It has been heard in Russia and in India,
in France and on the great plain of China,   120
but the news has not reached Scotland,
for she is deaf and blindfold,
and even if it is told in England,
the boors will not understand its significance.

They have taken his virtue from the poor beast,
they have taken his virtue from the beast,
they have taken his virtue from the poor beast;
and they knew the evil they did.

The Skyemen are all wounded
after what happened to that brute;   130
the men of Alba are all distressed
in spite of their ignorance of the tale;

the men of England are a laughing-stock
since they do not understand the case;

bha iomadh bùirdeasach is bàillidh
ga chumail fodha anns a' chàthar:
sgaradh a chlachan agus eanchainn,
rinneadh droch dhìol air an ainmhidh; 100
rinn iad mèilich de 'shitrich;
dh'fhàgadh e air an t-sitig.
Thugadh bhuainn ar n-each iomraidh;
bàthaidh a' bhoglach ud an t-iomlan;
tha i 'g èirigh 's tha i dannsa,
tha i dol am barrachd annsachd,
's i cur thairis le a ruaimlich
agus a' sìor fhàs am buadhan.
Ràinig i Sgùrr nan Gobhar
a chionn gun d' fhuair i an còrr todhair; 110
ma chuireas i an Cuilithionn fòidhpe,
feumaidh sinne dèanamh rèite
ris a' mhòintich mhòir sheannsail,
sleuchdaidh sinn ri Mararabhlainn.

An deach innse do na Dalaich
mar thachair don each lùthmhor, allail?
An deach innse anns a' Bhràighe
dìol an ainmhidh mheanmnaich, làidir?
Chualas an Ruisia is sna h-Innsean,
san Fhraing 's air magh mòr na Sìne, 120
ach cha d' ràinig am fios Alba,
oir tha i bodhar 's i fo dhalla-bhrat;
's ged a dh'innsear e an Sasann,
cha thuig na h-ùmpaidhean 'fhathann.

Thug iad a' bhrìgh bhon ainmhidh bhochd;
thug iad a' bhrìgh bhon ainmhidh;
thug iad a' bhrìgh bhon ainmhidh bhochd,
's bha fhios air an lochd a dhearbh iad.

Tha na Sgitheanaich uile ciùrrte
an dèis mar thachair don bhrùid ud; 130
tha fir Albann uile breòite
a dh'aindeoin aineolas an sgeòil ud;

tha luchd Shasainn 'nan cùis-bhùrta
a chionn nach tuig iad a' chùis ud;

fools are all the men of Europe
despite their understanding of that tale.

The Skyemen are all oppressed
though they themselves do not understand that case;
think you is there anyone in Glasgow
who understands and interprets the news?   140

Have you heard of the manly work
done for us by the bourgeoisie?
Far went the name of their exercise:
they took from the animal his substance.

I ascended early on a Sunday morning
to the summits of the misty battlements,
I saw the bourgeoisie in array,
Clan Donald and Clan Leod without victory.

Going up the spur of Corrie Each
I knew your cheer and your hue;   150
my country was a desert
and that deed was no reparation for it.

Have you heard the foul tale
of what was done to the Glendale Stallion?
That's little of their filthy acts,
work of landlords and their pimps.

Here's to you, Mararaulin,
you are overflowing the causeways;
if it is caught beside your banks
the bourgeoisie will geld the world.   160

I am pained for the victorious horse
who lifted his high head over the seas,
who challenged with his neighing
the mountain-surge of the western ocean rising.

Once I heard with exultation
of the dancing of bristles on his head,
when there was raised in the Island a banner
dappled with wounds and with the scarlet of wrath.

'nan amadain tha luchd na h-Eòrpa
a dh'aindeoin tuigse an sgeòil ud.

Tha na Sgitheanaich uile brùite
ged nach tuig iad fhèin a' chùis ud:
saoil sibh a bheil fear an Glaschu
a thuigeas 's a mhìnicheas am fathann?   140

An cuala sibhse an obair dhuineil
a rinn na bùirdeasaich dhuinne?
'S fhada chaidh ainm air an iomairt;
thug iad bhon ainmhidh a bhunait.

Dhìrich mi moch madainn Dòmhnaich
gu mullaichean nam baideal ceòthar:
chunnaic mi a' Bhùirdeasachd an òrdugh,
Dòmhnallaich gun bhuaidh is Leòdaich.

Dìreadh a-mach glùn Choir' Each,
dh'aithnich mi bhur sùrd 's bhur dreach.   150
Bha mo dhùthaich 'na fàsaich
's cha b' èirig air a' chùis an càs ud.

An cuala sibhse an sgeul salach
mar rinneadh air an Àigeach Dhalach?
Beag siud den gnìomharan trùillich,
obair uachdaran is fhùidsean.

Siud ort fhèin, a Mhararabhlainn,
tha thu a' taomadh thar nan cabhsair.
Ma ghlacar e ri do thaobh-sa,
claonaidh na Bùirdeasaich an saoghal.   160

Tha mi cràiteach mun each bhuadhmhor
a thogadh a cheann àrd thar chuantan,
a bheireadh an dùbhlan le shèitrich
do ghailebheinn a' Chuain Shiair ag èirigh.

Bha uair a chuala mi le annsachd
mu dhannsa fhrioghan air a cheann-san,
nuair thogadh anns an Eilean meirghe
breac le lot is sgàrlaid feirge.

God, had I been in his saddle
when the clangour of that year came,   170
I should have overtaken MacDiarmid
though hard his tempest across the firmament;
I should have caught MacDonald,
despite the lightning-fire of his glory.

But I have not seen the majesty
and I must stay where I may,
a Skyeman by the side of great Mary.

But I shall not tell her strong spirit
that no turn has come on that ebb-tide;
I shall avoid her brave forehead   180
since my tale is of our Island's glory subsided.

From the summits of the antlered Cuillin
has been seen many a lovely image,
some stalking over the high mountains
and others who had descended, drowned.
Even in the ugly bog
I saw the shadow of loveliness;
I saw youth, music and laughter,
I saw valour, wisdom, honour;
I saw generosity of heart,   190
heroism and unattained spiritedness;
I saw every flower that grew,
even the wounded, tortured side;
but in one was never seen there
the intellect of Lenin and the red side of Christ;
those two may not be seen together,
despite the spaciousness of the morass.
Oh God, they are not seen in one place
except on the bare top of the high mountains.

My chill heart was anguished   200
when I thought I saw
even your face in that foolish bog;
my darling, my delight, my white love,
you did not deem its black banks worthy;
my heart filled with a flame
to see you on the exultant mountain.

A Dhia, nach robh mi fhìn 'na dhìollaid
nuair thàinig faramachd na bliadhna,   170
bha mi air beireachd air MacDhiarmaid
ge cruaidh a dhoineannachd thar iarmailt;
bha mi air beireachd air MacDhòmhnaill
a dh'aindeoin beithir-theine 'ghlòir-san.

Ach chan fhaca mi a' mhòrachd
's feumar stad far na dh'fhòghnas,
Sgitheanach ri taobh Màiri Mòire.

Ach chan inns mi da spiorad làidir
nach tàinig tilleadh air an tràigh ud:
seachnaidh mi clàr treun a h-aodainn   180
's mo sgeul air buaidh ar n-Eilein traoighte.

Bho mhullaichean a' Chuilithinn chràcaich
chunnacas iomadh ìomhaigh àlainn,
cuid ag èaladh thar nan àrd-bheann,
cuid eile, theirinn, air am bàthadh.
Eadhon anns a' bhoglaich ghrànda
chunnaic mise faileas àilleachd,
chunnaic mi òige, ceòl is gàire,
chunnaic mi gaisgeachd, gliocas, nàire,
chunnaic mi fialaidheachd a' chridhe,   190
treuntas is aighear do-ruighinn.
Chunnaic mi gach flùr a dh'fhàsadh,
eadhon an taobh gonte, cràiteach,
ach an aon chan fhacas riamh ann
tuigse Lenin is taobh dearg Chrìosda;
chan fhaicear an dithis ud còmhla
a dh'aindeoin farsaingeachd na mòintich;
a Dhia, chan fhaicear an aon àit' iad
ach air mullach lom nan àrd-bheann.

Bha deuchainn 'na mo chridhe aognaidh   200
nuair smuainich mi gum b' e t' aodann
a chunnaic mi sa mhòintich bhaoith ud:
a luaidh, m' annsachd 's mo ghaol geal,
cha bu diù leat a thaobh dubh.
Lìon mo chridhe 'na lasadh caoire
ri t' fhaicinn air a' mhullach fhaoilteach.

Many a drowning of loveliness
has been made by the quagmire of that bog;
but it could not drown my white love,
sign that its triumph will end.   210

Day will fade on Mararaulin
though it is great and fortunate;
evening will darken on its braes,
its scum will subside and fall;
its great surging high-tide will ebb,
the plain will take another hue;
drowning and anguish will be abated
and day will rise on the Cuillin.   218

Part IV

Long and distant it is from the heights of the mountains
down to the depths of Mararaulin,
but the higher goes the ascent,
the deeper and longer one sees
through the scum and the bog,
through the heart of the drowning morass.
Why did I take hope
that the morass would change,
that its might and virtue would leave it,
that its scum would ebb and subside?   10
Is great proud Scotland not
already submerged in the mire?
Are not Spain and Italy,
France, Germany and Britain?
Has it not drowned all
good and evil in its floods?
Has it not overcome the world,
overflowing on all sides?
Has it not made a Dachau of the world?
Has it not spoilt heroism and white love?   20
There was seen on the streets of Glasgow
and on the streets of Edinburgh
and on the streets of London
the ultimate consequence of its filth;
poverty, hunger and prostitution,

'S iomadh bàthadh de nì àlainn
a rinn a' mhòinteach mhòr 'na càthar,
ach cha do bhàth i mo ghràdh geal:
an comharradh gun ruig i fàilling.   210

Ciaraidh an latha air Mararabhlainn
ged a tha i mòr, seannsail;
dubhaidh am feasgar air a bruachan,
traoghaidh is tuitidh a ruaimleach;
tràghaidh a muir-làn mòr, bàrcach,
thig coltas eile air an àrainn.
Leasaichear bho bhàthadh 's duilghinn
is èiridh latha air a' Chuilithionn.   218

Earrann IV

'S fhada cian bho àird' nam beanntan
sìos gu grunnd Mararabhlainn,
ach mar as àird' a thèid an dìreadh
's ann as doimhne 's fhaide chì neach
tro an ruaimleach, tro a' chàthar
tro chridhe boglach a' bhàthaidh.
Ach carson a ghabh mi dòchas
gun tigeadh caochladh air a' mhòintich,
gum fàgadh a treòir 's a buaidh i,
gun tràghadh 's gun traoghadh a ruaimleach?   10
Nach eil Alba mhòr ghràdhach
cheana fodha anns a' chàthar,
nach eil an Spàinnt is an Eadailt
nach eil an Fhraing, a' Ghearmailt 's Breatainn,
nach do bhàth i na h-uile,
olc is mhath, anns na tuiltean?
Nach tug i aon bhuaidh air an t-saoghal,
a' cur thairis thar uile thaobhan?
Nach d' rinn i Dachau den t-saoghal,
nach do mhill i gaisge is gaol geal?   20
Chunnacas air sràidean Ghlaschu
agus air sràidean Dhùn Èideann
agus air sràidean Lunnainn
ceann buileach a brèineid.
A' bhochdainn, an t-acras, an t-siùrsachd,

fever, consumption and disease.
They all grew on its side.
It went to seed with sores.

I have a foot in Mararaulin
and a foot on the Cuillin,   30
my hands bound beneath the dunghill
and my eyes on the many-headed swiftness.

Hardly shall I ever ascend
to the high hunting-ground of the mountains,
hardly shall I be found on the hills
where the stars are dwelling.

My spirit is weak and base,
defiled and oppressed
and my faint heart is without hope
that I may see the band of the wise.   40

Too much of the bog in my spirit,
too much of the moss in my heart,
too much of the red scum in my talents:
on my courage has lain the grey hue.

I shall make no struggle nor lonely wrestling
ever with that morass;
I shall not escape its horrible quagmire
through the restless exercise of wise spirit.

I shall not reach the summit of Bidean,
not to mention Blaven   50
I shall not be seen on the pinnacled height
between Sgurr nan Gillean and Garsven.

The night of the morass is on my eyes
and has penetrated my vision;
I have no hope of new bloom
nor of new whiteness of sun.

Distant, far distant,
distant the day that has not come.
Long the night on the Cuillin

an fhiabhrais, an eitig, an èislean –
dh'fhàs iad uile air a taobh-se:
rinn i laomadh le creuchdan.

Cas agam am Mararabhlainn
agus cas air a' Chuilithionn,   30
mo làmhan ceangailte san òtrach
's mo shùil ri tòrachd an iomaluais.

'S gann gun dìrich mi chaoidh
dh'ionnsaigh frìth àird a' mhunaidh,
's gann gum faighear mi air slèibhtean
air am bi reultan a' fuireach.

Tha mo spiorad lag suarach,
air a thruailleadh 's air a chlaoidh,
's tha mo chridhe fann gun dòchas
gum faic mi còmhlan nan saoi.   40

Cus den bhoglaich 'nam spiorad,
cus den mhòintich 'nam chridhe,
cus den ruaimlich 'nam bhuadhan:
air mo mhisneachd laigh an tuar glas.

Cha dèan mi gleac no carachd ònrachd
ris a' mhòintich ud a-chaoidh:
cha thàrr mi às a crithich uabhais
le iomairt luasgan aigne saoi.

Cha ruig mi mullach a' Bhidein
gun tighinn idir air Blàbheinn,   50
chan fhaicear mi bho Sgùrr nan Gillean
air àird nam binnean gus a' Ghàrsbheinn.

Tha oidhche na mòintich air mo shùilean
's i air drùdhadh air mo lèirsinn;
chan eil mo dhòchas ri ùr-dhreach
no ri ùr-ghile grèine.

'S fhada, cian fada,
's fhada 'n latha nach tàinig;
's fhada 'n oidhch' air a' Chuilithionn

that rocks in its anguish.   60
Long the night on the mountains
that shriek with a hard cry.
Long the evening has greyed
on the desired mountain of my love.   64

Part V

I heard that a breaking was seen
and a startling on the horizon,
that there was seen a red, fresh rose
over an oppressed, maimed world.
I heard about the River Clyde
being of the hue of scarlet;
I heard about Maclean
making an undying knot
of every brain and heart,
with spirit over agony.   10

A great portent and a monster has been seen,
the Stallion neighing on the Cuillin,
rising of the bubbling rocks
which the spirit made to rock.
The choice of the craggy steeds
was bounding on Sgurr a' Ghreadaidh;
the great wild Stallion leaped
across the remote lands;
he put his foot on Sgurr nan Gillean
while prancing on the Bidein;   20
he jumped with might and pride
from Sgurr na h-Uamha to Blaven
and thence he took a stride
to the horned top of Garsven.
He took one bound off Sgurr an Fheadain
leaving the wild, lonely cliff
until he reached the quagmire
which he stamped into a rutting bog.
Here's to you, fresh Stallion,
you will smash the pimps' bourgeoisie;   30
you will stretch the great pace across the morass;
no longer are you on the dungheap;

's e ri tulgadh an àmhghair; 60
's fhada 'n oidhch' air na slèibhtean
's iad ri èigheachd cruaidh-ghàireach;
's fhada 'm feasgar air ciaradh
air beinn iargain mo ghràidh-sa. 64

Earrann V

Chuala mi gum facas bristeadh
agus clisgeadh air an fhàire,
gum facas ròs dearg, ùrail
thar saoghal brùite, màbte:
chuala mi mu abhainn Chluaidh
a bhith air tuar na càrnaid;
chuala mi mu MhacGill-Eain
bhith dèanamh ceangal neo-bhàsmhor
air gach cridhe agus eanchainn
le meanmnachd thar cràdhlot. 10

Chunnacas manadh mòr is uilebheist,
an t-Àigeach a' sèitrich air a' Chuilithionn,
èirigh nan creagan a bha builgeadh,
air an tug an spiorad tulgadh.
Bha roghainn nan steud-each creagach
a' bocail air Sgùrr a' Ghreadaidh;
leum an Eist mhòr fhiadhaich
tarsainn iomallachd nan crìochan,
chuir e a chas air Sgùrr nan Gillean
's e prannsail air bàrr a' Bhidein, 20
leum e le lùth is àrdan
bho Sgùrr na h-Uamha gu Blàbheinn
agus à sin thug e gàmag
gu mullach adharcach na Gàrsbheinn.
Ghearr e boc de Sgùrr an Fheadain
's e fàgail uamhaltachd na creige,
gus an d' ràinig e an càthar,
's dh'fhàg e e 'na aon pholl-dàmhair.
Siud ort fhèin, Àigich ùrail,
prannaidh tu bùirdeasachd nam fùidse; 30
nì thu sìnteag thar na mòintich;
chan eil thu tuilleadh air an òtrach:

you are no more a poor gelding.
Great Mararaulin has lost its charm.

Grey horse, grey horse
of the high steep head,
of the chest of pride,
of the impetuous career,
joyous your leaping,
joyous your neighing,   40
joyous your incitement
and your restless feet.

Flawless Stallion
of the great grey flank,
of the bold heart
with the might of wings;
my love your leaping,
my love your snorting,
I loved your joy
that roared in my ear.   50

Great horse of the sea,
my love your gloom,
spirited horse
of the old hard-head,
comely grey horse
of the brindled sides,
great wild Stallion,
you were always our love.

Great horse, your bridle
is flawless steel,   60
your head iron-tempered,
my delight its look.
Your mighty motion
and your featsome body
have ever given us
our exultation and pride.

Skye Stallion,
you are before me,
my jealous choice,

chan eil thu nis 'nad thruaghan gearrain;
chaill Mararabhlainn mhòr a mealladh.

Eich ghlais, eich ghlais
a' chinn àird, chais,
an uchd uabhair,
an deannain bhrais,
ait do leumraich,
ait do shèitrich, 40
ait do bhuaireadh
's do luasgan chas.

Àigich gun ghiamh
led shlios mòr liath,
a' chridhe euchdaich
le èifeachd sgiath:
mo ghaol do leumraich,
mo ghaol do shèitrich,
b' ait leam t' èibhneas
bu bheucail fiamh. 50

Eich mhòir a' chuain,
mo ghaol do ghruaim,
eich mheanmnaich
an t-seana chinn chruaidh:
eich ghlais sgiamhaich
nan slios riabhach,
Eist mhòr, fhiadhaich
b' thu riamh ar luaidh.

Eich mhòir, do shrian
stàileann gun ghiamh, 60
do cheann cruadhach,
mo luaidh am fiamh:
's e t' iomairt lùthmhor
's do chorp lùth-chleas
a thug ar sùgradh
's ar cliù dhuinn riamh.

Àigich Sgitheanaich,
's tu th' air mo bhialaibh,
mo roghainn iadaich

my yearning of desire;   70
steed of the oceans,
you have provoked me,
and my heart is restless
with the restlessness of your eyes.

Great loved horse
of the mantling mane,
you heard the appeasement
of the angry 'Caogach';
great horse of the waves,
heroes' mount,   80
you heard the melody
of piercing 'Maol Donn'.

Rugged Stallion,
you heard the storm
and shouting cry
of brisk impetuous drone
from Patrick Mor
and Patrick Og,
love and grief
and great joyous pride.   90

Great horse of the horizon,
my heart of laughter,
you heard the pride
of the great, generous one;
you heard MacPherson
from your mountain battlement;
you heard the hero
who did the guiding.

Grey, awful steed,
you heard the bellowing   100
when came a striking
with a great year:
you heard MacCallum,
the great militant,
and MacPherson
with flame in his path.

is m' iargan dùil.   70
A steud nan cuantan,
's tu th' air mo bhuaireadh,
's mo chridhe luaineach
led luasgan shùl.

Eich mhòir ghaolaich,
na muinne craobhaich,
chual' thusa faochadh
a' Chaogaich chais.
Eich mhòir nan tonn,
a mharcachd shonn,   80
chual' thu fonn
Maol Donn nan gath.

Àigich ghairbh,
chual' thu an stoirm
is glaodhaich gairm
duis fhoirmeil bhrais
bho Phàdraig Mòr
's bho Phàdraig Òg:
an gaol 's am bròn
's a' phròis mhòr ait.   90

Eich mhòir na fàire,
mo chridhe gàire,
chual' thu àrdan
an t-sàr-fhir chòir;
chual' thu MacMhuirich
bhod bhaideal munaidh,
chual' thu an curaidh
dan tugadh seòl.

Eich ghlais iargalt,
chual' thu 'n t-sianail   100
nuair thàinig stialladh
le bliadhna mhòir:
chual' thu MacCaluim,
an gaisgeach allail,
is Mac a' Phearsain
le las 'na thòir.

Stallion of the mountains,
you will be there
when the time comes
to be commanding, in concord,   110
on the Cuillin
awaiting a hope,
and [a] joyous heart
glorious in the east.

Men of Europe
raised, erect
to the heart of justice
which was wounded and oppressed;
men of the world
welcoming   120
a fire spreading
in the east with its glow.

Love of horizon,
darling of the high mountains,
my treasure of shade,
my love your beauty;
girdling summit
of philosophers and heroes,
treasured hills,
your strife may not cease.   130

Love of Scotland,
the blind mantle will lift
that has killed
with the force of vain talk;
hope of Europe,
the help will come,
the living red flame
that will expunge the ash.

The Cuillin will be seen
a multi-swift eagle,   140
an affable lion,
a red dragon;
Scotland will be seen
a white-branded side,

Àigich nam beann,
's tu bhios ann
nuair thig an t-àm
a bhith ceannsail còrdt',   110
's tu air a' Chuilithionn
a' feitheamh muinighin
is cridhe suilbhir
san ear le glòir.

Sluagh na h-Eòrpa
togte, stòite
gu cridhe còrach
bu bhreòite creuchd;
sluagh an t-saoghail
a' cur faoilte   120
air teine sgaoilidh
san ear le leus.

A luaidh fàire,
a ghaoil nan àrd-bheann,
m' eudail sgàile
mo ghràdh do lì:
a chearcaill mullaich
nan saoi 's nan curaidh,
a bheanntan ulaidh,
cha sguir bhur strì.   130

A ghaoil Albann,
togaidh dalla-bhrat
a tha air marbhadh
le arraghloir lùiths.
A spèis na h-Eòrpa,
thig an còmhnadh,
an lasair bheò-dhearg
a sgriosas smùr.

Chithear an Cuilithionn
'na iolair iomaluath,   140
'na leòmhann suilbhir,
'na bheithir dheirg.
Chithear Alba
'na slios geala-chrios

a fire moving
on plain in wrath.

Long, long distant,
long the way of the ascent;
long the way of the Cuillin
and the rocking of your strife;   150
long the way of the mountains,
many a deed they require;
hard the ascent of the hills,
and toil is not lacking on them.

Great the war and wounded blood
that is in the ransom of Europe;
hard the agony's wrestling,
in the realisation of justice;
long, long the perplexity
and the manifold wretchedness,   160
long the night of longing
before the red-gold sun comes.

Long, but come it will,
the gold sun will come to us;
the Cuillin will rise
affable in his white glory;
bitter the night to us
that put your beauty under a dark shadow,
but morning will break
on glorious battlements.   170

Hard the extremity of China,
of India and Scotland,
bitter the loss of Spain,
field of the great dead;
hard the case of Italy,
of Germany and of France,
and the folly of England
that puts the poor to extremity.

Connolly is in Ireland
rising above agony,   180
Maclean in Scotland

'na teine falbhaidh
air magh le feirg.

'S fhada, cian fada,
's fhad' slighe an dìridh,
's fhada sligh' a' Chuilithinn
is tulgadh bhur strì-se: 150
's fhad' slighe nan slèibhtean,
's iomadh euchd a tha dhìth orr',
's cruaidh dìreadh nam beanntan –
cha ghann a tha strì orr'.

Mòr am blàr 's an fhuil chreuchdach
tha an èiginn na h-Eòrpa;
cruaidh a' ghleac iomagain
tha an tuigse na còrach;
cian fada 'n imcheist
is iomaluas na breòiteachd, 160
fad' an oidhche iargain
mun tig grian dhearg òraidh.

Fada, ach thig i,
thig dhuinn an òr-ghrian:
èiridh an Cuilithionn
gu suilbhir 'na ghlòir geal:
searbh dhuinn an oidhche
chuir an loinneas fo sgleò dubh,
ach bristidh a' mhadainn
air baidealan glòrmhor. 170

Cruaidh càs na Sìne,
nan Innsean 's na h-Albann,
searbh call na Spàinnte,
àrainn nam marbh mòr';
cruaidh càs na h-Eadailt,
na Gearmailt 's na Frainge;
is baothaireachd Shasainn
cur a bochdan fo ghanntachd.

Tha an Connollach an Èirinn
ag èirigh thar àmhghair; 180
MacGill-Eain an Albainn

a pillar on the heights;
Liebknecht in Germany
dead but undying,
and Lenin in Russia,
destination of great judgements.

"If there are bounds to any man
save those himself has set
to far horizons they're postponed
and none have reached them yet.   190

"And if most men are close curtailed
and keep a petty groove
'tis their own sloth that is to blame,
their powers they will not prove.

"Preferring ease to energy,
soft lives to steel-like wills,
and mole-heaps of morality
to the eternal hills."   198

Part VI

I knew hardship without respite
from the day when I was put on the Ship of the People.
I was in Gesto gathering shellfish
when I was seized, being alone.
I endured slavery with stripes,
"black-labour" and a sun of heat
that withered my flesh on my bones
and harried the young bloom
that was in my cheeks and forehead
before misery came on my world.   10
Many a trial I heard of
before that time in the Island;
but who got so much, or half of it?
God's curse on the Laird of Dunvegan
and on MacDonald of Sleat
and on Norman of Unish,
the skipper of the brutes' ship.
God of graces and Christ,

'na chalbh air na h-àirdean;
Liebknecht sa Ghearmailt
marbh ach neo-bhàsmhor,
is Lenin an Ruisia,
ceann-uidhe nan sàr-bhreith.

Ma chuireadh crìochan ro neach
ach iad a chuir e fhèin,
don fhàire far an ruigear iad
cha tug aon neach a cheum.   190

'S ma tha mhòr-chuid gu fangte teann,
a' leantainn slighe chrìon,
's e 'n leisg fhann fhèin as coireach air,
an lùths cha dhearbh iad fìor.

'S fheàrr leò 'n t-seasgaireachd na 'n treòir,
buigead thar stàilinn bhuadh,
is dùintean beaga moraltachd
os cionn nam beann biothbhuan.   198

Earrann VI

Fhuair mise deuchainn gun fhaochadh
bhon là chuireadh mi air Long nan Daoine:
bha mi an Geusto a' buain maoraich
an uair a ghlacadh mi 's mi 'm aonar.
Dh'fhuiling mi daorsa nan stràc,
an dubh-chosnadh is grian le àin
a shearg m' fheòil air mo chnàmhan,
's a rinn leathar den bhlàth òg
a bha 'nam ghruaidhean 's an clàr m' aodainn
mun tàinig dunachd air mo shaoghal.   10
'S iomadh deuchainn mun cuala
mi fhìn san Eilean ron uair ud;
ach cò fhuair uiread rium no leth dheth?
Mallachd Dhè air Fear Dhùn Bheagain
agus air Dòmhnallach Shlèite
agus air Tormod Ùnais,
sgiobair soitheach nam brùidean.
A Dhia nan gràs agus a Chrìosda,

my asking was not great,
but I did not get as much little kindness   20
as that I might see on the horizon
Ben Duagraich where the shieling was
in my youth, nor the graveyard of my kin.
Many a thing comes on the poor,
but no-one has suffered my woe,
though I was happy in my youth,
in spite of poverty, in the Land of MacLeod.
When I rise in the morning
I see only the grey fields
where is toil and anguish   30
and the soil itself is almost splitting
with the murdering heat of the sore sun.
Toil, hunger, faintness, shame,
those were the portion in fate for me
and never may I reach a horizon
whence I may see Loch Harport, or my mother's house,
where was heartiness and laughter
at waulkings in the time of my kin,
and I may not see the horned Cuillin
rising over Minginish of my love-fullness.   40

My fullness of grief
is my case tonight,
and the poor's dispensation in my mind.

It is not the death of chiefs
that ever pained me,
but the case and lot of those I love.

The language and music
I knew when young,
gone like a film off my eye.

And my joy of thought,   50
of reason and love,
over the race of the seas beyond my hope.

In Bracadale
of the steep braes,
of the green meadows, my desire.

cha bu mhòr m' iarrtas
ach cha d' fhuair mi de bhàidh bhig   20
am fiù 's gum faicinn air fàire
Beinn Dubhagraich far robh an àirigh
'nam òige, no cladh mo chàirdean.
'S iomadh nì thig air na bochdan
ach cha d' fhuiling neach mo lochd-sa,
ged bha mi sona nuair bha mi òg
a dh'aindeoin bochdainn an Dùth' MhicLeòid.
An uair a dh'èireas mi sa mhadainn
chan fhaic mi ach na raointean glasa,
far a bheil saothair is ànradh   30
's am fonn e fhèin an impis sgàinidh
le teas murtail na grèine cràitich:
saothair, acras, fannachd, tàmailt,
b' iadsan an cuibhreann a bha 'n dàn dhomh
agus a-chaoidh cha ruig mi fàire
bhom faic mi Loch Harport 's taigh mo mhàthar
far an robh cridhealas is gàire
aig luaidhean ri linn mo chàirdean;
agus chan fhaic mi an Cuilithionn cràcach
ag èirigh thar Minginis mo shàth-ghaoil.   40

Mo shàth-ghal goirt
mar tha mi nochd
is dàl nam bochd rim dhùil:

cha bhàs nan triath
a chràidh mi riamh
ach càs is dìol luchd-rùin.

A' chainnt 's an ceòl
a chleachd mi òg
air falbh mar sgleò bhom shùil:

is èibhneas smuain   50
mo chèille 's luaidh
thar rèis a' chuain bhom dhùil.

Am Bràcadal
nam bruthach cas,
nan cluaintean glas, tha m' ùidh:

In Minginish
of most graceful hill-slopes.
of greenest bushes, my love.

In Skye Island
of the splendid hills,   60
of the brindled moors,
my delight and thought.

In the proud Island
of the surly Cuillin,
of the winding lochs,
my glory and love.

In the topmost Island
of the cold mountains,
of the restless streams,
of the tender meadows.   70

In the joyous Island
of the rich hearts,
of the kindly spirits
where generosity is art.

Exile is a wretched thing
when hardship of poverty goes with it.
I learned that for myself
when I sailed on the *Annie Jane*.
We lifted sails in the Bay of Barra,
a wild day, destruction's night,   80
and the sails went out in pieces
at the back of Vatersay with the drift
and whirling spray of a wild sea.
The *Annie Jane* went in pieces
with myself and her cargo of my kin.
I did not see distant America,
for the sea swallowed me with its gills.
Drowning was a miserable thing
when it was neither useful nor necessary.

I am the great Clio of Skye: 90
I am known above hundreds,

am Minginis
as grinne slios,
as guirme pris, mo rùn.

An Eilean Sgitheanach
nam beann sgiamhach,   60
nam monadh riabhach,
mo chiall 's mo smaoin;

an eilean uallach
a' Chuilithinn ghruamaich,
nan lochan suaineach,
mo luaidh 's mo ghaol;

an eilean uachdrach
nam beann fuara,
nan sruth luaineach,
nan cluaineag caomh;   70

an eilean aoibhneach
nan cridhe saidhbhir,
nan spiorad coibhneil,
le loinn-chruth faoil.

'S e gnothach bochd a tha san fhògradh
nuair tha an cruadhchàs an tòir air:
dh'fhoghlaim mise siud dhomh fhèin
nuair sheòl mi anns an *Annie Jane*.
Thog sinn siùil am bàgh Bharraigh
latha fiadhaich, oidhche a' challa,   80
is chaidh ar siùil a-mach 'nan stiallan
air cùl Bhatarsaigh le siaban
agus cathadh-mara fiadhaich.
Chaidh an *Annie Jane* 'na clàran
leam fhìn agus luchd mo chàirdean;
chan fhaca mi Ameireaga chianail,
oir shluig a' mhuir mhòr 'na giall mi.
'S e gnothach bochd a tha sa bhàthadh
an uair nach robh feum no stàth ann.

'S mise a' Chlio mhòr Sgitheanach: 90
tha mi ainmeil thar chiadan;

I am well-informed throughout the world,
and I know the fate and dispensation of mankind.
I was one day in Strath Swordale
and a tingling came to my ears:
I heard the coronach of the wretches
whom the Baron was driving
from Borreraig and green Suishnish
to the other side of the seas.

I am the great Clio of Lewis: 100
I walked as far as was required
on that ready keen way
from Bernera to Stornoway.
I am the Clio that does not lack pride,
for I have seen the hunt of Park;
I am the shrewd Clio,
I know whence the Revival.

I am the Clio of Harris:
I nibbled among those eastern rocks.

I am the sorrowful Clio of Mull: 110
I have seen bracken in floods.

I am the Clio of the Hebrides:
I have seen suffering and loss;
I have heard the great music of MacCrimmon,
and the hornless sheep cropping.

I am the Clio of Scotland:
I know wretchedness and illusion's binding cloak;
I have seen the miner a bonded slave,
but I have seen the red rose of Clyde pouring
in its great mighty flood of anger   120
when Maclean raised a standard.

I am the Clio of Ireland:
oh God, I was desolated
by the famine of the potato year,
by violence, poverty and anguish,
but despite misery
I am the great, proud Clio,

tha mi fiosrach feadh an t-saoghail,
's eòl dhomh dàn is dàl nan daoine.
Bha mi latha an Srath Shuardail
agus thàinig gaoir gum chluasan:
chuala mi corranach nan truaghan
a bha am Morair a' ruagadh
à Boraraig is Suidhisnis uaine
gu taobh eile nan cuantan.

'S mise Clio mhòr Leòdhais: 100
choisich mi cho fad' 's a dh'fhòghnadh
air an t-slighe ealamh dheònach ud
à Beàrnaraigh gu Steòrnabhagh.
'S mise Clio gun chion àrdain,
oir chunnaic mi Fiadhach na Pàirce:
's mise Clio geur-chùiseach,
tha fhios a'm cia às an Dùsgadh.

'S mise Clio na Hearadh:
phioc mi anns na creagan sear ud.

'S mise Clio bhrònach Mhuile: 110
chunnaic mi fraineach 'na tuiltean.

'S mise Clio Innse Gall:
chunnaic mi allaban is call,
chuala mi ceòl mòr MhicCruimein
agus a' chaora mhaol a' criomadh.

'S mise Clio na h-Albann:
's aithne dhomh breòiteachd is dalla-bhrat;
chunnaic mi am mèinnear 'na thràill daorsa,
ach chunnaic mi ròs dearg Chluaidh a' taomadh
'na thuil cumhachdach mòr feirge   120
is MacGill-Eain togail meirghe.

'S mise Clio na h-Èireann:
a Dhia, fhuair mise mo lèireadh
le gort Bliadhna a' Bhuntàta,
le fòirneart, bochdainn is ànradh:
ach a dh'aindeoin na truaighe
's mise a' Chlio mhòr uallach,

for I have seen Connolly and Pearse,
Wolfe Tone, Fitzgerald and Emmet.

I am the great Clio of England,   130
my lot has been no easier:
I have seen Tyler and John Ball
and Robert Kett and more;
I have heard Shelley in his glory
and Byron in the Lords;
I have seen snobbery and art
and Paul Robeson singing.

I am the great Clio of Spain:
it is I who know anguish;
I was in Madrid and Barcelona,   140
I saw heroism and oppression,
suffering and misery,
despite the struggle of the proud heart.

I am the Clio of Germany:
God, it's I who saw the troubled mist
on the condition and heart of mankind,
Liebknecht, Thaelmann and slavery.

I am the Clio of France:
I saw the Revolution lost,
and I saw the Commune with its glory,   150
its suffering, heroism and grief.

I am the Clio of Italy:
I saw a terrible sight
when the Via Appia was under the crosses
of Spartacus and the militant slaves;
there I saw what sufficed,
and also the death of Matteotti.

I am the Clio of Greece:
I have seen maimed slavery
and false Metaxas,   160
in spite of poetry and philosophy.

I am the Clio of India:

oir chunnaic mi an Connollach 's am Pearsach,
Wolfe Tone, Fitzgerald agus Emmet.

'S mise Clio mhòr Shasainn: 130
cha b' e mo chuibhreann-sa a b' fhasa;
chunnaic mi Tyler is John Ball,
is Robert Kett agus an còrr;
chuala mi Shelley 'na ghlòir
agus Byron anns na *Lòrds*;
chunnaic mi fearas-mhòr is loinn
agus Paul Robeson a' seinn.

'S mise a' Chlio mhòr Spàinnteach:
's ann agamsa tha fios air àmhghair;
bha mi am Madrid 's am Barsalòna,   140
chunnaic mi gaisge agus fòirneart,
an t-allaban agus an truaighe,
a dh'aindeoin spàirn cridhe an uabhair.

'S mise Clio na Gearmailt:
a Dhia, 's mise chunnaic alla-cheò
air cor is cridhe nan daoine,
Liebknecht, Thaelmann is daorsa.

'S mise Clio na Frainge:
chunnaic mi an t-Ar-a-mach caillte;
's chunnaic mi *La Commune* le glòir,   150
le h-àmhghar, le gaisge, le bròn.

'S mise Clio na h-Eadailte:
chunnaic mise sealladh eagalach
nuair bha am Via Appia fo chroisean-ceusta
Spartacus 's nan tràillean euchdach;
chunnaic mi an siud na dh'fhòghnadh,
agus cuideachd bàs Mhatteotti.

'S mise Clio na Grèige:
chunnaic mi daorsa le creuchdan,
agus Metaxas na brèige   160
a dh'aindeoin gliocais is èigse.

'S mise Clio nan Innsean:

I have seen untold shame,
I have seen exploitation and lies,
Nehru and Gandhi in extremity;
I have seen poverty beyond thought,
the misery of mankind.

I am the Clio of China:
I got my own share of it;
but I grasped a chain on the Tatu Ho   170
and the misery turned to glory.

I am the Clio of the world:
I have traversed mountains, glens and plains,
towns and empty moors,
but I have not seen much respite.
I have read Plato and Rousseau,
Voltaire, Condorcet and Cobbett,
Leonardo, Schopenhauer, Hume, Fichte,
Blok, Lenin, Marx, Nietzsche.

I am the Clio of the world: 180
I worked my passage on the Slave Ship,
I was at the Battle of the Braes,
and in Leningrad at the Winter
Palace when a torrent
of Bolshevik warriors came pouring.

A mavis I on the floor of Paible,
but I have not got much sleep.

Look out and see if it is day,
and I waiting for the horizon,
and I waiting for the Cuillin   190
until the rocking is appeased.
Look out and see if it is the morning
that is dappling the skies,
and if it is the red rose
that is gilding the mountains.

I am the Clio of the world:
my wandering is eternal, constant.

chunnaic mi tàmailt gun innse,
chunnaic mi spùilleadh is breugan,
Nehru is Gandhi 'nan èiginn;
chunnaic mi bochdainn do-smaointinn,
allaban a' chinne-daonna.

'S mise Clio na Sìne:
fhuair mise mo chuid fhìn dheth;
ach ghlac mi slabhraidh air Tatu Hò   170
's chaidh an truaighe 'na glòir.

'S mise Clio an t-saoghail:
shiubhail mi beanntan, glinn is raointean,
bailtean agus monaidhean faoine,
ach chan fhacas mòran faochaidh.
Leugh mi Plato is Rousseau,
Voltaire, Condorcet is Cobbett,
Leonardo, Schopenhauer, Fichte,
Blok, Lenin, Marx, Nietzsche.

'S mise Clio an t-saoghail: 180
dh'obraich mi *passage* air Soitheach nan Daoine;
bha mi aig Batal a' Bhràighe
agus an Leningrad aig a' Phàileis
Gheamhraidh, nuair thàinig maoim-shruth
de churaidhean Boilseabhach a' taomadh.

Smeòrach mis' air ùrlar Phabail,
ach cha d' fhuair mi mòran cadail.

Seall a-mach an e 'n là e,
's mi ri feitheamh na fàire,
's mi ri fuireach a' Chuilithinn   190
gus an tulgadh bhith sàsaicht';
seall a-mach an e a' mhadainn
a tha a' balladh nan speuran;
agus faic an e an ròs dearg
a tha 'g òradh nan slèibhtean.

'S mise Clio an t-saoghail:
tha mo shiubhal sìorraidh, daonnan:

I was present in the castle
when monks came in a band
to question Galileo;   200
I heard the ready answer:
"It moves all the same".
I was in Leipzig with full desire
when Dimitrov stood before the court,
and there I heard more
than I had ever heard before.
I saw all in one living flame
the surging spirit of man,
the spirited hero-soul,
the exact brain of the summit,   210
ever-victorious irrepressible intellect,
the white-darting philosophic heart –
"The wheel of history going round,
over it the universe will not prevail".

The wheel will go round
and the distress will turn to triumph.
Lo, I shall one day see
the surging of the ebbless sea,
the rising of the waves
and a swell with its great high gloom;   220
that day will be lasting
and the mountains will be under a war-cry of joy.

Clio did not leave the Dun
despite faint misery from time immemorial,
though her joy was swift-going
on heights beyond thought, [on] a mountain.
She spoke to me saying:
There is no doubt that the hope and the expectation
will be seen in their truth,
joy's head and desire of the poets.   230

I saw the rising and falling of poor faces
in the sea's motion, dismayed:
at the Mound in Edinburgh
I marked the hand rising
above the welter of the sea
to clutch at the flitting thing,

bha mi 'n lathair sa chaisteal
nuair thàinig manaich 'nam prasgan
a chur ceist air Galilei.   200
Chuala mi an fhreagairt ealamh –
"Tha e gluasad a dh'aindeoin".
Bha mi an Leipzig le ùidh
nuair sheas Dimitrov air beulaibh cùirt,
's chuala mi barrachd na chuala
mi riamh roimhe an uair ud.
Chunnaic mi 'na chaoir bheò uile
spiorad beadarrach an duine,
anam aigeannach a' churaidh,
eanchainn eagarra nam mullach,   210
spiorad sìor-bhuadhach gun chlaoidh,
cridhe geal-ghathach an t-saoi.
"Cuibhle na h-Eachdraidh a' dol mun cuairt,
oirre cha toir an domhain buaidh."

Thèid a' chuibhle mun cuairt
is tionnda'idh gu buaidh an càs:
nàile, chì mise uair
onfhadh a' chuain gun tràigh;
chì mi bàrcadh nan stuadh
agus bàirlinn le gruaim mhòir àird;   220
bidh an latha sin buan
's bidh na beanntan fo nuallan àigh.

Cha d' fhàg Clio an dùn
dh'aindeoin truaighe gun lùths bho chian;
ged bu fhalbhach a mùirn
air àirdean thar dùil 's air sliabh;
's ann a labhair i rium:
Chan eil teagamh nach fhaicear fìor
an dòchas 's an dùil,
ceann aighir is ùidh nan cliar.   230

Chunnaic mi bogadaich aodann bhochd
an iomairt na fairge fo lochd:
aig a' Mhound an Dùn Èideann
mhothaich mi an làmh ag èirigh
os cionn plubartaich na fairge
a dhèanamh grèim air an fhalbhan,

the straw of expectation that was passing,
while the empty heart was bursting.

I have seen on the streets of Glasgow
and on the streets of Edinburgh   240
and on the streets of London
the ultimate course of the spirit's way:
arising from poverty and hunger,
from suffering and wounds,
the great red standard of the spirit
that will not be cast down after rising.

Dimitrov brandished in Leipzig
the high-willed banner that will come
to waken each sick spirit,
to put courage in the feeble.   250

The Hammer and the Sickle
golden on the red,
the mantling blood of Fate's spirit
that will raise the flood-tide bitterly.

Blood and sweat of toilers,
the scarlet that will give freedom,
brain's blood of poor and sage
that will overcome perverse wealth.

I looked on the Cuillin
on which another rocking was come;   260
excelling Dimitrov, your face
was cut in the face of the ancient summits;
the spirited blast of your heart
made Sgurr nan Gillean heave;
the surging of the hopes of humanity
made the mountain shake.

"If a limit has been set to man
beyond that which he has put himself,
and if living man has reached it,
it has known your step."   270

an sop fiughair bha dol seachad
's an cridhe falamh a' spreadhadh.

Chunnaic mi air sràidean Ghlaschu
agus air sràidean Dhùn Èideann   240
agus air sràidean Lunnainn
ceann buileach slighe an spèirid;
ag èirigh à bochdainn is acras,
à allaban is creuchdan,
meirghe mhòr dhearg an spioraid
nach leagar an dèis èirigh.

Chrath Dimitrov an Leipzig
a' bhratach aigeannach a thig
a dhùsgadh gach spioraid eucail,
a chur misneachd an èislean.   250

An Corran agus an t-Òrd
gu òraidh air an dearg,
fuil chraobhach spiorad an dàin
thogas a' mhuir-làn gu searbh.

Fuil is fallas luchd-saothrach,
an sgàrlaid a bheir saorsa,
fuil eanchainn nam bochd 's nan saoi
a bheir bàrr air airgead dhaoi.

Choimhead mi air a' Chuilithionn
air an tàinig caochladh tulgaidh: 260
a shàir Dhimitrov, bha t' aodann
gèarrt' an gnùis nam mullach aosta;
bha sgal aigeannach do chridhe
toirt luasgain air Sgùrr nan Gillean;
bha bàrcadh spèis a' chinne-daonna
a' toirt a' chrathaidh air an aonach.

Ma tha crìoch air a cur ro neach
ach ise chuir e fhèin,
's ma ràinig duine beò i,
gun d' fhoghlaim i do cheum.   270

Part VII

Many a turn the world has taken
since Aeschylus saw the likeness
of hero-man-god hanged, lacerated
on Caucasus of the dangerous peaks:
the god fashioned after man's image,
barbarous Jupiter, with oblique jealousy
sending the hungry, trained vultures
to rend and eat his liver;
humanity on the rocks
crucifying his own soul, to the screeches   10
of birds and savage animals
that profiteer from the feeding.
Jupiter, the brutal coward, has gone,
and barbarous Jewish Yahweh,
but a time has never come
when [the] ruling class has not found a god
who hangs on pious mountains
the sacrificed body of surpassing men.
Christ was hanged on a cross,
and Spartacus with his hundreds,   20
and there were many god-vultures in Britain
to tear the flesh of Connolly and Casement,
and many a French and Spanish Christ
has been crucified in a hundred years.

Shelley said that the Caucasian summit
started at the pain of the hero,
and I saw a leaping
in the breast of the Cuillin for joy
to see Dimitrov alone
making the human spirit   30
leap out of its shell, unhusked,
to stop the breath of the world.
In that stoppage died
ancient, little, paltry bourgeois gods;
they fell from the awful summits
down to the abysses, shrieking.

I saw Dimitrov with his emblem
overcoming horror.

Earrann VII

'S iomadh car a chuir an saoghal
bhon chunnaic Aeschylus aogas
suinn-dia-duine crochte, màbte
air Caucasus nan sgùrr gàbhaidh:
an dia fhuair dealbh air cruth daonda,
Iupiter borb, le iadach claoine
a' cur nam biatach acrach, mùinte
a shracadh 's a dh'ithe a ghrùdhain.
An cinne-daonna air na creagan
ag ithe anama fhèin ri sgreadan   10
nan eun is nam brùidean fiadhaich
a fhuair an toirt fhèin bhon bhiathadh.
Dh'aom Iupiter, an gealtair brùideil,
agus Iahweh borb Iùdhach
ach cha tàinig àm riamh
nach d' fhuair uachdarain dia
a chrochadh air na beanntan cràbhach
colann iobairt nan sàr-fhear.
Chrochadh Crìosda air crois-ceusaidh
agus Spartacus le 'cheudan: 20
bha iomadh biatach dè am Breatainn
a shrac feòil Chonnollaigh is Chasement,
agus cheusadh iomadh Crìosda
Spàinnteach is Frangach an ciad bliadhna.

Thubhairt Shelley gun do chlisg am mullach
Caucasach ri pèin a' churaidh;
agus chunnaic mise leumraich
air cliabh a' Chuilithinn le èibhneas
ri faicinn Dhimitrov 'na aonar
a' toirt air an spiorad dhaonda   30
leum à chochall le faoisgneadh
gu stad analach an t-saoghail.
Anns an stad ud bhàsaich diathan
beaga, bùirdeasach, crìona;
thuit iad bho na mullaichean cianail
sìos gu glomharan le sianail.

Chunnaic mi Dimitrov le 'shuaithneas
a' toirt bàrr air uabhas.

But the vulture and the buzzard
are yet on the sides of the savage mountain.   40

My love went with me on the mountain
so that she might hear the singing
of the peaks of dangerous steps.
She heard and half-understood the melody,
and straight the form of the vulture
had taken her white sad beauty
and she holed my side.

There are many birds on the hills,
some dumb and some singing.

I went out on the uplands of the high mountains   50
and I took with me my kin.
They heard the theme of the crying melody
and they took to lacerating
the great alien famous form
that was hanging to the precipice.

The bird's beak will tear the blasphemy
that is in the heart of holy knowledge.

I walked on the height of the mountains
and two loves were fighting in my head;
white vultures and the foul ones   60
were torturing my heart with devastation.

I am not the Clio of the world
and I found the summit death-chill.

I am the Clio of the world:
I saw enough toil-suffering;
I enjoyed poverty with Lenin
and Krupskaya before now.

I saw Eliot in Bloomsbury,
anguished prosperously
and Ezra Pound in Italy –   70
he got a happy drubbing.
If I were an "aesthete"

Ach tha a' bhiatach 's an clamhan
fhathast air sliosan nam beann allaidh. 40

Chaidh mo ghaol leam air a' bheinn
fiach an cluinneadh i an t-seinn
a bh' air stùcan nan ceum gàbhaidh;
chual' is leth-thuig i 'm mànran,
agus air ball bha cruth na biataich
air a bòidhchid ghil chianail
agus 's ann tholl i mo chliathaich.

Tha iomadh eun air a' bheinn,
cuid dhiubh balbh is cuid a' seinn.

Chaidh mi mach air frìth nan àrd-bheann, 50
thug mi leam mo chuid chàirdean;
chual' iad ùrlar a' ghàir-chiùil
agus 's ann shìn iad air màbadh
a' chrutha mhòir, làidir, allail
a bha an crochadh ris an stalla.

Reubaidh gob an eòin an toibheum
a tha an cridhe an naomh-oilein.

Choisich mi air àird nam beann
is dà ghaol a' sabaid 'nam cheann:
bha biataichean geala 's breuna 60
a' pianadh mo chridhe le lèirchreach.

Cha mhise Clio an t-saoghail
agus fhuair mi am mullach aognaidh.

'S mise Clio an t-saoghail:
chunnaic mise gu leòr saothrach;
mheal mi bochdainn còmh' ri Lenin
agus ri Krupskaya cheana.

Tha Eliot beag am Bloomsbury
air a chràdh gu h-iunntasach;
agus tha Ezra Pound san Eadailt – 70
fhuair esan sonas leadairt.
Nam bu mhise eisteiteach

vulture and buzzard would avoid me.

Great MacDiarmid is in Shetland,
taking the width of a hungry sea:
what Lenin did he will sing;
God's vultures will not be stronger.

The monster has been lifted out of the sea
and put on the height of the Cuillin;
it was coiled when routed   80
out of the depth of the oceans,
but now it is straight,
leaping windward against elements;
I saw the serpent leaping,
striking heaven's face with its fangs.

I saw Christ going round
on the bare cold summit.

I saw Lenin who had ascended
no small peak.

I saw Dimitrov on heights   90
and the mountain shaking with laughter-music.

A day and I in the rocky Cuillin,
I heard the great pipe incited,
roaring of mankind answering,
brain and heart in harmony.

I heard a cry on the mountains,
the liberty-shout of the people rising.

On the peaks around
were the living dead and their triumph:
Toussaint, More, Lenin, Marx,   100
Liebknecht, Connolly, Maclean,
and many a proud spirit
extinguished in the extremity of Spain.

A thousand years was like a drift
of mist lost in the firmament.

sheachnadh biatach 's clamhan mi.

Tha MacDhiarmaid mòr an Sealtainn
a' gabhail farsaingeachd cuain acraich:
na rinn Lenin seinnidh esan;
cha bhi biatach dè nas treasa.

Thogadh às a' mhuir an uilebheist
's chuireadh i air àird a' Chuilithinn;
bha i cearclach an àm ruagaidh   80
a-mach à doimhne na cuantan,
ach a-nis tha i dìreach
a' leum ri gaoith an aghaidh sìne;
chunnaic mi an nathair a' leumraich
le gathan aodann nèimh a' beumadh.

Chunnaic mi Crìosda dol mun cuairt
air a' mhullach lom, fhuar.

Chunnaic mi Lenin 's e air dìreadh
sgurra nach robh idir ìseal.

Chunnaic mi Dimitrov air àirdean   90
's a' bheinn a' crith le ceòl-gàire.

Latha dhomh sa Chuilithionn chreagach
chuala mi a' phìob ga spreigeadh,
nuallan a' chinne-daonna 'freagairt,
an eanchainn is an cridhe leagte.

Chuala mi iolach air na slèibhtean,
gàir shaorsa an t-sluaigh ag èirigh.

Air na sgurrachan mun cuairt,
bha na beò-mhairbh a thug buaidh:
Toussaint, Marx, More, Lenin,   100
Liebknecht, Connollaigh, MacGill-Eain
agus iomadh spiorad àrdain
a chuireadh às an càs na Spàinne.

Bha mìle bliadhna mar shiaban
ceò air a chall san iarmailt;

The great Clio was ever rising,
a hundred thousand years paltry in her sight.
It was she who saw the Cuillin
rising on the other side of anguish.

Landauer, Liebknecht, Eisner, Toller   110
walking, walking on the mountain;
the Commune of France arisen,
ever walking on the summits;
Connolly and the company of Ireland
taking the way of the hills;
Thomas Muir and Maclean
in death, not sleeping nor lying;
MacCallum, Donald MacLeod, Macpherson,
always walking on the moorland;
Dimitrov in the court forever,   120
defying terrible vicissitude;
the funeral of Maclean in Glasgow
winding through the streets of steep mountains,
the soldiers of the people pouring
over the peaks and glens of the mountains,
thousands nameless without history,
heroes flawless, unyielding,
who looked on death and agony
in the ramparts in the great hills.

The chains of the Tatu Ho swinging   130
in steel between perilous peaks.

The balance of the mountains weighing together
the brain of Einstein and the live-red spirit,
the understanding of a universe and the changing of a world
meeting on the bareness of the mountains.

The Cuillin will be purged with fire
to the steel of the spirit's rocks;
the synthesis raised up
beyond agony, travail and victory;
the frailty of a harlot in her disease   140
and Dimitrov adding to the great-spirited
mountains of man's consciousness,
and a little, fat, vapid bourgeois.

bha a' Chlio mhòr ag èirigh,
ceud mìle bliadhna crìon fa lèirsinn:
's ise chunnaic an Cuilithionn
ag èirigh air taobh eile duilghe.

Landauer, Liebknecht, Eisner, Toller   110
a' coiseachd, a' coiseachd air a' mhonadh;
Commune na Frainge air èirigh,
a' sìor choiseachd air na slèibhtean;
Connollaigh is comann Èireann
a' gabhail rathaid an t-slèibhe:
Tòmas Muir is MacGill-Eain
am bàs gun chadal gun laighe:
MacCaluim, Dòmhnall MacLeòid, MacMhuirich
a' sìor choiseachd air a' mhunadh;
Dimitrov sa chùirt gu sìorraidh   120
toirt a dhùbhlain do chàs iargalt.
Tiodhlacadh MhicGhill-Eain an Glaschu
a' suaineadh thar sràidean chas-bheann;
saighdearan an t-sluaigh a' taomadh
thar bheanntan is ghleanntan aonaich:
mìltean gun ainm no eachdraidh,
curaidhean gun ghiamh gun sheachnadh
a choimhead air a' bhàs 's air àmhghar
'nam ballachan dìon nan àrd-bheann.

Slabhraidhean an Tatu-Hò an stàilinn   130
a' riaghan eadar sgurrachan gàbhaidh.

Tomhas nam beann a' tomhas còmhla
eanchainn Einstein 's an spiorad beò-dhearg:
tuigse na cruinne is tionndadh saoghail
a' coinneachadh air lom nan aonach.

Glanar an Cuilithionn le teine
gu stàilinn creagan an spioraid.
An co-chur air a thogail suas
thar àmhghair, allabain is buaidh:
breòiteachd siùrsaich 'na h-eucail   140
is Dimitrov a' cur ri slèibhtean
meanmnach na h-aigne daonda
is bùirdeasach bog, reamhar, baothail.

The edge of man's spirit will be ground
on the sharp tops of a mountain;
the heart that cannot be torn
and the brain that cannot be choked
are walking, ever walking together
over the black peaks of grief.

The distant, dim course of the stars   150
being ever measured on the mountains;
the great consciousness in the exercise of a poem,
the hard strife of a wrestling soul,
the heroism of the spirit that will cause to turn
the multi-swift misery of the wheel;
Einstein high, but higher
Dimitrov wrestling with agony,
man's spirit putting his seal
to the difficult eternity of the mountains.

Rising on the other side of sorrow   160
there are seen more than one Cuillin,
there are seen the blue Cuillin of the Island
and two other Cuillins:
the Cuillin of ancient Scotland
and the Cuillin of mankind,
a Cuillin trinity pouring
its surge of peaks on the world;
a Cuillin trinity rising
above the lasting misery of the hills.
The black rose of the sharp-wounding Cuillin   170
red with the blood of man's heart;
the dim rose of the grey brain
red with the hue of the impetuous blood;
the white rose of philosophic intellect
red with the unoppressed blood;
the red rose of hero courage
aflame above mountains' summit.

A black ooze on the rock-face,
"black labour" and the sweat of blood;
a black ooze on the firmament,   180
the misery of millions making it dim;
the lasting misery that has come

Bleithear roinn an spioraid dhaonda
air mullaichean geura aonaich.
Tha an cridhe nach gabh sracadh
agus an inntinn nach gabh tachdadh
a' coiseachd, a' sìor choiseachd còmhla
thar sgurrachan dubha na dòrainn.

Cùrsa cian, mòr nan reultan   150
ga shìor thomhas air na slèibhtean,
an aigne mhòr an iomairt dàin,
cruaidh-ghleac anama a' spàirn,
gaisge an spioraid a bheir tionndadh
air ànradh iomaluath na cuibhle;
Einstein àrd, ach nas àirde
Dimitrov a' gleac ri àmhghar,
spiorad an duine a' cur a sheula
ri biothbhuantachd dhoirbh nan slèibhtean.

Ag èirigh air taobh eile duilghe   160
chithear barrachd na aon Chuilithionn.
Chithear Cuilithionn gorm an Eilein
agus dà Chuilithionn eile:
Cuilithionn na h-Albann aosta
is Cuilithionn a' chinne-daonna,
trianaid Cuilithinn a' taomadh
onfhaidh sgurraich air an t-saoghal;
trianaid Cuilithinn ag èirigh
thar àmhghar buan nan slèibhtean.
Ròs dubh a' Chuilithinn ghuinich   170
dearg le fuil cridhe an duine;
ròs ciar na h-eanchainne glaise
dearg le tuar na fala braise;
ròs geal tuigse nan saoi
dearg leis an fhuil gun chlaoidh;
ròs dearg misneachd nan laoch
thar mullach shlèibhtean 'na chaoir.

Snighe dubh air an stalla,
an dubh-chosnadh is fallas fala;
snighe dubh air an iarmailt,   180
ànradh nam milleanan a' ciaradh;
an t-ànradh buan a thàinig

and the misery that is to come,
and the misery that is with us,
the sore, killing, long misery;
Christ hanging on the cross
and Spartacus by him;
each millenium of slow toil-suffering,
the bitter leaves of the salt rose;
"black-labour" a nightmare,   190
humiliation, fever, consumption,
leaves of the terrible rose
a nightmare on the firmament.

Nevertheless, the Cuillin is seen
rising on the far side of agony,
the lyric Cuillin of the free,
the ardent Cuillin of the heroic,
the Cuillin of the great mind,
the Cuillin of the rugged heart of sorrow.
The variations of "Cumha na Cloinne" are seen   200
marching on a clear summit;
and the theme of "Maol Donn"
walking on the bare height.
Lucretius, Beethoven, Christ,
Lenin, Liebknecht traverse it,
Connolly and Maclean,
their flesh kindling a heath bonfire,
the great serpent stiff and straight,
to Heaven's height its striving,
the gold-lit eagle of the hills,   210
the wild Stallion of the glens.

Skye Cuillin,
awesome Cuillin,
savage mountains,
how vehement the cry of your weeping.

Rocky Cuillin
of the unoverthrown peaks,
wanton mountains
of the shrill-screeching din.

Horizon Cuillin,   220

agus an t-ànradh nach tàinig,
agus an t-ànradh a tha againn,
an t-ànradh goirt, marbhteach, fada;
Crìosda a' crochadh air a' chrois
agus Spartacus 'na chois;
gach mìle bliadhna saothrach maille,
duilleagan searbha an ròis shaillte;
an dubh-chosnadh 'na throm-laighe,   190
an tàmailt, an fhiabhrais 's a' chaitheamh;
duilleagan an ròis iargalt
'nan trom-laighe air an iarmailt.

A dh'aindeoin chithear trianaid Cuilithinn
ag èirigh air taobh eile duilghe,
Cuilithionn beadarrach nan saor,
Cuilithionn togarrach nan laoch,
Cuilithionn na h-inntinne mòire,
Cuilithionn cridhe garbh na dòrainn.
Chithear siubhail Cumha na Cloinne   200
a' màrsail air mullach soilleir
agus ùrlair Maoil Duinn
a' coiseachd air an àirde luim;
Lucretius, Beethoven, Crìosda,
Lenin, Liebknecht a' triall air,
an Connollach is MacGill-Eain,
am feòil a' losgadh falaisg aighir,
an nathair mhòr rag, dìreach,
ri àirde nèimhe a strì-se,
iolair òr-laist nam beann,   210
Àigeach fiadhaich nan gleann.

A Chuilithinn Sgitheanaich,
a Chuilithinn iargalt,
a bheannta fiadhaich,
glaodh dian bhur rànaich.

A Chuilithinn chreagaich
nan sgùrr do-leagte,
a bheannta beadarr'
nan sgread cruaidh gàirich.

A Chuilithinn fàire,   220

sharp girdle of high hills,
strong Cuillin,
end of hope's agony.

Summit wall
of man's spirit,
dangerous rocks
for the "élan" of desires.

Beloved Cuillin,
topmost mountain-height,
unblemished, undeviating,   230
without obliquity of eye.

Glorious Cuillin
of the luminous bare summits,
noble precipice,
head of love-talk's ecstasy.

Ancient Cuillin
of the trouble and agony,
surging Cuillin,
your pride is erect.

Wooing mountains   240
of the unresting minds,
naked white body,
strength beyond grief.

Naked brain
beyond the misery of woes,
beyond the agony of poverty,
beyond extreme vicissitude.

Soul of steel
beyond laughter's pulsing,
beyond distress's gloom,   250
beyond strife's outrage.

Heart of iron,
eternal mind,
ruling brain
above jealous vehemence.

crios geur nan àrd-bheann,
a Chuilithinn làidir,
crìoch ànraidh dhùilean.

A ghàrraidh mullaich
do aigne an duine,
a chreagan cunnairt
do spionnadh rùintean.

A Chuilithinn ghaolaich,
fras-mhullach aonaich,
gun ghais gun aomadh,   230
gun chlaonadh shùilean.

A Chuilithinn ghlòrmhoir
nan creachann lòghmhor,
a stalla òirdheirc,
ceann sòlais sùgraidh.

A Chuilithinn àrsaidh
na trioblaid àmhghair,
a Chuilithinn bhàrcaich,
tha t' àrdan stòite.

A bheannta sùgraidh,   240
nan aigne siùbhlach,
a chuirp ghil rùisgte,
a lùiths thar dòrainn.

Eanchainn nochdta
thar ànradh lochdan,
thar àmhghar bochdainn,
thar torchairt èiginn.

Anam stàilinn
thar plosgadh gàire,
thar dosgainn ànraidh,   250
thar màbadh streupa.

A chridhe 'n iarainn,
inntinn shìorraidh,
eanchainn riaghlaidh
thar dianais eudmhoir.

Lowering Cuillin,
dark mountain of dead winter,
smoking blackness
beyond the sun's white strength.

Whiteness in blackness,   260
light of the wise,
unoppressed mountain,
torrent-flood of deeds.

Cuillin, Cuillin,
heart of sorrow,
spirit kindly
above a mountain of wrong.

The Ship of the People
taking the torrent stream
over ancient barenesses   270
of the torn mountains.

The vessel of a great nation
going to windward
over ocean rocks
with blue roaring waves.

The great ship of newness,
and her rudder-stream
raising billows
above the black rock of a mountain.

The ship of the world   280
without deviation of surrender,
without veering of obliquity
before a great wind of heroism.

The restless Cuillin,
both notch and oceans,
both ditch and wavetop,
locked, well-founded rocking.

The summit Cuillin
a destination of genius,

A Chuilithinn mhùgaich,
meall dorcha dùdlachd,
a dhuibhread smùidrich
thar lùths ghil grèine.

A ghile an duibhreid,   260
a sholais shaoidhean,
a bheinn neo-chlaoidhte,
a mhaoim-shruth euchdaich.

A Chuilithinn, Chuilithinn,
a chridhe duilghe,
a mheanmna shuilbhir
thar thulchann eucoir.

Long nan Daoine
a' gabhail maoim-shruth
thar loman aosta   270
nan aonach reubte.

Soitheach sluaigh mhòir
a' gabhail fuaraidh
thar creagan chuantan
nan stuadh gorm gleusta.

Long mhor na h-ùrachd
's a h-uisge stiùrach
a' togail shùghan
thar dùbh-chreag slèibhe.

Long an t-saoghail   280
gun fhiaradh aomaidh,
gun shiaradh claonaidh
ro ghaoith mhòir treuntais.

An Cuilithionn luaineach
'na eag 's 'na chuantan,
'na chlais 's 'na stuadh-bhàrr,
'na luasgan stèidh-ghlaist'.

An Cuilithionn uachdrach
'na cheann-uidhe bhuadhan,

an august hardness,   290
a pure-white paean.

The ancient Cuillin
a growing soul,
a teeming brain,
a white agony of ecstasy.

Cuillin Stallion,
utmost rock-steed,
giant horse,
your multi-swiftness is stayed.

Welcoming Cuillin,   300
you are my thoughts,
you are the divulged, secret desire
of glorious mankind.

Mountain Stallion,
great unbound horse,
unstinted ocean,
slender-bellied, blood-red deer.

Cuillin Trinity,
great Stallion,
eternal steed-mountain,   310
great, powerful reason.

Cuillin of history,
great-spirited, wise,
rock unwithered
in the bitter strife of sorrow.

Naked brain,
naked heart,
naked spirit,
nakedness of ecstasy.

Ocean-smouldering,   320
fire of rough hills,
flame-sorrow of rugged mountains,
glorious journeying one.

'na chruas suaimhneach,   290
'na luathghair glè-gheal.

An Cuilithionn àrsaidh
'na anam fàsmhor,
'na eanchainn lànmhoir,
'na chràdh geal èibhneis.

Àigich Cuilithinn,
a chreag-steud iomallach,
Eistir fhuirbidh
an iomaluais stòlda.

A Chuilithinn fhaoiltich,   300
's tu mo smaointean,
's tu rùn sgaoilidh
chloinn-daoine glòrmhor.

Àigich bheanntan,
eich mhòir gun bhann ort,
a chuain gun staing ort,
a sheang-fhiadh chròdhant.

A Chuilithinn trianaid,
àigich mhiadmhoir,
a steud-bheann shìorraidh,   310
a chiall mhòr threòirmhor.

A Chuilithinn eachdraidh
mheanmnaich, bheachdail,
a chreag gun sheacadh
ri gleac geur dòlais.

Eanchainn nochdta,
a chridhe nochdta,
a spioraid nochdta,
a nochdachd sòlais.

A smùidrich fairge,   320
a theine garbhlaich,
a chaoir-ghal gharbh-bheann,
fhalbhain glòire.

Far, far distant, far on a horizon
I see the rocking of the antlered Cuillin;
beyond seas of sorrow, beyond morass of agony,
I see the white felicity of the high-peaked mountains.

Who is this, who is this on an evil night?
Who is this walking on the moor?
The steps of a spirit by my side   330
and the soft steps of my love.

Footsteps, footsteps on the mountains,
murmur of footsteps rising,
quiet footsteps, gentle footsteps,
footsteps stealthy, mild and disciplined.

Who is this, who is this on a night of woe?
Who is this walking on the summit?
The ghost of a bare naked brain,
cold in the chill of vicissitude.

Who is this, who is this in the night of the spirit?   340
It is but the naked ghost of a heart,
a spectre alone, going in thought,
a skeleton, naked of flesh, on the mountain.

Who is this, who is this in the night of the heart?
It is but the inaccessible thing,
the ghost seen by the soul,
a Cuillin rising over the sea.

Who is this, who is this in the night of the soul,
following the veering of the fugitive light?
It is only, it is only the journeying one,   350
seeking the Cuillin over the ocean.

Who is this, who is this in the night of mankind?
It is but the ghost of the spirit,
a soul alone, going on mountains,
longing for the Cuillin that is rising.

Beyond the lakes of blood of the sons of men,
beyond the frailty of plain and the labour of the mountain,

Fada, cian fada, fada air fàire
chì mi tulgadh a' Chuilithinn chràcaich;
thar marannan dòlais, thar mòinteach àmhghair,
chì mi geal-shuaimhneas nan stuadh-bheann àrda.

Cò seo, cò seo oidhche dhona,
cò tha coiseachd air a' mhonadh?
Ceumannan spioraid ri mo thaobh   330
agus ceumannan ciùin mo ghaoil.

Ceumannan, ceumannan air na slèibhtean,
monmhar cheumannan ag èirigh:
ceumannan fiata, ceumannan ciùine,
ceumannan èalaidh, socair, mùinte.

Cò seo, cò seo oidhche dunaidh,
cò seo a' coiseachd air a' mhullach?
Tannasg eanchainne luime, nochdta,
fuar ri aognaidheachd an torchairt.

Cò seo, cò seo oidhche spioraid?   340
Chan eil ach tannasg lom cridhe,
manadh leis fhèin a' falbh a' smaointinn,
cliabh feòil-rùisgte air an aonach.

Cò seo, cò seo oidhche cridhe?
Chan eil ach an nì do-ruighinn,
an samhladh a chunnaic an t-anam,
Cuilithionn ag èirigh thar mara.

Cò seo, cò seo oidhche 'n anama,
a' leantainn fiarachd an leòis fhalbhaich?
Chan eil, chan eil ach am falbhan   350
a' sireadh a' Chuilithinn thar fairge.

Cò seo, cò seo oidhche 'chinne?
Chan eil ach samhladh an spioraid,
anam leis fhèin a' falbh air slèibhtean
ag iargain a' Chuilithinn 's e 'g èirigh.

Thar lochan fala clann nan daoine,
thar breòiteachd blàir is strì an aonaich,

beyond poverty, consumption, fever, agony,
beyond hardship, wrong, tyranny, distress,
beyond misery, despair, hatred, treachery,   360
beyond guilt and defilement, watchful,
heroic, the Cuillin is seen
rising on the other side of sorrow.   363

thar bochdainn, caithimh, fiabhrais, àmhghair,
tha anacothruim, eucoir, ainneirt, ànraidh,
thar truaighe, eu-dòchais, gamhlais, cuilbheirt,   360
thar ciont is truaillidheachd, gu furachair,
gu treunmhor chithear an Cuilithionn
's e 'g èirigh air taobh eile duilghe.   363

COMMENTARY

The Cuillin

Although well over a century has passed since its first publication. Francis Groome's discussion of the hills which provided the core imagery for MacLean's poem can still function as an effective presentation.[1] In his view 'the group consists of two distinct portions totally different in both rock formation and external appearance'. The Red Hills are

> composed of rock which weathers and decomposes with great readiness, their slopes... formed by masses of bright red detritus – whence the name – only relieved here and there by strips of bright green sod.

The Cuillin proper, however, are constituted by the second group, consisting of 'rocks of Laurentian age'. Groome gives no source for the evocative description he then quotes at length which, in its latter part, demonstrates beyond doubt that the impulse to imbue one's experience of, and relationship to, the hills with moral and ethical values predated MacLean's poem:

> The darkness of that mass is indeed extraordinary, and adds much to the wildness of aspect and grandeur of effect produced by the rugged and bold outlines of the mountains of which it is formed. No light seems to harmonise their colour to its place in the general landscape; perpetual shadow seems to cover them in every state of the atmosphere, and when the clouds involve their summits a deep and dark abyss seems opened beneath into which the eye vainly endeavours to penetrate. Their exterior outline is equally remarkable, as well for the contrast it presents to the tame and smooth boundary of the Red Hills as for its peculiarly rugged and serrated form. Pinnacles and projecting crags darkly indenting the sky rise along the whole line, marking by their acuteness and permanence the durability of the rock of which they are composed... The

enormous bulks, their gradual receding to invisible crests, their utter movelessness, their austere silence daunt you. You are conscious of their presence, and you hardly care to speak lest you be overheard. You can't laugh; you would not crack a joke for the world. Glen Sligachan would be the place to do a little self-examination in. There you would have a sense of your own meannesses, selfishnesses, paltry evasions of truth and duty, and find out what a shabby fellow you at heart are; and, looking up to your silent father-confessors, you would find no mercy in their grim faces.

During a series of conversations with Donald Archie MacDonald recorded in Edinburgh in September 1982,[2] MacLean described himself as

> very much affected by what one calls physical beauty. I think I have always been, and Skye, of course, is an island of an amazing variety of beauty, but, above all, apart from the great sea cliffs of Biod an Adhar in Diùrrinis and the cliffs of Bioda Ruadh and of Minginnis and so on, you get the great winding sea lochs and you get a lot of the high green, like the green dome of the Storr suddenly plunging into pretty well perpendicular cliffs of 500–600 feet and then, but above all, the Cuillins. It's a very, very spectacular landscape and it is the kind of landscape that easily resolves itself into what you might call heroic symbols.

He notes that the landscape of his native island, Raasay, lying directly E of Skye, offers a gentler and more luscious contrast to both the Cuillins and the Red Hills on the bigger island. It was true that

> from most parts of Raasay we could only see part of the Cuillins, the Sgurr nan Gillean to Bruach na Frìthe group, but you have the great landscape of Blàbheinn and the Garbhbheinn further to the south-east.

MacLean's more intimate acquaintance with these hills dates from the years immediately preceding the composition of the poem. In 1935

> I went to teach in Portree School and started going to the Cuillins. In those days I could get very few people to

go with me, practically nobody in those days, and I used to wander about alone on them, ridge-wandering and doing some rock-climbing to avoid detours and being there in all kinds of conditions.

A crucial element in these solitary expeditions, whether in the Cuillin proper or on Dùn Cana, the highest point in Raasay, was ruminating on the people who once populated this area of the Hebrides. MacLean's father was of Raasay stock. His mother, however, a Nicolson, came from the village of Braes across the sound in Skye.

> To me the whole thing was bound up with the history of Skye and Raasay, as I knew it. Because, you see, I was of that, in every way... And also, you see, even at my youngest and most... what you might call politically radical time of my life, I had this sense of continuity. And when I was up on top of the Cuillins or on Dùn Cana I mean, it wasn't just a case of scenery, but it was always very much intermingled with the people.

The conversation was recorded more than four decades after the writing of 'An Cuilithionn'. What comes next reads like a posterior justification, or explanation, of the poem's emergence, one whose cogency and relevance is not diminished by its later dating:

> I came to maturity at the time of the great symbolist movement in European poetry, which you've got in Yeats, Eliot, MacDiarmid, Blok in Russia and Paul Valéry in France, and my symbols came mostly from my immediate environment, because in many ways my immediate physical environment was very varied. The Cuillins naturally became a symbol of difficulty, hardship and heroic qualities as against, as it were, the softness and relative luxury of the woods of Raasay with all their own contradictions.

MacLean's words offer a key to what rendered his appearance on the literary scene, not only in Scotland, such a unique phenomenon: his combination of profound familiarity with, and attachment to, the natural setting, as well as the oral and written traditions, of Gaelic-speaking Scotland with an instinctive grasp of the Symbolist tradition in the arts and

literature which preceded the modern movement in so
many European countries. The poet evokes, no doubt un-
consciously, a specific passage in the poem:

> When I was younger, I wasn't affected so much by
> colour as I was by outline in landscape, and, of course
> the outlines of Skye are spectacular and even heroic... I
> remember an evening being on Sgurr Alasdair, a
> summer evening, and seeing glitter – the glitter of the
> sun, west of Barra. And another day, for instance, being
> on the Cuillins, with swirling mist on the narrow top of
> Sgurr a' Ghreadaidh, and the mist suddenly clearing
> and there was a glint of sun on the wings of a golden
> eagle standing on a ledge about twenty feet below me.

The relevant lines come from Part I:

> Latha dhomh air Sgùrr a' Ghreadaidh
> 'nam sheasamh air an roinn àird, eagaich,
> ag amharc sìos air Coire an Uaigneis
> tro bhàrcadh a' cheò mun cuairt orm,
> ann am bristeadh an t-siabain
> dheàlraich aiteal òir air sgiathan
> iolaire dol seachad shìos ann
> tarsainn nam ballachan cliathaich.
> Is dhòmhsa thar glòir gach ianlaith
> aiteal òir an eòin Sgitheanaich... (I: 152–161)[3]

His concluding words sum up the crucial elements which
went into the making of 'An Cuilithionn':

> I grew up at that time, when symbolism was such a
> thing in European poetry and I was affected a lot by...
> people, more by MacDiarmid and Yeats, and my
> symbols almost automatically became the landscape of
> my physical environment. But, of course, that was
> always affected, blended with what I knew of the history
> of my people.

Dedication

The heading 'dedication' is present in the English translation
but has no equivalent in the Gaelic text. A pencil note in the

Edinburgh typescript, as well as on Douglas Young's copy of MacLean's English translation in St Andrews has 'based on the "Elegy to Ian Lom"'.[4]

1 MacLean opens with an instance of the traditional modesty topos, by which the writer invokes help in his undertaking from other writers he admires whose gifts he claims to look upon as superior to his own. He was introduced to MacDiarmid by George Davie in Rutherford's Bar, Edinburgh in May 1934, while completing his training as a teacher at Moray House. He then prepared versions of both 'Birlinn Chlann Raghnaill' and 'Moladh Mòraig' as a basis for translations by MacDiarmid intended for *The Golden Treasury of Scottish Poetry* (published in 1940). 'The Birlinn of Clanranald' was published in the *Modern Scot* in January 1935. At the end of July and beginning of August that year MacLean visited MacDiarmid in Whalsay, Shetland, without fully grasping the precarious state of the older man's health, which led to him being admitted to hospital in Perth on August 17th. MacDiarmid finally took advantage of MacLean's invitiation to visit Raasay and Skye in September 1937, when he was accompanied by W. D. MacColl, who would subsequently offer detailed comments on MacLean's draft English version of 'An Cuilithionn' which are preserved in the National Library of Scotland.[5] A poem by MacLean appeared in the first issue of MacDiarmid's magazine *Voice of Scotland* (June-August 1938) and a cordial relationship between the two continued until MacDiarmid's death in September 1978.[6] Even many years afterwards, MacLean credited MacDiarmid with having inspired 'An Cuilithionn':

> It was in Mull in 1938 that I conceived the idea of writing a very long poem, 10,000 words or so, on the human condition, radiating from the history of Skye and the West Highlands to Europe and what I knew of the rest of the world. Its symbolism was to be, mostly, native symbolism. I started it in Edinburgh in the summer of 1939. The idea came from *The Drunk Man*.[7]

Despite this indication, however, there is every reason to maintain that *To Circumjack Cencrastus* (1930) exercised a more consistent and more telling influence on 'An Cuili-thionn' than MacDiarmid's earlier poem. MacDiarmid wrote to MacLean on February 11th 1940 that

> I will look forward very keenly to the eventual publication of the whole Cuillin poem you have so kindly dedicated to myself, coupling my name with the great name of Alexander MacDonald...

and announced on May 13th that

> The typescript of your big poem has just arrived. Glory be! I'll write you about it as soon as I hear from you.[8]

Issues of literary filiation aside, MacLean's attitude to the older poet was certainly not one of unmixed adulation. Their correspondence never attains the ease of self-disclosure which marks the letters to Douglas Young,[9] though even with the latter it would still be unwise to speak of intimacy. MacLean wrote to Young on November 23rd 1940 that

> If a poem is to be bare and forthright it must be such and also be distinguished and heightened in style but I am afraid that something or everything has gone out of Grieve's poetry. I suppose it indicates that Grieve's Anglophobia strikes me as a bit hollow. That may be because for a long time I have not paid much atten-tion to his politics. As early as the *Drunk Man* I had resented an arty attitude to politics, and I gave up paying much attention to his utterances on politics when he began to use the *Voice [of Scotland]* largely to fulminate against his literary enemies in imaginary quarrels.

Having seen MacDiarmid's *Golden Treasury of Scottish Poetry*, MacLean pronounced himself 'much disappointed with it', adding 'what a bad judge he evidently is of his own poetry' (letter of December 7th 1940). The note of impatience recurs in a letter of February 22nd 1941: 'He should really stop his pose as interpreter of Gaelic Scotland but perhaps it is not really a pose but honest boosting'.

5   Here and subsequently, MacLean speaks of Skye quite simply as 'an t-Eilean', 'the Island' par excellence, as is habitual in Gaelic. Note the capitalisation in the English text.

9 In an interview with Aonghas MacNeacail published in 1979, MacLean again tellingly pairs MacDiarmid with his illustrious Gaelic predecessor. In *To Circumjack Cencrastus*, the later poet

> had paid a great tribute to Alexander MacDonald. He had sensed something in Alexander MacDonald, he had sensed this tremendous energy, this verve in Alexander MacDonald, and I recognized that he was right in that. When I met him in 1934 I agreed to help him (I was a student in Moray House then) in translating MacDonald's "Birlinn" and Macintyre's "Ben Dorain" and a few other Gaelic poems, but especially the "Birlinn". I always felt that Hugh MacDiarmid did better with MacDonald than he did with Macintyre.[10]

Along with a persistent fondness for heaping at times scurrilous invective on their enemies, both poets confronted hardship and ostracism in their personal lives, not least in consequence of doggedly maintaining commitment to a losing or controversial political cause.

Alasdair Mac Mhaighstir Alasdair (Alexander MacDonald, c.1695-c.1770) was a great-grandson of Ranald MacDonald of Benbecula and claimed, through his mother, descent from King Robert II. He is believed to have studied at the University of Glasgow and appears in the records from 1729 onwards as teacher and catechist for the Society in Scotland for Propagating Christian Knowledge, an organisation originally hostile to both Gaelic and Catholicism (to which Mac Mhaighstir Alasdair converted during the build-up to the second Stewart rebellion).[11] Nevertheless he prepared a Gaelic-English vocabulary for it, which was published in 1741. In 1744 he is said to have deserted his post in order to help rally the clans, and he held a Captain's commission in the Jacobite army in 1745. Derick Thomson credits him with 'the prime literary oeuvre in Gaelic in the eighteenth century' and offers the following summing up in his entry for the *Companion to Gaelic Scotland*:

> He was a man of strong views and violent emotions but with a hard intellectual cast of mind also; he was learned in the Gaelic tradition and open to influence from his other reading; he was an innovator and a

conservative; and his poetry is full of the stimulating contradictions that proceed from these diversities.[12]

A reference to MacDonald's participation in the 1745 rebellion occurs at III: 170 where, interestingly, the same threefold relationship adumbrated at the start of 'An Cuilithionn' recurs.

At I: 25 Skye poet Màiri Nic a' Phearsain (Mary MacPherson, 'Màiri Mhòr nan Òran') is introduced, separately from MacLean's announced models and, as it were, in a more subdued tone. At III: 169ff., after evoking both MacDiarmid and MacDonald, Maclean announces ''s feumar stad far na dh'fhòghnas,/ Sgitheanach ri taobh Màiri Mòire'.[13] Writing to Young (letter dated September 7th 1941), he explains that Neil MacLeod (see note to I: 112) 'is just a symbol in the "Cuillin"', whereas Màiri Mhòr influenced the poem

> a great deal. A huge deal of her stuff is just comical in its padding but there is a great deal of extremely moving clean-cut stuff, strong, tender feeling. She has influenced 'The Cuillin' quite a lot [–] especially the expressions of blood kinship are not unlike things in Mary... In fact the most easily distinguished stylistic influences in 'The Cuillin' are those of MacDonald e.g. the opening of Parts I and II and those of Mary MacPherson appearing *passim* in simple expressions of simple feeling.

11 In version C MacLean renders what is here treated as a trope for Skye (note the phonetic parallel of 'Sgìth – Sgitheanach') as 'our noble Cuillin'. In either case, the image is of a helmsman directing the island unerringly towards the heart of the imminent conflagration on mainland Europe.

Part I

1–2 The main ridge of the Cuillins describes a rough semicircle whose westernmost point falls more or less in the centre, at Sgurr na Banachdaich (965 metres).[14] Sgurr nan Gillean (also 965 metres) is to the north, where the ridge starts, while the highest peak, Sgurr Alasdair (991 metres), lies in the more southerly segment, where the ridge turns eastwards again. Having opened with the highest, the poet turns to his favourite, 'the lads' peak', which 'actually consists of five peaks, or pinnacles like needles, and furnishes a wonderful echo'.[15] See l. 16 'do choigeimh bidean'.[16] Dwelly's first meaning for 'sgùrr' is 'high, sharp-pointed hill'.

Here, as in the 'dedication', MacLean uses a line with four stresses. In modern Gaelic verse, rhyme involves the stressed vowel but not the consonant or consonants immediately following. The number of possible rhymes is thus limited to the number of stressed vowels present in the language. As a consequence, whole paragraphs may feature the same, repeated rhyme, as here at ll. 1–10.

In C, 'Sgùrr Alasdair' becomes 'an Sgurra Biorach' (literally the 'sharp-pointed' sgurr). MacLean may have learned in the interim that the peak had been named after the first man to ascend it in 1873, Sheriff Alexander Nicolson, the other name being used by local people, according to guide John MacKenzie of Sconser (for whom see also note to I. 100). Perhaps MacLean believed the earlier form to be more authentic, even if, by introducing it, he severed a possible, probably unconscious, link with the earlier of the poem's two dedicatees.

Interestingly, MacDiarmid's 'Dìreadh III', first published in the *Voice of Scotland* in December 1938, opens with 'a glorious description of the poet standing on the summit of Sgurr Alasdair looking at the Cuillin peaks of Skye'.[17]

18 The *Oxford English Dictionary* glosses 'gabbro' as 'a dark, coarse-grained plutonic rock of crystalline texture, consisting mainly of pyroxene, plagioclase feldspar, and often olivine'. MacLean speaks of the rock formation as waves, as a heaving or jolting ocean, initiating what is referred to in the 'Introduction' as a 'choreography' of the Cuillin. Perhaps the climber's sensation of his own movement is projected onto the hills he is ascending. It may not be unreasonable to discern, in passages such as this one, the opening of Part II and the close of the whole poem, an influence from the remarkable opening and closing passages of MacDiarmid's long poem 'On a Raised Beach', published in *Second Hymn to Lenin and Other Poems* in 1935.[18]

24 Another trope for Skye: 'sàr' is 'an augmentative prefix, expressing a great degree of any quality' but, as a noun, also means 'hero, brave warrior'.

25 Mary MacPherson (Màiri Mhòr nan Òran (1821–1898)), was born Mary MacDonald in Skeabost, Skye and moved to Inverness when she married in 1847. Her husband's death in 1871 left her with four children to care for. She was imprisoned briefly in 1872 on a charge of theft, and claimed that the injustice visited upon her on this occasion had spurred her to become a poet.[19] Upon release she moved to Glasgow, trained as a nurse and worked until 1882, a regular attender of Highland Society ceilidhs, familiar with leading figures in the land reform movement. Her political involvement was expressed in active support for MP Charles Fraser Mackintosh, and she became the unofficial bard of the Land League agitation. MacLean's generic reference here could be applied to several of her songs, including 'Eilean a' Cheò' where the poetess, having passed her 50th year, looks back on the island of her birth with fondness and nostalgia. The island is described as 'nan siantannan 's a' cheò', ('of the storms and the mist').[20] Politically radical, of humble origins and outspokenly polemical, Mary MacPherson fittingly completes the trio of poets elected to preside over MacLean's own poem.

31 Glossed by Dwelly as a 'circular hollow surrounded by hills', in the vicinity of the Cuillin 'coire' denotes an opening onto lower ground bounded by two outcrops of the ridge, usually with a stream running down it. Coire Làgan ('corrie of the hollow'), where the stream issues from a small loch, is bounded by Sgurr Dearg and its westward ridge Sgurr Mhic Coinnich, by Sgurr Thearlaich, Sgurr Alasdair and Sgurr Sgumain.[21]

32 To NW of the main ridge, Coire na Creiche ('corrie of the spoil', commemorating a clan fight between the MacLeods and the MacDonalds[22]) is divided by Sgurr an Fheadain into two distinct corries, Coir' a' Mhadaidh ('corrie of the fox') and Coir' a' Tairneilear ('the thunderer'). Given that 'the latter leads up to Sgurr a' Mhadaidh', Humble presumes the Ordnance Survey to have named these corries in the wrong order.

34 The 'fair corrie' is the next one N from Coire na Creiche, between Sgurr a' Bhàsteir and Bruach na Frithe.

35 A deft pun on 'fuaran' and 'fiùran' allows MacLean to make a seamless transition from the landscape he is observing to the people who once inhabited it, but are no longer to be found there. The blending of the natural and the human (from which one element is now lacking) is all the more cogent in that 'fiùran' has as first meaning 'sapling, branch', as second 'straight, free-growing young tree' and only as third 'blooming or handsome youth'.

43–46 An annotation by Douglas Young conserved in St Andrews identifies the first hoodie crow mentioned in these four lines (omitted in C) as Flora MacLeod, while the second, who would appear to be described at greater length in ll. 133ff., is said to be the headmaster of Portree High School.

Dame Flora Louisa Cecilia MacLeod of MacLeod was born in 1878 at 10 Downing Street, the home of her grandfather, then Chancellor of the Exchequer. In 1901 she married Hubert Walter, son of the principal owner of the London *Times*. Starting in 1921 she began to spend more time on Skye and was elected a district councillor in 1929, the year in which her father Reginald became clan chief. She succeeded him as 28th chief in 1935, not long before the composition of 'An Cuilithionn', thanks to an entail which allowed the title to pass to the eldest daughter should the male line fail. She took a lively interest in tourism in the postwar years and succeeded in turning Dunvegan Castle – whose demise the speaker of 'An Cuilithionn' so ardently desires – into one of Scotland's most popular tourist attractions. A portrait by Dennis Ramsay is in the Scottish National Portrait Gallery. A mischievous rumour claims that, when a German invasion was feared, she proposed waving the famed Fairy Banner from the cliffs of Dover in order to deter Hitler's forces. A note by Douglas Young in St Andrews indicates that ll.172–173 again refer to 'Flora Macleod, whom Lady Glen-Coats[23] calls "a Piccadilly Highlander"'.

When MacLean joined the staff of Portree High School in autumn 1934, the headmaster was Alexander Tait, who in 1935 became Rector of Stirling High School. His re-placement was Ian Murray, who died in post in 1962, shortly in advance of the date planned for his retirement. Difficult relations with Murray led not only MacLean, but also his close friend Jack Stuart to seek employment elsewhere. In a letter to MacDiarmid dated November 8th 1937 the poet writes:

We are in for some changes at Portree. Jack Stuart is going away in a fortnight; he is going to Aberfeldy. His going away will make Portree a very much less pleasant place for me... I do not like the idea of leaving Skye but things have changed for the worse in the school of late... Of course I shall never get a fellow like Stuart to teach with again and without him I am afraid of the prospect of Portree High School.

More is revealed in a letter to the same correspondent from Tobermory, dated February 27th 1938:

But about that time when I decided to leave Portree and got the job here I was in a strange mood. I was in a terrible state of anger against things done against me by a certain gent in Portree and I could not do anything about [it] as I had pledged myself not to use openly the inside information I did get. Being in such a mood I wasted about six weeks, November and December... I was obsessed with my own private affairs and feeling in such a mood of impotent wrath that I was unfit for anything in the way of work after school... I felt pretty bad about leaving Portree. In the circumstances I could do nothing else as I could not have waited there longer without throttling the headmaster of the school. Besides Stuart had left and Swanney, who was a very fine chap, was leaving too and I would have been badly isolated.

Two months later (April 28th) he concludes 'Almost the whole male staff has cleared out of Portree School in disgust at developments'.[24]

For Murray, see also ll. 133–151, where 136 would seem to express MacLean's execration of the man's hobnobbing with the local aristocracy. It seems likely that the epigram 'Dithis' ('Unpublished poems' 11) contains a further reference to MacLean's unpopular superior, the 'fear eile briagha bialach' (i.e. suffering from a degree of verbal diarrhoea). The image of the hooded crow returns in 'Mi fhìn agus feannag fhireann air sràid am Port Rìgh' ('Myself and a male hoodie-crow on a Portree street', 'Unpublished Poems' 26).

MacLean wrote to MacDiarmid on May 25th 1940 (year conjectural), with reference to a planned anthology to be published by the Hogarth Press, that 'If you think any part of "The Cuillin" will do you can use it provided you tell me beforehand as a good deal of it is libellous and I can't afford a libel action.'[25] The lines concerning the hoodie crows may well have been among those he had in mind.

In Douglas Young's 'projection',[26] these lines are rendered:

> a flabby hoodie-crow is crouching
> on the slippery roosts of a certain tower,
> a lying hoodie down in Portree there
> smarmily flatters that sleekit female.

47ff. MacLean's account of the Skye clearances shows a clear indebtedness to the history of the island published by his mother's eldest brother Alexander Nicolson in 1930, and specifically to the chapter 'The Clearances and Emigration'. As a boy, the poet was regularly sent with his elder brother John to spend summers on Skye, at his mother's original home in Braes, where they would have met up with this uncle, on holiday from Glasgow. There would have been much discussion of the history and genealogy of the island during these summers, which the poet no doubt also draws on here.[27]

The pairing of outrages perpetrated by the two principal landowning families of Skye, the MacLeods of Dunvegan and the MacDonalds of Armadale, is corroborated in a passage relevant to the treatment of the clearances throughout Part I of the poem:

> The grassy slopes on the west side of the island being considered to be eminently suitable for the rearing of Cheviots, clearances on a wholesale scale were there effected. From Duirinish, Bracadale, and Minginish people were evicted. The population of Bracadale in 1841 was 1824. By 1881 it had dropped to 929. The whole of the land in this fertile area was divided among six tenant farmers... Glenbrittle, which was occupied by crofters in fairly comfortable circumstances, was now converted into a sheep-run. The flats and the slopes of Eynort, and of Tuasdale, two of the most picturesque spots in Skye, bear the records of the clearances in unmistakable characters even to this day. A large community was driven off the former, and the manse was converted into a shepherd's cottage; from the latter

about a dozen families were cleared away. Sixteen families were expelled from the adjoining lands of Krakinish, and as many as thirty were forced to evacuate Fernilea. All these took place in Minginish; but a similar tale could be told of Bracadale, from one district of which, namely, Feorlig, seventeen families were removed in 1840.

And Trotarnish did not escape. The populous district of Scorrybreck was cleared from end to end. The fertile south end of Raasay suffered a similar fate, and numerous townships there were wholly given over to the rearing of sheep. Indeed, few districts escaped the effects of the change. The work of devastation was carried into Strath, where, among other districts, two populous townships, Boreraig and Suisnish, were ruthlessly cleared by the notorious Ballingall, Lord MacDonald's factor. This was in 1852; and, as some of the crofters offered resistance, they were forcibly evicted, their dwellings being razed to the ground in order to prevent their return... It has been said that as many as 2000 were dispossessed of land and home on the estate of MacLeod, and that the number for the whole island amounted to 3500 persons.

The evicted were in some cases provided with alternative accommodation; but invariably on those parts of the estate where the soil was inferior or exhausted. Hundreds were intruded on the crofting areas, where extreme overcrowding, with all its attendant evils, soon prevailed. A few instances will suffice to show the extent to which this congestion had been allowed to go. Two of the townships of Braes, namely, Penichorran and Achnahanaid, were divided among four and five tenants, respectively, about the year 1823. By 1883 the number of crofters had been increased to twenty-six in the former, and in the latter to seventeen, exclusive of several squatters.[28]

In the second chapter of his history of the island of Soay, Laurence Reed offers detailed information about the clearances in Minginish. Around 1724

it became the practice for all the farms on the Macleod estate to be let at a given date and for a fixed period of years... in 1754 the farms at the Rhu and Leasol were merged together to form one large unit... thus began a series of mergers which were to culminate 75 years later in south Minginish being organised as a single sheep farm. The man who oversaw these changes was Kenneth MacAskill...

Wholesale evictions on the Macleod estates can be dated from the "set", or renewal of rentals, of 1792:

it was decided to enlarge many of the farms so that they could be let at higher rents. In preparation for the change decrees of removal were taken out against about 150 tenants in Skye. Among those affected in the district of Minginish were nine joint-tenants at the Glenbrittle township which in this year was joined to Rhundunan. Some of the families were found alternative holdings up at Carbost; others were removed to Soay... At Whitsunday 1825 Carbost, Trien and Sataran became part of the Rhundunan farm. Macleod had bound himself to deliver them free of 'present possessors' and the small tenants involved now applied to the Government for grants of land in Canada and assistance to emigrate. In their petition they stated that they and their fathers had occupied small farms in the parish which the landlord had now consolidated as sheep walks. They had no place to remove to and deprived of land they were unable to support themselves.

The years 1810 and 1811 were especially crucial:

at the 'set' of 1810 Macleod sought a substantial increase in rents. This drew protests from every quarter. These, however, were ignored... Kenneth... chartered a ship and set sail for America with a large party of his own tenants. The ship sailed in 1811 and, running the blockade of American ports, docked safely in Wilmington. Some of the party stayed in North Carolina; others went to South Carolina where they joined MacAskill kinsmen who had emigrated to America before independence. Many years later Kenneth MacAskill was to be accused of taking these people away against their will and under false pretences. John Mackenzie, factor of the estate... replied, 'I believe they went of their own accord. It may or may not have been the case. I cannot say...'

The 'Slave Ship' to which MacLean refers repeatedly in his poetry in fact made it no further than Donaghadee in Ulster (see note to VI: 14–18). It is tempting to conclude that confused memories of Kenneth MacAskill's enterprise may lie behind the role it plays in 'An Cuilithionn'.

Reed quotes a correspondent to the *Oban Times* issue of April 24th 1886 who offers an interesting overview of events in Minginish:

When about 15 years of age, and that is now 60 years since, I accompanied the Sheriff Officer. My duties were to help in filling up each notice to quit and witness each being served upon the tenant. I cannot now remember the number but it must have been considerable when it took us fully three weeks to serve them all. I can well recall that in Minginish it was a wholesale affair... doubtless these evictions served still more to increase the poverty existing in already too much congested districts on the sea shore.[29]

James Hunter has the following to say concerning the clearances in Bracadale:

vast tracts of the Dunvegan estate, especially the parts of it contained by the parish of Bracadale, were put under sheep. Bracadale's population in 1821 was 2,103. Ten years later it was 1,769, and the decrease, according to the parish minister, was 'solely to be ascribed to the system of farming which has for some time been adopted, viz., throwing a number of farms into one large tack for sheep grazing and dispossessing and setting adrift the small tenants'. The number of tenants 'set adrift' in this way can be gauged from the fact that, in 1826, no fewer than 229 people from Bracadale, all of whom had received notices of eviction from MacLeod's estate managers, applied for assisted passages to Canada – their applications being accompanied by a similar set of requests from the neighbouring parish of Duirinish.[30]

The Dunvegan chiefs during the relevant period were Norman (d. 1801); John Norman, his son by a second marriage (d.1835); and this man's son in turn, also Norman (d. 1895). By the 1880s

> the estates of MacLeod of MacLeod, once extensive, had been considerably reduced in size through the extravagance of previous chiefs and the misfortunes of the destitution years in the 1840s.[31]

For the MacDonalds of Sleat, the corresponding figures are Alexander Wentworth (d. unmarried 1824); his younger brother Godfrey (d.1832); and the latter's son, also Godfrey (d.1863), who was succeeded by his own sons Somerled (d. unmarried 1875) and Ronald. Alexander Wentworth's father Alexander received a peerage in 1776, which then passed to his successors.

50   Again according to Nicolson

> emigration was considered to be the only expedient for relieving the difficulties of the situation, and many philanthropically-minded people formed associations for the purpose of raising funds in order to help those who might be induced to go abroad. By many the action of these agencies was thought to be a most com-mendable one, most of the ministers of Skye giving it their blessing.

He quotes the Rev. Coll MacDonald of Portree, 'enthusiastic in his praise' when writing in 1841, as follows:

> It cannot fail... to afford the highest satisfaction to every well-regulated mind to see the efforts now made by noble men, proprietors, and others connected with the Highlands of Scotland, for transferring the poor and labouring classes of the community to the British colonies... The highest praise is due to Lord MacDonald for his liberality in this beneficent work and patriotic enterprise, he having expended large sums of money, both this year and last, in conveying the poor people on his property to America.

A view more diametrically opposed to the poet's would be hard to imagine.

52   The 'same one' referred to euphemistically is the Devil, evoked at l. 47. One can perhaps see an anticipation of the diabolical 'ceilidh' which will ensue at I. 202.

53   In the neighbouring parish of Strath to the east, Loch Slapin forms a deep indentation of the coast, hidden by Blaven (927 metres) from the point where the poet imagines himself standing.

54   Lord MacDonald, referred to as 'morair' ('lord', 'earl') in the following line.

57   MacLean's use of district names is more evocative than precise. Presumably intended here is the Duirinish peninsula in Duirinish parish (of which Waternish also forms part), the easternmost part of Skye, nearly separated from the main body of the island by the inlets of Loch Dunvegan, to the N, and an arm of Loch Bracadale, to the S. Though both officially fall into the parish of Bracadale, in referring to Minginish MacLean generally has in mind the area immediately west of the Cuillins, including Glen Brittle and Glen Eynort but without arriving quite to Talisker. According to Groom, Minginish 'is prevailingly hilly and mountainous, and... terminates, at the SE, in a portion of the unique, curious, darkly sublime groups' of the Cuillins. Strictly speaking the latter lie in Minginish, which extends S from Loch Harport and W from River Sligachan. Groom adds that 'several vales in Minginish, and several detached fields in other parts on the coast, are almost the only low flat lands'. By Bracadale, he tends to understand the land east of Loch Bracadale and Loch Harport. Narrowing its range further still, the Ordnance Survey Explorer Map inserts the word 'Minginish' across the lower slopes of Sgurr Thuilm, S of Coire na Creiche, on the upper, E side of Glen Brittle.

59   To the paired oppressors of the people, MacLeods and MacDonalds, MacLean opposes two instances of vindicated resistance. The colourful description of events in Glendale and Edinburgh given in the chapter 'Black Winter in the Islands' from J. Cameron's *The Old and the New Highlands and Hebrides* is worth quoting at length, though not always factually reliable:

    ... the Braes dispute was hardly settled when the Glendale men came prominently to the front. This

beautiful glen, with its rich, loamy soil, is situated on
the western seaboard of the island, about ten miles from
Dunvegan, and nearly forty by road from Portree. It
contains one of the largest and most prosperous crofter
colonies in the Western Isles. The land is well cultivated,
the habitations of the people are more modern, the
people themselves are active, intelligent, and with a
reputation for hospitality to the stranger who finds
himself in these remote regions. The Glendale crofters in
1882 permitted their cattle and sheep to wander on the
farm of Waterstein in the teeth of an interdict against
them in the Court of Session. The officer of the Court of
Session duly proceeded to Glendale to serve the order,
but on arriving there the people refused to receive the
writs. It was stated that he was roughly handled by the
crowd, and that the following day some 2000 people
had travelled into Dunvegan, a distance of two miles, to
make certain that he had quitted the district. Immedi-
ately after his deforcement the county authorities
applied to Government for a gunboat or a military
force. The end of it was that on Monday, 5th February,
a gunboat, the *Jackal*, arrived in the North of Skye.
On Friday, the 9th, she anchored in Poltiel opposite
Glendale and sent an officer on shore. It was then
arranged that the people should meet Mr Malcolm
MacNeil, of the Board of Supervision, and Captain
Macdonald, of Waternish, in the Free Church at two
o'clock the same afternoon. Mr MacNeil told them
that the offence of which they had been guilty could
only be forgiven when four offenders – John
Macpherson, Malcolm Matheson, Donald Macleod,
and John Morrison – had surrendered themselves to
receive the punishment they deserved.

In the event five men stood trial at the Court of Session in
Edinburgh and were given a prison sentence of two months.

The Glendale "martyrs" were liberated on the 15th
May, when they were met at the prison door by about
1500 people headed by two pipers, who marched to the
Ship Hotel, where the liberated men were entertained to
breakfast. The same evening John Macpherson pro-
ceeded to Skye by Strome Ferry. As the *Clydesdale*, by

which he travelled, approached the Braes, three bonfires
were noticed ablaze and several flags were flying. When
the steamer rounded into Portree Bay, a large crowd
congregated on the pier. Before Macpherson could place
his foot on shore he was raised on the shoulders of four
stalwart fellows, who carried him aloft, hat in hand,
bowing to the crowd, to the Portree Hotel, a piper
leading the way. Macpherson, on reaching the hotel,
addressed the people.[32]

It is worth nothing, and may not be entirely accidental,
that the image of a stallion which plays such an important
role in the development of 'An Cuilithionn' is derived from
the rock formation on the coast of Waterstein, the area
whose grazing rights lay at the origin of the dispute in
Glendale.

60   Consistent with the general softening of satirical attack,
this line was rendered vaguer in C: 'gu caistealan mòra
leagail' ('to bring down big castles').

61ff.   Nicolson describes the antecedents of what became
known as the 'Battle of Braes' in the following terms:

In the district of Braes a crisis was approaching. The
grazing of Ben Lee was due to run out of lease in 1882,
and the crofters of the three southern townships were
negotiating for its restoration to themselves. Time and
again they declared their willingness to pay, in the
aggregate, a higher rent than that paid by the 'sitting'
tenant; but their plea went unheeded.

When redress was denied them, they took matters into
their own hands. They allowed their sheep to stray over
the whole range of the mountain, and some went so far
as to refuse to pay rent until their claims should be
recognised.

Certain men amongst the agitating crofters were
marked out for punishment. In order to have them
evicted from their holdings, the Sheriff's officer in
Portree, with two assistants, went to the Braes to serve
notices of ejectment. The officials were met on the way
to Braes by the women and children, who forced them
to burn the documents on the public highway, in
addition to heaping other indignities upon them.

Sheriff Ivory, the chief legal authority in Inverness-shire, had recourse to the Chief Constable of Glasgow who, according to Nicolson, sent men northwards without so much as informing the city magistrates. The battle proper commenced at 6am on April 17th 1882, when the local people observed the policemen approaching in the company of ten local constables, two sheriffs and their officers:

> the invading force was met by a hurriedly summoned body of the people of Balmeanach and Penichorran, about one hundred strong, many of them dishevelled and in a state of deshabille; for news of the invasion had come to most of them whilst they were still in bed... most of the able-bodied men of the district had already left home for the Irish fishing... if they had been present that day a situation fraught with alarming consequences would have developed.
>
> As it was, matters soon assumed an ugly aspect; for no sooner had certain men been arrested, and a start made by the police to return, than, at the instigation of the women, a general attack was launched against the expeditionary force... The road goes through a narrow gorge at a place called Allt na Gobhlag, and there the police were assailed on both flanks with relentless vigour... the worst was yet to come. About 300 yards to the north, the road is cut along the face of a steep declivity...
>
> The race for this strategic point started in deadly earnest, and a small body of the natives having secured it first... An avalanche of boulders was sent hurtling down the precipitous slope, so that several of the policemen were grievously injured...
>
> Having now gained the more open ground, the constables, who had hitherto used their batons only, began to retaliate with stones also; and the crofters, incensed to fury for having lost their position, closed with the police in grim hand-to-hand strife... the marvel is that all escaped with their lives. The women fought like Amazons...[33]

It should not be forgotten, where the emergence of determined resistance on the part of the crofters is concerned, that

the most important factor influencing the course of
events in the Highlands and Islands in 1881 was the
emergence of the Irish question – first, agrarian reform,
followed by the demand for self-government.[34]

64   The poet's claim that resistance at the Braes woke the
entire country from its torpor may seem hyperbolical, but is
justified in view of the course events took. Warships having
arrived in the lochs of Skye, troops were sent onshore. The
longer-term outcome was the setting up of a Royal
Commission whose report led to the passing in 1886 of the
Crofters' Holdings Act, which introduced fair rentals and
security of tenure for the smallholders.

65   From here as far as I. 114 comes the first sizeable
excision practised in C. Lines with three stresses indicate the
intervention of a more lyrical and reflective tone.

67   Trotternish is the northernmost part of Skye, a peninsula
lying between Loch Snizort and the Sound of Raasay,
containing the parishes of Kilmuir and Snizort.

69   Waternish (also Vaternish) is the peninsula bounded by
Loch Snizort, to the E, and Loch Dunvegan, to the W, in the
parish of Duirinish.

74   Waterstein (also Vaterstein), the 'water stone' is the
westernmost spot in Skye, Neist Point, also known as 'an
eist fhiadhaich' or 'the wild stallion', a denomination
which, according to Forbes, is particularly apt when a
southerly or south-west wind is blowing. He also gives the
forms 'feist', 'an fheist'. The snorting MacLean refers to
could be associated with the impact of the sea at this spot
during storms. Again according to Forbes, 'an t-Aigeach' is a
striking rocky outcrop facing NW half a mile away. The
closeness of the two, and the association with horses, may
justify seeing this reference as introducing the stallion which
will become a central symbol of the poem. Forbes derives
'eist' from Norse 'hestr' meaning a horse, but also cites the
words 'eist', 'eitionach' for 'a gelded horse'.[35] If MacLean
were aware, however dimly, of this further nuance, could that
have helped to suggest the passage at III: 94ff. where the
stallion is gelded by the bourgeoisie and their minions?

75   Sleat is the peninsula forming the southernmost part of
Skye, separated from the mainland by the Sound of Sleat to
the E. The W coast faces onto the Atlantic, and offers fine

views of the Cuillins (see l. 78). Groom comments that 'the soil of much of the arable land on the SE side is a deep and not unproductive clay' while, with 'its larch plantations and trim hedgerows' the district 'has been termed "the best wooded, the sunniest, and the most carefully cultivated part of Skye"'.[36]

78   Blaven (927 metres), not part of the main Cuillin ridge, but some distance to the E, is nonetheless composed of gabbro and can be viewed from Sleat rising above Loch Slapin.

79   Dwelly refers 'guala' to 'gualann' ('shoulder'), listing as second meaning 'elbow or corner of a mountain'. The valley known as Glen Brittle lies immediately to the W of the Cuillins.

81   The point here is that the speaker's affection for the barren terrain around the Cuillins is such that he would be willing to pay for it three times what was disbursed for infinitely more fertile terrain. Scorrybreck (or Scorrybreac) near Portree would have considerable resonance for MacLean as the ancestral home of his mother's people, the Nicolsons (Clann Mhic Neacail).[37] The old house there was most likely abandoned in 1825, when the last Nicolson chief to live on Skye emigrated to Tasmania. His creditors gave up Scorrybreck in 1827 and, after the estate had been cleared, a handsome new building was erected.[38] The transfer of evicted tenants from Scorrybreck to Braes is referred to in 'Am Putan Airgid' ('The Silver Button', 'Unpublished Poems' 40):

> Clann is mnathan is fir mhòra
> Sgoirebreac am faing 'sa Bhràighe,
> a' bhochdainn 's an t-anacothrom 'gan cràdhadh.
>
> Agus raointean gorma brìoghmhor
> Sgoirebreac gun dad brìgh dhaibh.[39]

Concerning 'fiachan an uasail', literally 'the nobleman's debts', geologist Archibald Geikie prefaces his account of the clearance of Kilbride, in Strath parish, with the following observation:

> The land belonged to the wide domain of Lord MacDonald, whose affairs were in such a state that he

had to place himself in the hands of trustees. These men had little local knowledge of the estate; and though they doubtless administered it to the best of their ability, their main object was to make as much money as possible out of the rents, so as, on the one hand, to satisfy the creditors, and, on the other, to hasten the time when the proprietor might be able to resume possession...[40]

85 The speaker surveys the ridge of the Cuillins from what now appears on the Ordnance Survey maps as Coire an t-Seasaich (earlier maps preserve the form with 'g'), just north of the Mararaulin bog which will play such a major role in the development of the poem.

87 Sgurr Sgumain (946 metres) lies SW of Sgurr Alasdair on the outcrop of the main Cuillin ridge (whence 'sròn', literally 'nose', with second meaning in Dwelly 'promontory, headland running from a mountain to a "strath"') between Coire Làgan (to the N) and Coir' a' Ghrunnda (to the S).

88 The poet's gaze pans round Nwards to the point where the pass of Bealach na Glaic Moire cuts into the main ridge SW of Sgurr an Fheadain (688 metres) and Bidein Druim nan Ramh (896 metres).

89–90 The archangel Michael, traditionally leader of the heavenly hosts, is named in the last vision of Daniel (Dan. 12.1) and also appears several times in the Hebrew apocrypha. Gabriel bears the word of God to Daniel (Dan. 8.16, 9.21) and, in the gospel of Luke, announces the births of both John the Baptist and Christ (1: 10–20, 26–37). Given MacLean's atheistic stance at the time of writing, it comes as a surprise to find him invoking the names of two archangels. The paragraph where they appear constitutes a fantasy of buying back, of reacquisition and repopulation. The speaker desires to be rid of these heavenly beings, who are invited to take 'sheep, cattle and sheep-pens' along with them.

99 The return to quatrains marks the arrival of a more prosaic tone. In 1989 ll. 99–114 were omitted, along with the further attack on Kennedy-Fraser at 127–132 and the return of the hoodie-crows at 133–151, according to a general tendency in C to eliminate topical or personal references, thus softening the poem's satirical edge.

100   Not only Dame Flora MacLeod, but the Prince of
Wales and the Archbishop of Canterbury counted among the
associates of naturalist, photographer and folklorist Seton
Paul Gordon (1886–1977), born in Aberdeenshire, educated
at Oxford and later a resident of Aviemore and Duntulm in
Skye. Of private means, he was able to devote his life to his
twin passions – piping, and the landscape and wildlife of the
Scottish Highlands. Of a prolonged stay in Skye between
August and November 1925, biographer Raymond Eagle
observes that

> The Gordons were fast being accepted into island
> society and soon were at Dunvegan again and at
> Armadale Castle for tea, then the home of the
> MacDonalds of Sleat. On both occasions Seton joined
> in piping after tea.

Again according to Eagle, Gordon

> stressed that, contrary to popular belief, these hills are
> not just the preserve of rock climbers, and with common
> sense the climbing is very easy. Up to that time he had
> been on the summit of six peaks without once needing a
> rope. On an ascent of Sgurr Alasdair he was accom-
> panied by John MacKenzie of Sconser, a fascinating
> figure who was the only full-time professional guide in
> the Cuillins. He died in 1933 well into his eighties and
> climbed almost to the end of his life.[41]

Gordon's most productive period, during which he published
16 popular titles, came in the 1920s and 1930s, and he was
awarded the C.B.E. in 1939, the very year in which MacLean
composed 'An Cuilithionn'.
   Aside from the class animosities evident at this point,
MacLean is also engaging in a competition for representa-
tion, entering into a polemical relationship with other figures
who have attempted to purvey the culture and the
background of Gaelic Scotland to a broader public. An
impression of Gordon's approach as a writer, and a sense of
how strongly it differs from MacLean's, may be gained from
the following extract, quoted in Raymond Eagle's biography:

> Beneath an overhanging boulder I lay awaiting the
> coming of the storm. The clouds now approached more

slowly, and the moon sailed into view from behind the rocks of Sgurr an Sgumban. She moved, an orb of glowing bronze, serenely across the velvet starless sky like some friendly beacon. A thundercloud crept slowly, relentlessly, across her face. Distant sheet lightning played upon the horizon and it was not long before the thunderstorm drew near. Momently the lightning flickered more brightly, but the bursting of the storm over Coire Lagan at midnight was dramatic in its swiftness. The dusk of a summer's night changed quickly to the blackness of a midwinter's evening. This pall was suddenly rent by a blinding flash. The lightning appeared to strike Sgurr Alasdair. A glowing halo for a moment surrounded the hilltop. Almost on the instant came the thunder, followed within a second by a second report as Sgurr Dearg threw back on the pulsating night the echo of that fearsome peal. Flash succeeded flash, peal succeeded peal. The sky glowed. The corrie was illuminated so that each stone was clear. Once forked lightning sped across the heavens from behind Sgurr Dearg. Quivering and changing colour like some living creature the lightning hastened across the sky. It was as though some mighty being had struck the rocks with a stupendous hammer, causing the sparks to fly.[42]

103 MacLean never made a secret of his hostility to the turn of the century revival of interest in Gaelic folklore and music known as the Celtic Twilight, despite his evident respect for the poetry of Yeats. Writing of the work of William Sharp (Fiona MacLeod) (1856–1905), Derick Thomson observes that

> the 'Celtic Twilight' style derived from a false idea of Gaelic literature... In place of the robust heroes of Gaelic mythology and tales, 'Celtic Twilight' writing gives us the rather wan and ethereal young men and women who appear in Pre-Raphaelite paintings.[43]

Referring specifically to Kennedy-Fraser's compilations, MacLean writes in his essay 'Old songs and new poetry' (first published in 1970) that

> The Celtic Twilight of the 1890s and its product, *Songs of the Hebrides*, were to the realities of Gaelic song

poetry as Victorian Gothic is to the North French cathedrals. There is, however, in Gaelic song such an intrinsic quality of poetry that it could not fail to come through again and again, even in the *Songs of the Hebrides*, just as there is such a quality in Gothic architecture that it often shines through sham Gothic. In the 1920s, therefore, much "educated" Gaelic opinion was right in preferring the *Songs of the Hebrides* to almost all 19th-century Gaelic song, which now seems, to me at any rate, to have been a natural product of the Clearances, the Evangelical Revival and the Education Act of 1872.[44]

Marjory Kennedy-Fraser (1857–1930) was the daughter of celebrated Scottish singer David Kennedy (1825–1886). Three of her siblings died when fire consumed the municipal theatre of Nice, France, in 1881. Her father died five years afterwards. She herself was left to care for two small children when her husband died in 1890. A visit to Eriskay in 1905 at the prompting of painter John Duncan, a close friend, coincided with the last year of the life of folklorist and poet Father Allan McDonald. Kennedy-Fraser made recordings, using a wax cylinder phonograph, in Eriskay in 1907 and on Barra in 1907–8 and later. She published her arrangements for voice and piano (sometimes harp or clàrsach) as *Songs of the Hebrides* (three volumes, 1909 to 1921). In a paper read to the Gaelic Society of Inverness on March 27th 1925 Malcolm MacFarlane observes that her collection

> is also marred by the tunes being adapted to English words and by the liberties taken with their original forms... they have, in cases, to be timed anew for the Gaelic singer... the new words are often conceived in a false Gaelic spirit for which there is no valid excuse.[45]

MacLean's less than generous epigram ('Unpublished Poems' 34) interestingly uses the imagery of gelding which will be so important in Part III of 'An Cuilithionn'.

109 The capitalisation of 'terror' in MacLean's English version has been reproduced in the Gaelic, implying as it does a reference to the mass executions of June 1793 to July 1794 which followed on the French Revolution of 1789.

110 Tobar nan Uaislean (the 'spring of the nobles') rises in Bealach a' Mhàim, at the foot of Fionn Choire. Presumably

MacLean is playing sarcastically with the meaning of the toponym, contrasting the willingness of Seton Gordon and Kennedy-Fraser to mix in aristocratic circles with his own stubborn avoidance of them.

112   Neil MacLeod (1843–1924) was the most popular Gaelic poet of the 19th century. His verse is gathered in *Clarsach an Doire* (1883 and subsequent editions). Born in Glendale, son of the poet Dòmhnall nan Òran, he moved to Edinburgh aged 22 and stayed there for the remainder of his life, working in the tea business. Thomson finds MacLeod guilty of 'invented detail and spurious emotion', of 'simulated emotion issuing in sentimentality'. MacLean told MacDiarmid that 'I don't like his stuff in general',[46] yet MacLeod may have evoked his sympathy with a song like the celebrated 'An gleann san robh mi òg' ('The glen where I was young'), which refers, in muted terms, to the tragedy of the evictions. Thomson concedes that in 'Na croitearan Sgitheanach' ('The Skye crofters') McLeod

> does come to grips with the situation of eviction, and the question of human rights, as actuality, but only in some stanzas, while others slide into the grooves of jingoism or braggadocio.[47]

117–122   The speaker moves into prophetic mode, indicating that the fate visited on the dwellings of the Gaelic peasantry in turn awaits the homes of those responsible for evicting them. There can be little doubt that, had the wholesale communist revolution repeatedly adumbrated in the course of the poem ever taken place, the resulting climate would have been far from hospitable to either the Dunvegan MacLeods or the MacDonalds of Sleat. The image of castle and residence buried beneath luxuriant vegetation is an oneiric one, in line with the visionary tone which increasingly come to dominate 'An Cuilithionn'. A fire which destroyed the south wing of Dunvegan Castle in 1938 elicited the following biting quatrain from MacLean:

An Dùn 'na theine

> Ged theab gun do loisgeadh Dùn Bheagain
> cha robh "theab" an losgadh nan taighean
> a loisg MacLeòid a chum Dùn Bheagain
> a chumail uasal air a chreagan.[48]

123   Glen Eynort, with a river feeding into Loch Eynort, is
the next glen W of Glen Brittle in Minginish. MacLean
probably has in mind the ruined settlement E of Biod Mòr
(384 metres).

133–151   See note to I. 45 for a possible identification of this
figure, who articulates explicitly the speaker's irrevocable
exclusion from bourgeois circles. He would write to Douglas
Young (letter dated October 1st 1940), shortly after arriving
at Catterick Camp in Yorkshire to begin training as a
signaller, that

> I can't pronounce on the English yet but my first
> impression is that I do not at all dislike the proletarian
> Englishman much as I loathe the bourgeois English-
> man... I am not sensitive to material *differentia* but very
> to class *differentia*. I loathe the English bourgeois and
> more so the Anglo-Scot bourgeois but honestly I like
> the English privates here. Most of them too I suppose
> are not proletarians but petty-bourgeois, people of the
> same class as that in which I am at present myself but
> some are genuine proletarians.

The uninterrupted series of adjectives at ll. 139–142, with
their luscious invective, may be a conscious gesture in the
direction of Mac Mhaighstir Alasdair, though in a letter to
Douglas Young dated September 7th 1941 MacLean would
complain, referring to the Gaelic poetry he studied at school,
about 'the heavily adjectival stuff of which we got a
plethora'.

152   Sgurr a' Ghreadaidh (973 metres) ('the peak of mighty
winds or clear waters') stands above the W facing corrie of
the same name, between the outcrops of Sgurr Thuilm (881
metres) and Sgurr nan Gobhar (630 metres), slightly N and E
of the point at which the main ridge turns E after Sgurr na
Banachdach (965 metres). Coire an Uaigneis ('the corrie of
loneliness or privacy') descends to the E.

167   Here and in the following passage, MacLean repro-
duces in his English version the typical Gaelic word order,
with the verb preceding its subject.

168–169   This is one point where MacLean's trimming,
cutting and pasting of the A text for his C revision issued
in a moment of high poetry. A detached leaf in National
Library of Scotland ms 29560, f1, shows the poet working over

ll. 163–170. There is no clear evidence for dating this sheet, which may come from as late as the mid 1980s. One wonders if the revision was prompted in part by the desire to eliminate the highlighted term 'bùirdeas'. Beginning with 'ciamar a chumas beò an smuain seo', MacLean thought of 'mhaireas beò', then 'sheasas brìgh na smuain seo/ air rathaidean sleamhna an t-saoghail?'[49] Then the brilliant notion of the bullet (recalling the close of 'Hallaig') produced 'dhiùchd ach thàinig sian a' pheileir' for l. 167 (now l. 88 in C), with the following line proceeding through 'ciamar a sheasas leis an smaoin seo' to 'ciamar a chumas leis an smaoin seo' then finally 'ciamar chumas an gaol seo/ grèim air creig dheighe 'n t-saoghail?'[50] The reference to 'creig dheighe' (the 'icy rock') is apposite in a poem whose central image is a mountain, while the phonetic echoing of 'grèim', 'creig' and 'dheighe' gives overall cogency to the new solution.

170ff. MacLean wrote to Young in a letter dated March 30th 1942 that 'Of "The Cuillin" the first thing was the "Ann an talla" lyric written in Mull in the spring of 1938'. Whether this applies to all eight quatrains or just the first seven is unclear. A letter to Young from Raigmore Hospital in Inverness dated April 20th 1943 warns that 'your version of the "rant" [a nickname for 'An Cuilithionn'] misses out one quatrain of the London ball-room scene viz. "Agus fear eile a bha caoidh... tràigh" but I haven't the Gaelic to check the whole version'. This indicates both the nature of the social gathering in question and that the quoted stanza may not be the last. One can discern here the beginning of the diabolical ceilidh of clearers which is developed more fully at ll. 202ff., and balanced at VII: 86ff. by an assembly on the Cuillins of the poem's intellectual and political heroes.

175 Sgùrr Thuilm (881 metres) is an outcrop of the Cuillins lying N and E of Sgùrr a' Mhadaidh, between Coire a' Mhadaidh and Coire a' Ghreadaidh. The two mountains of Healaval More (469 metres) and Healaval Beg (actually slightly higher, at 488 metres), also known as MacLeod's Tables, are near Dunvegan in Duirinish.

182–189 An instance of careful planning in 'An Cuili-thionn' is the way the voice and the bones referred to here anticipate the two monologues at the beginning of Part VI, from a girl supposed to have been forced onto the Slave Ship at Gesto, and a man drowned in the *Annie Jane*

off Vatersay in the Outer Hebrides. Duagraich is referred
by Forbes to 'a loch and hill in Bracadale'.[51] In a letter to
Douglas Young dated August 19th 1940, MacLean speaks
of 'the rhymed list of Skye place names of which I have two
lines in "The Cuillin"...'. A second quatrain on the 1938 fire
at Dunvegan Castle ironically links it with the fate of the
Annie Jane:

> *Air an adhbhar cheudna*

> Cà bheil Leòdaich gu cur às
> smùidreach gharbh na h-aitreibh seo?
> Chuir an cuan Barrach iadsan às
> air cùlaibh Caolas Bhatarsaigh.[52]

191 For Neil MacLeod and 'An gleann san robh mi òg'
('The glen where I spent my youth') see note to l. 112.

194–197 A note by Douglas Young in St Andrews refers
these lines to the Jura-born poet Donald MacKechnie
(Dòmhnall MacEacharn) (1836–1908), who spent the latter
part of his life in Edinburgh, mixing with figures such as
Donald Mackinnon, Alexander Carmichael and Sheriff
Nicolson. In Thomson's view, his

> verse as a whole is dull and pedestrian, in distinction to
> his prose, which has humour, gaiety and a sense of style.
> Perhaps several of his poems suffer from being com-
> petition pieces. The jingoist strain appears in his verse
> also.[53]

198 Note the surprisingly short line.

199–200 The 'Glendale martyr' (see note to l. 59) John
Macpherson is buried in St Congan's chapel. Given his
proximity to Dunvegan Castle and the MacLeod landowners,
it is fitting that he should rise from the grave to express
displeasure at the social goings-on in London.

202ff. Note how the use of rhyming couplets gives energy
and verve to this paragraph.

208 Am Bàsteir (glossed by Humble as 'the executioner')
(934 metres) lies W of Sgurr nan Gillean where the N
extremity of the Cuillin ridge peters out. The denomination
'fiacail' ('tooth') could suggest that MacLean has in mind
Sgùrr a' Bhàsteir (898 metres), W of Loch a' Bhàsteir and of
Coire a' Bhàsteir, which opens to the N of the main peak.

210ff. The targets of MacLean's attack at this point include several tacksmen (from Gaelic 'fear-taic', 'supporting men'), intermediary figures who stood between the landlord and more lowly tenantry, and were frequently entrusted with the business of carrying out evictions.[54]

211 A descendant of Martin Martin, who wrote around 1695 a celebrated *Description of the Western Islands of Scotland* first published in 1703, Dr Nicol Martin

> acquired Boreraig and Husabost... from the Nicolson family in 1840, and owned only a small part of Glendale proper but held a tack of the Waterstein grazing on the far side of the township of Upper and Lower Milovaig.[55]

His lands lay on the west side of Loch Dunvegan. Martin told the Glendale hearing that

> The crofters are getting indolent and lazy besides. Look at this winter: they did nothing but go about with fires on every hill and playing at sentinels to watch for fear of the sheriff's officer coming with warnings to take their cattle for rent... I would give £500 today if all the crofters on my place went away.[56]

His nephew Donald Archibald threatened to resettle 'the whole of the Glendale people'.[57]

212 An Alexander MacAllister was in the 1880s the laird of Strathaird, the Mackinnon homeland.[58] The family originated from Kintyre. Dymock refers the passage to an earlier laird with the same name (1744–1831).

214, 216 In 1853 Hugh MacAskill ceded the northern or Glenbrittle division of his farm to Donald C. Cameron from Barcaldine in Argyllshire. On Hugh's death in 1864, Cameron combined this with the other division, known as Rhundunan, and held both for a further 20 years. According to John MacInnes, Cameron's grandson, the last of the family, died in the 1930s. Kenneth MacAskill, who farmed Glenbrittle from 1775 to 1841, employed a certain Ewen Macmillan from Lochaber as his farm manager.[59] Douglas Young, however, in his English 'projection' of 'An Cuilithionn', has at this point 'big Ewen MacAskill'. Could MacLean's memory have slipped up here? Reed lists no Ewen among the MacAskill farmers of Glenbrittle.[60] For more on

the clearances of Minginish, and on Kenneth MacAskill's
role in them, see note to ll. 47ff.

219 Captain, later Major William Fraser of Kilmuir, came
of the Frasers of Culbokie in the Black Isle and was a Liberal
in politics. In the 1880s he was the third most important
landowner on Skye. The crofters on his Kilmuir estates,
purchased from the trustees of Lord MacDonald in 1855,
were particularly discontented. He was described variously as
'the rack-renter, the process server, the persecutor of "the
brave old crofter"' and 'a greedy and grasping Highland
laird... the most conspicuous example of a ferocious and
peremptory land merchant, hungering for a large return upon
his capital'.[61] The mansion house in Uig where Fraser was
in the habit of spending half the year was destroyed by a
flood in 1877, Màiri Mhòr composing a song on the subject.[62]
Press coverage of the disaster led to a libel action against
John Murdoch of *The Highlander* for £1000 damages, at the
conclusion of which Major Fraser was awarded £50. See
further note to l. 275.

221 Ballingall figures more than once in Alexander Nicol-
son's account:

> ... the wicked work of eviction went relentlessly on.
> The veriest pretext was often considered sufficient
> justification for turning a whole community adrift.
> When Lord MacDonald's factor, Ballingall, wished to
> extend the deer forest of Sconser, in 1853, two families
> of crofters and seven of cottars were cleared off Arich-
> arnach, eight from Moll, and sixteen crofters, in
> addition to several squatters, were removed from Ceann
> nan Creagan and Tormicheag...[63]

In evidence to what is commonly referred to as the Napier
Commission, after its chairman Francis, tenth Lord Napier,
Ballingall is described as 'threatening to cut the couples from
above our heads if we would not quit'.[64]

A certain Gibbon(s), factor to MacLeod of Dunvegan, 'an
Englishman, and... not a good one', crops up several times in
the evidence given to the commission. John McPhee, a crofter
from Harlosh, speaks of him removing seventeen families:

> He placed these families as close together as the sea
> would allow him; and we have but very little land, and

it will not support us; and some of those he took from
Minginish were placed upon peat soil, which had never
previously been cultivated...[65]

Donald Campbell of Struanmore tells how, having added five
townships to the tack of Ulinish and Ebost

Gibbons... put away the tenants out of the glens. They
were in very comfortable circumstances, with cattle and
sheep and horses. He sent them away at the term of
Whitsunday... There were plenty of people at that time
in Ebost and Ulinish. He sent five of the remaining
families to a wet black place called Garamore, which
had not been inhabited before. Of those who were in
Ulinish he sent twenty families to Struanmore. He there
gave them the corner of a piece of ground plotted out
among them all, and none of them had a cow but one.
He was a merchant. That was in 1841... He compelled
them to give him four days' work cutting peats each
year, and for which he was giving them a lippie of meal.
Mr Gibbons was fifteen years in possession of the
place.[66]

223 Neil Shaw, who had been moved from Bracadale to
the lower part of Duirinish, was a cottar in Lowergill when a
Macdonald of Tormore in Sleat, who acted as factor to both
the MacLeod and the MacDonald estates, made his
appearance on the scene:

he never rested, and nothing would do until he became
possessed of our lands. He removed the five families of
us, and I believe that they did not owe a sixpence of
arrears among them.[67]

Donald McGillivray read to the commission a paper dated
May 14th 1883, concerning Lower Breakish:

We still had a right to keep sheep or cattle on the hill
pastures until Tormore, the late factor, deprived us of
all the hill, and ordered our sheep to be gathered to
Kinloch sheepfold, where we had either to kill them at
once, or sell them for half price. He left us a patch of
the hill for a shift for our cattle twice a year... In the
second year of his factorship he (Tormore) added to our

rent from 3s. to 16s. per lot. Moreover, he charged the township £28 extra for the patch of hill pasture.[68]

In B, Tormore becomes 'Fear a' Choire', which is also the reading of C. On the basis of family name and farm it is not always possible to pin down a reference to a single individual. This vagueness, or inclusiveness, can of course be looked on as an advantage in MacLean's treatment of the class of tacksmen. A MacKinnon of Corrie was factor to MacLeod of Raasay in the 1840s. MacLean is presumably referring to Lord MacDonald's factor in the Braes area, who cleared Ferindonald in the late 1860s, and of whom John Mathieson observes wrily that 'he was not very easy. We had not much to say in his praise.'[69]

Alasdair Roy MacDonald of Bernisdale in Snizort was a solicitor and factor popularly regarded as a demon. He administered a whole range of Skye estates in the 1880s. At a meeting in 1884, crofters specifically requested his dismissal in favour of a replacement with a better understanding of agriculture. MacDonald resigned most of his duties in 1886 on the grounds of ill health.[70]

224–225 MacLean switches the focus briefly to his native island of Raasay. In 1842–1843 the factor for the island's last MacLeod proprietor 'began to clear people from various parts of the island'. Some 'were cleared to improve the leasable value of land, particularly on the east coast between Eyre and Screapadal. Many of the writs of removal survive'. Bankrupted, the chief was forced to sell up and emigrated to Tasmania (see note to l. 81, also 'Unpublished poems' 40). Having bought the island in November 1843, George Rainy took possession at Whitsuntide 1846 and cleared fourteen townships, converting arable land to sheep farming. A John MacLeod of Arnish is said to have disobeyed a rule of Rainy's that no-one on the island was to get married. When Rainy's son died aged 27 in 1872 the island was bought by George G. MacKay, whose 'main achievement was the raising of all the rents', and who 'took a bad name away with him' when he left, selling the island in 1874.[71] According to Norma MacLeod, Rainy 'drastically reduced the population', with 'approximately 330 people leaving Raasay for Skye and the mainland between 1848 and the early 1850s'.[72]

246–254   These lines are omitted from C. The Gaelic spelling of foreign toponyms is taken from National Library of Scotland ms 29558 f27, where another hand, probably John MacKechnie's, has inserted them into the typescript.

247–248   The Spanish Civil War began when a group of army generals launched an insurrection against the government of the Second Republic on July 17th 1936. Barcelona (see I. 251) fell to the so-called "nationalists" on January 26th 1939, Madrid on March 28th. Valencia surrendered the following day. The end of the war was marked on April 1st by a victory speech broadcast on the radio by Francisco Franco, who would retain effective control of the country till his death in 1975. The Spanish Civil War figures repeatedly in MacLean's poetry (see e.g. 'Dàin do Eimhir' XVIII, XXII, XXXV).

Pope Pius XI (Ambrogrio Damiano Achille Ratti) died on February 10th 1939 aged 81. It was he who concluded the Lateran Treaty or Concordat with Mussolini's regime in Italy in 1929. Similar negotiations with Hitler's government in Germany were entrusted to Eugenio Pacelli, who succeeded Ratti as Pope Pius XII. Hitler became German chancellor on January 30th 1933, and the relevant treaty was signed in June of that year. The encyclical 'Dilectissima nobis', issued on June 3rd 1933, spoke out against the Spanish Republican government's expropriation of church properties. In 1937 Pacelli issued a further encyclical, in German, entitled 'Mit brennender Sorge' ('With acute concern'), condemning Nazi racist ideology and violations of the concordat.

For an epigram on the Vatican's reaction to the fall of Barcelona, whose third line indicates a dating towards the very start of 1940, see 'Unpublished Poems' 2.

249   Conservative politician Arthur Neville Chamberlain (1869–1940) was prime minister of Great Britain from May 1937 to May 1940, when he resigned in the wake of the Allied retreat from Norway. As part of a policy of appeasing the increasingly aggressive claims of the Nazi leader, on September 29th 1938 Chamberlain put his name to an agreement in Munich (see l. 254) which forced Czechoslovakia to cede the border regions known as the Sudetenland. An initial capitulation on the Czechoslovak side on September 21st had produced increased demands from Hitler, upon which a new cabinet under General Jan Surov announced a general mobilisation. The attitude of the Western powers, however, was decisive. The Czech provinces of Bohemia, Moravia and Silesia lost some 38% of their territory, with a population of around 750,000 Czechs and 3.2 million Germans. After a declaration of independence by the Slovak diet on March 14th 1938, Czech president Hácha surrendered to Hitler. German troops occupied the remaining Czech territories, including Prague, the following day. Chamberlain is the target of a brief satirical poem from MacLean's 1943 volume:

Do Mgr. Niall Mac an t-Seumarlain

Leanaidh t' aodann-sa na h-àlan,
brath nan Teacach 's nan Spàinnteach
air a dhealbh nad smuiseal grànda.[73]

250   A simple internet search will show how the supposed war cry of Odin has been revived by more than one latter day enthusiast of radically right wing and racist ideology.

251   Though the treaties concluded at Versailles and St Germain specifically vetoed any union between the two countries, Austria was annexed to the Third Reich with the so-called 'Anschluss' of March 12th 1938. Hitler's triumphant entry into the country climaxed in a rally held in the Heldenplatz in Vienna on April 2nd. The response of the population was jubilant. A plebiscite held on April 10th was claimed to have indicated support for the annexation from 99.73% of those who voted.

252   Capital of Heilongjiang province at the NE extremity of China and renowned for its extremely harsh winters, Harbin was captured in February 1932 when Japanese forces invaded Manchuria and set up the puppet state of Manchukuo. Protests against the invasion on the part of Chinese students were cited as the pretext for a Japanese bombing raid on Shanghai at the end of January 1932. After a three-month battle beginning in August 1937, Shanghai fell to attacking Japanese forces. Chinese hopes of provoking international intervention were shattered. Might MacLean have perceived a parallel with what was happening in Spain?

If the poet singles out Hamburg among German cities, this may be because elections to the German Reichstag held on November 6th 1932, from which the Nazis emerged as the largest single party with 33.1% of the vote, produced a victory for the Social Democrats there.[74] Another, more likely explanation lies in the attempted Communist uprising in Hamburg of October 23rd to 25th 1923, which Ernst Thaelmann (see note to l. 261) both took part in and helped to organise.

253 It is hard to locate specific historical events which would explain the inclusion of Calcutta (Kolkota) in West Bengal, India, of London and of Naples at this point in the poem. MacLean aims to create as panoramic an impression as possible of the political and social catastrophe which he sees approaching at an international level.

258 The account given by writer and geologist Archibald Geikie (1835–1924) of the clearances in Strath is quoted at length in Nicolson's *History of Skye* and may usefully be excerpted here:

> One of the most vivid recollections I retain of Kilbride is that of the eviction, or the clearance of the crofters of Suisnish. The corner of Strath between the two sea-inlets of Lochs Slapin and Eishort had been for ages occupied by a community that cultivated the lower ground, where their huts formed a kind of scattered village. The land belonged to the wide domain of Lord MacDonald...
>
> ... as I was returning from my ramble, a strange wailing sound reached my ears at intervals on the breeze from the west. On gaining the top of a hill on the south side of the valley, I could see a long and motley procession wending along the road that led from Suisnish. It halted at the point in the road opposite Kilbride, and there the lamentation became long and loud.
>
> As I drew nearer, I could see that the minister, with his wife and daughters, had come out to meet the people, and bid them all farewell. It was a miscellaneous gathering of at least three generations of crofters. There were old men and women, too feeble to walk, who were placed in carts, the younger members of the community on foot were carrying their bundles of clothes and household effects, while the children, with looks of alarm, walked alongside.
>
> There was a pause in the notes of woe as the last

words were exchanged with the family of Kilbride. Every one was in tears; each wished to clasp the hands that had so often befriended them; and it seemed as if they could not tear themselves away. When they set off once more, a cry of grief went up to heaven; the long plaintive wail, like a funeral coronach, was resumed; and, after the last of the emigrants had disappeared behind the hill, the sound seemed to re-echo through the whole wide valley of Strath in one prolonged note of desolation. The people were on their way to be shipped to Canada. I have often wandered since then over the solitary ground of Suisnish. Not a soul is to be seen there now; but the greener patches of field, and the crumbling walls, mark where an active and happy community once lived.[75]

Eric Richards' account of events in Boeraig and Suisnish in 1853 offers additional details, including the participation of Ballingall:

It was, in winter, bleak country: the people involved were, like those from Benbecula, the remants of previous clearances on the Macdonald estates. They had been shifted at least twice before, in 1849 and 1852; they were greatly in arrears of rent ad unable to support themselves by their crofts. In 1853 the tenants were offered the choice of assisted emigration to Australia or removal to yet another part of the estate. None of the people would accept emigration, but eight out of eighteen families chose to shift to the other location on the estate. The remaining ten families were ordered out in October 1853... Macdonald's factor, Balli[n]gall, removed the people from Suishnish and Boreraig in the last part of 1853. Resistance was quickly suppressed, prisoners were taken, and the old dwellings were razed to the ground to prevent their return. It was a time of snowfall, and one man, who returned to his home in Suishnish, was found dead the following morning at the door of his ruined house, having perished in the night from exposure and cold... During the actual clearances the officers had first removed the furniture from the houses... Some of the people were more than eighty years old, and one was ninety... There was much criticism of the fact that the evicting ground officer was also the Poor Law inspector. Pluralism of this kind, with its attendant allegation of corruption, was rife in the Highlands in the mid-nineteenth century... Resistance during the Suishnish and Boreraig Clearances had been relatively slight but three of the people were brought to trial in November 1853... in the dramatic outcome the jury returned a verdict of 'not guilty' by a majority decision.[76]

Suishnish is at the tip of the promontory separating Loch Slapin from Loch Eishort, while Boraraig lies to the W, in a more sheltered position on the north shore of Loch Eishort.
260 The technique of interweaving references to Skye, Scotland and Britain with references to the wider world (of linking 'microcosm' and 'macrocosm', see the 'Introduction'), previously applied to placenames, is now applied with equal intensity and effectiveness to personal names.

Vladimir Ilyich Lenin (1870–1924) masterminded the Bolshevik seizure of power in the revolution of October 1917. Between May 1922 and March 1923 he suffered a series of three strokes which left him bedridden and unable to speak. His leadership, however, was crucial during the civil war and the initial phase of establishing a communist regime in the country. The ideology propounded by the Bolsheviks was heavily indebted to the writings of Karl Heinrich Marx (1818–1883), who interpreted the history of society primarily in terms of class struggle and published *The Communist Manifesto* in 1848. The first volume of Marx's major text, *Das Kapital*, partly edited by Friedrich Engels, was published in 1867. What became known as Marxism-Leninism was the prevailing orthodoxy in the Soviet Union, as well as in those European nations falling within its sphere of influence, until the dismantling of the Berlin Wall in November 1989. It also provided, and continues to provide, inspiration for regimes in other parts of the world.

Further mentions of Lenin in the 1939 version of 'An Cuilithionn' can be found at III: 195 (where it is opined that 'an aon chan fhacas riamh ann/ tuigse Lenin is taobh dearg Chrìosda'[77]), V: 185, VI: 179, VII: 66, 76, 88, 100 and 205, while his wife Nadezhda Krupskaya is named at VII: 67. Marx recurs at VI: 179 and VII: 100. In 'Dàin do Eimhir' III the speaker laments that his beloved beauty 'chuir... sgleò/ air bochdainn 's air creuchd sheirbh/ agus air saoghal tuigse Lenin, air fhoighidinn 's air fheirg.'[78] MacLean's lionising of Lenin may well have been influenced by MacDiarmid, who produced no fewer than three 'Hymns to Lenin', the first of which is especially memorable for its advocacy of police terror as a means to achieving the desired social order:

> As necessary, and insignificant, as death
> wi a' its agonies in the cosmos still
> the Cheka's horrors are in their degree;
> and'll end suner! What maitters 't wha we kill
> to lessen that foulest murder that deprives
> maist men o' real lives?[79]

MacLean would express a more nuanced approach to the notion of political terror in a letter to Douglas Young dated February 22nd 1941:

> I myself can only work it out by thinking that the sum of all human suffering is not greater than the suffering of one individual, that hence human suffering in mass does not matter more than the inevitable suffering even of a comparative few and that therefore the evolutionary urge must work itself out even with the deaths of thousands of kulaks or of western European people of high or low place. And all my own instincts are to loathe and fear the Nazis more than anyone or anything else, because I feel that their victory would make human slavery more permanent than anything else would. If it were not for the existence of Russia and China I should despair of all politics.

The two poets were also linked by their admiration for schoolteacher and Scottish socialist John Maclean (1879–1923). MacLean wrote to Douglas Young that 'I occasionally heard hints from two of my uncles that they had come into contact with a saint and a hero – John Maclean'.[80] Grandson of a crofter evicted from Mull at the time of the Clearances and of migrants to industrial Strathclyde, Maclean was born in Pollokshaws, Glasgow, trained as a schoolteacher and graduated M.A. from Glasgow University in 1904. His opposition to Britain's involvement in the First World War led to both imprisonment and loss of employment, after which he became a full-time Marxist propagandist and educator. Appointed Bolshevik consul in Scotland in February 1918, he attempted to set up a consular office in Glasgow. Arrested on charges of sedition in April, Maclean conducted his own defence in an impassioned manner which offers certain parallels with Bulgarian communist Dimitrov (see following line). He received a five-year prison sentence but was released in December 1918. His desire for a separate, Scottish formation alienated him from the British Communist Party, formed in 1920, which could not tolerate Maclean's combined commitment to Marxism-Leninism and the cause of Scottish independence. His health was severely impaired as a result of hunger strikes during which he had been force-fed in Peterhead Prison. A crowd of several thousands turned out to pay its respects at his Glasgow funeral in 1923 (an occasion to which 'An Cuilithionn' makes specific reference at VII: 121).

At III: 80 MacLean refers (with a deft pun) to 'Glaschu,/ uaigh MhicGhill-Eain ann a' glasadh',[81] pairing him with the 'Glendale martyr' John Macpherson (for whom see above ll. 199–200), while at VII: 114 his associate is Thomas Muir; at V: 3–10 'ròs dearg, ùrail'[82] is introduced as a symbol of the Red Clydeside movement associated with his name, and at VI: 119–121 the poem's speaker sees 'ròs dearg Chluaidh a' taomadh/ 'na thuil cumhachdach mòr feirge/ is MacGhill-Eain togail meirghe'.[83]

Indicative of MacLean's strikingly idiosyncratic use of proper names throughout 'An Cuilithionn' as a species of historical or political shorthand, as if these could form a signifying system on their own, is the quartet introduced at V: 181 (where John Maclean is ''na chalbh air na h-àirdean'[84]), the other members being Connolly, Liebknecht and Lenin. The four, so to speak, stick together, or cohere, once the basis of their association has been established, recurring at VII: 100–101 and 205–206. The strategy may not be immediately appealing in aesthetic terms, indeed it may strike some readers as unpoetic. Yet it is a crucial element in the poem's 'ways of meaning', effective in its uncompromising originality.

The avenue in central Leningrad named after Maclean has now reverted to its original denomination 'English' or 'Angliysky'. A scornful satire on the judge who pronounced

Maclean a coward for his opposition to war appears in the poet's 1943 volume:

> *Don bhritheamh a thubhairt ri Iain MacGill-Eain*
> *gum b' e gealtair a bh' ann*

> Chuala mi gàireachdaich nan reultan,
> lasganaich gealaich agus grèine,
> mothar a' chruinne-cè 's e 'g iathadh
> luime 's farsaingeachd na bliadhna.
> Gàireachdaich, lasganaich is èisgeachd
> bho mhullaichean gorma anns na speuran,
> mothal gàire aig na bèistean
> a' magadh ortsa, mo cho-chreutair.[85]

In his poem 'Clann Ghill-Eain' ('The Clan MacLean') MacLean hails the Marxist agitator and educator as 'ceann uachdrach ar sgeula... ursann-chatha nam feumach',[86] superior to the heroes who fought at the Battle of Inverkeithing waged by English Parliamentarians against a force of Scottish Covenanters in July 1651.

MacDiarmid's poem 'Krassivy, krassivy' plays on the twin Russian meanings of 'beautiful' and 'red' and specifically likens the Scottish Marxist to Lenin.[87]

261 Originally a socialist, Ernst Thaelmann (1886–1944) joined the German Communist Party at the end of 1920, becoming its chairman in October 1925. He stood for president in the same year, in elections where a split in centre-left votes allowed Hindenburg to emerge victorious. Hindenburg would subsequently appoint Hitler as chancellor. Arrested in 1933, Thaelmann was never put on trial, possibly out of fear that Dimitrov's heroic stand, and the international attention it attracted, might be repeated. After eleven years in solitary confinement, he was shot on orders from Hitler in the concentration camp at Buchenwald.

Georgi Dimitrov Mikhaylov (1882–1949) trained as a compositor. Originally a Socialist, like Thaelmann, the group he belonged to founded the Bulgarian Communist Party upon affiliating to Bolshevism and the Comintern in 1919. Having fled to Yugoslavia after a failed uprising in June 1923, Dimitrov spent the years until 1929 in the Soviet Union. Arrested in 1933 as one of those allegedly responsible for setting the Reichstag on fire, his dignified and compelling self-defence won international attention. Allowed to depart for the Soviet Union along with two other Bulgarian communists as part of an exchange negotiated with Nazi Germany, Dimitrov was General Secretary of the Comintern from 1934 until its disbandment in 1943. His loyalty to Stalin did not waver during the period of the purges. Returning to Bulgaria to assume leadership of the communist party at the end of the war, he again sided with Stalin in the latter's disputes with Yugoslav leader Tito.

Dimitrov's name appears nine more times in the 1939 version of 'An Cuilithionn', at VI: 204, 247 and 261 and VII: 29, 37, 90, 120, 141 and 157. One of the manifestations of Clio, the muse of history, tells how she was present at the Leipzig trial (VI: 204, 'Bha mi an Leipzig le ùidh/ nuair sheas Dimitrov air beulaibh cùirt'[88]), while the banner he brandishes at VI: 246 offers a clear parallel to the standard John Maclean has lifted earlier, at VI: 121 (see also the 'suaithneas' ('emblem') at VII: 37); Dimitrov's features are cut into the summits of the Cuillin at VI: 261–262; at VII: 29ff. MacLean finds powerful imagery for the Bulgarian man's conduct at his trial (' 'na aonar/ a' toirt air an spiorad dhaonda/ leum à chochall le faoisgneadh/ gu stad analach an t-saoghail'[89]). Two references were deleted at a relatively early stage in MacLean's revision of the poem (VII 90 & 156). In C, MacLean's 1987 revision of 'An Cuilithionn', Dimitrov is mentioned three times only.

John Murdoch (1818–1903) was born near Nairn and raised in a strongly Gaelic-speaking district of Perthshire, then in Islay, to which his family moved in 1827. He worked as an exciseman for thirty-five years, beginning in 1838, and was a total abstainer from both alcohol and tobacco. His career as a journalist, campaigning in support of the right of the people to own the land they lived on, began in 1851. A move to Dublin in 1853 intensified his political radicalism. Elected honorary secretary of the Gaelic Society of Inverness in 1871, he founded the magazine *The Highlander* in 1873 as a means of spreading his views. It ceased publication in 1881, when Murdoch moved to Glasgow where, in May 1888, he chaired the meeting at which the Scottish Labour Party was founded.

262   Son of a peasant who achieved prosperity as a farmer and a dealer in grain, Mao Tse Tung (or Mao Tze Dong)

(1893–1976) belonged to a group of Chinese intellectuals who, dissatisfied with the Paris peace conference's decision to hand German concessions over to Japan rather than restoring them to China, came to identify with Marxism-Leninism around the time of the foundation of the Chinese Communist Party in 1921. Though chief of state from 1949 to 1959, and chairman of the party until his death, at the time 'An Cuilithionn' was written Mao had not yet come to dominate the Chinese political scene.

In November 1931 a Chinese Soviet Republic, with Mao as chairman, was set up in a part of Jiangxi province. The troops of nationalist leader Chiang Kai-Shek forced Mao and the Red Army to set out on the Long March north-west in October 1934. In 1935 the Seventh Congress of the Comintern in Moscow proclaimed the desirability of forming alliances with other political formations in order to offer joint resistance to fascism. In September 1937 the communists reached a formal agreement with Chiang Kai-Shek so as jointly to oppose the expansionist aims of Japan. See also VI: 170, where the Clio of China refers to a specific incident on the Long March.

265 Iosif Vissarionovich Stalin (or 'steel' – Gaelic 'stàilinn' permits MacLean to transfer the implications to his poetry) (1879–1953) was the name adopted by Georgian Ioseb Dzugashvili. From 1922 until his death he was General Secretary of the Russian Communist Party's central committee. Notwithstanding explicit condemnation by Lenin from his deathbed, Stalin overcame all potential rivals, establishing a personal dictatorship practically without parallel in modern history.

Despite the fact that, by the time 'An Cuilithionn' was completed, the Molotov-Ribbentrop pact had allowed Stalin, as Hitler's ally, to overrun the Baltic Republics and enact a renewed partition of Poland, MacLean's faith in him had not yet wavered. Towards the close of the next paragraph, the speaker announces that 'gus am bi an t-Arm Dearg còmhla/ ri caismeachd tarsainn na Roinn Eòrpa,/ drùidhidh iorram na truaighe/ air mo chridhe 's air mo chluasan'[90] – in other words, only a triumph for Soviet forces at a European level can hope to compensate for, and in a sense nullify, the tragic consequences of the eviction of the Gaelic peasantry. These lines survived in the 1987 version of the poem, while the couplet which in 1939 closes the first paragraph of III was suppressed: 'Cò chuireas dhuinn a-mach am buachar/ mur teirinn Stàilin bho na cruachan?'[91] The reference to the Red Army in the lines immediately preceding was, however, retained. On October 27th, 1940 the poet wrote to Douglas Young that

> I do not see why I should excise Dimitrov from the 'Cuillin' or Jo [Stalin] either until history proves them wrong. Perhaps, however, I did underestimate the Red Army.

A poem written on Edinburgh University headed notepaper (see 'Unpublished Poems' 41) indicates that, in the last decades of his life, he once more came to take a positive view of Stalin's political astuteness and general conduct of affairs. Note, however, his statement in *O Choille gu Bearradh* that

> the behaviour of the Russian Government to the Polish insurrection in 1944 made me politically as well as aesthetically disgusted with most of ['An Cuilithionn'].[92]

The early copy of 'Dàin do Eimhir' I to XLI conserved in Aberdeen has a cancelled version of XVIII: 39, 'cho treun ri Dimitrov, cho glic ri Stàlain'.[93] Altering the end of this line to 'ri Connolly' involved rewriting the previous line so as to come up with a satisfactory rhyme. The reasons which led MacLean to suppress the Russian leader's name at this relatively early stage are not entirely clear. The copy was entrusted to Douglas Young in September 1940, before the poet departed for active service in north Africa. He did the same in l. 18 of '1939. Fuil' ("Unpublished Poems' 24), which was altered from 'Liebknecht, Lenin, MacGhill-Eathain, Stàilinn' to 'Blake, Liebknecht, MacGhill-Eathain, am Mùireach'.

273   See note to ll. 61ff. When news arrived in May 1887 that the crofters were to get the grazing rights at a reduced rent, Màiri Mhòr composed a song in celebration, 'Òran Beinn Lì'.[94]

275   The rocks of Valtos are situated near the fort of Dun Dearg in the parish of Kilmuir, on the east side of the Trotternish peninsula. Landlord Captain Fraser (see note to l. 219) doubled rents on the Kilmuir estate in 1877, on the basis of a revaluation carried out by an east-coast farmer.

Three years later tenants around Staffin refused to pay the additional sums being exacted. Their leader was a crofter and fisherman from Valtos, Norman Stewart, nicknamed "Parnell", who received a prison sentence for gathering materials on the moor with which to re-thatch his house. At a meeting held in Glasgow on April 18th 1881, given the threat of evictions on the Kilmuir estate, a pledge was made to support the crofters 'whatever form the struggle might ultimately assume'. A meeting between Fraser and his tenants held three days later at Valtos did not resolve the dispute.[95]

277–278 Beul Àtha nan Trì Allt (in 1989 the 'confluence' of the three burns) was important as a location for open-air preaching in 1843, when the evangelical revival or 'dùsgadh' had already been proceeding in Skye for two years:

> Shortly after the awakening began, the Rev. Roderick McLeod came from Snizort and preached at Fairy-bridge, at a place where three roads meet; and continued to do so weekly for a long while. On such occasions the gatherings were often very great: the numbers who left their work and came to hear were said to have been sometimes from five to nine thousand. The word was quick and powerful, and many who seemed to feel little while under it, were struck with convictions on their way home, and turned aside to pray.[96]

Known in English as the Fairy Bridge, the place also figures as the refrain of a song by Màiri Mhòr, 'Coinneamh nan Croitearan'.[97] Some 800 crofters from Snizort, Diurinish, Waternish and Bracadale attended a rally there on May 13th 1884 to discuss the findings of the Napier Commission. A letter was subsequently addressed to Prime Minister Gladstone asking that landlords should lose the power to evict. Donald MacCallum (see note to ll. 281–284) delivered a speech which later appeared in English in the *Oban Times*. Meek notes that a letter from MacLeod of Dunvegan was read out and aroused general indignation. The sheer weight of animosity against landlords at this time, powerfully expressed in MacLean's poem, does not always find its way into printed records of a more official nature.

281–284 Donald MacCallum (1849–1929) was born in Barravulin, Craignish, Argyll and served as a Church of Scotland minister in Morvern (as assistant), Arisaig and South Morar (1882–81), Waternish (Skye) (1884–87), Heylipol (Tiree) (1887–89) and Lochs (Lewis) (1889–1920). Meek sees MacCallum's 'preaching of the "land gospel"' as 'a form of what would now be termed "liberation theology"'. His behaviour incurred 'the wrath of many of his clerical contemporaries' and he was 'arraigned before the Presbytery of Skye in 1886 and censured'.[98]

In that year MacCallum was arrested for 'inciting the lieges to violence and class hatred'. His own account of the incident, written when he was minister of Lochs in Lewis, forms a chapter of Cameron's *The Old and the New Highlands and Hebrides* and may usefully be excerpted here:

On the night of the 13th November, 1886, I was sitting in the parlour of the schoolhouse, Valtos, Skye, conversing with Mr MacKenzie, the teacher, when suddenly there burst into the room a young man, flushed, excited, and soaked with rain, who, as hurriedly as he could, made this startling announcement: 'There are three great policemen over at Garafad searching Archibald MacDonald's house for Mr MacCallum, and while they were making sure that he was not hid in barrel, chest, or closet I ran across to inform you.'

Breaking in upon the silence that followed, I heard the voice of a little girl, the teacher's daughter, saying, 'I know of a cave on the seashore where Mr MacCallum can hide if he will go with me at once. I shall show it to him, and they can never find him there.'

Upon that the three great policemen made their appearance at the door, and one of them putting his right hand on my shoulder, said: 'Mr MacCallum, I have a warrant to arrest you on the charge of inciting the lieges to violence and class hatred.' 'All right, sir,' I replied, 'I am ready to go with you'...

We reached Portree Prison after 1 a.m., and there I was taken in charge by the jailor, who, to begin with, emptied my pockets and secured what they contained. He then took charge of my boots, and gave me a pair of slippers that I believe were white at some time in their career... Lastly, having spread a blanket on the wooden bed with the wooden pillow, he left me to my meditations, turning the key in the closed door of the cell...

I was alone indeed, but I did not feel down-hearted. I felt elated, and I can truly say that not since Skye was delivered over to the terrible sway of Sheriff Ivory, who most appropriately called himself "Old Nicholas," did I enjoy so much peace of mind.

I was put in touch with the sorely afflicted people, and the feeling that I was sharing their troubles seemed to put new life into me. The bed was hard, and I slept not, but visions of defenceless women, alarmed in their humble homes, under cover of night, and of good men and true shuddering and starving in caves, were more tolerable than when I lay on my accustomed comfortable bed...

The Sheriff asked me my name, my age, my birthplace, my profession, and having given him satisfactory answers, he asked me if I wished to make a statement. I told him that I reserved my statement for the day of my trial. Mr MacLachlan then stated he was my agent, and that he submitted I should be released on bail... Two Portree merchants who were present, Messrs John and Donald Kemp, offered to become guarantees. Their offer was accepted. They signed the documents and I was set at liberty.

My joy, however, was not full, as my comrade in arms, John Macpherson, was still held in durance vile.

There was a great concourse of people in the square as I stepped out, and they raised a hearty cheer in my honour...

On Tuesday morning three policemen made a raid on my manse at Waternish, to the great consternation of my sister Martha and widowed mother who lived with me... They made a minute search. They searched all my pockets, and under the very cushions of the sofa on which I rested. After they were satisfied that they had done their duty they walked proudly away.

In due course the Government sent in their warships some of the most famous lawyers of the day round the Island of Skye to precognise witnesses for the prosecution, but no evidence of my ever having incited the lieges to violence or class hatred was produced. I was never called to answer the charges made against me... I continued my warfare against the oppressors of my fellow-countrymen in the Highlands, and I was never further interfered with.

It is interesting, in terms of the poetics of 'An Cuilithionn', that in referring to the occasion on which he heard MacCallum speaking in Portree, MacLean momentarily identifies the speaker of the poem with his own biographical person. Even if it issues in an oneiric vision, the text is rooted at this point in actual experience.

287 Douglas Young notes 'iorram na truaighe' as a reference to an 'old Gaelic song'. An elegy with this title, and first line 'Gur i iorram na truaighe', is included in Mackenzie's *Beauties*, attributed to a certain Zachary MacAulay from Lewis, and said to concern the last McKenzie laird of Kildun, whose widow entertained Charles Stewart.[99]

Part II

34 Goll mac Morna lost one eye in battle with Cumhail, whom he killed. Cumhail's son Fionn later replaced Goll as head of the Fianna, the group of warriors and hunters at the heart of the Fenian or Ossianic cycle of Old Irish literature.[100]

37 One of three major heroes of early Ireland, Cuchulainn is the principal figure in the other major cycle of Old Irish literature, the Red Branch or Ulster cycle. His early boyhood deeds, recounted by Fergus mac Róich, occupy a sizeable chapter early in the *Táin Bó Cuailnge*, where Fergus also offers Queen Medb an extended account of his outstanding qualities as a warrior.[101] In l. 33, MacLean has playfully invented a new hero to match the ancient ones, son both of the Cuillin mountains and of Culainn, after whose 'hound' the Irish hero was named. Groom has 'the hills that may be spoken of collectively as the Cuillin (or CUCHULLIN) group'.[102]

47 Sgùrr Dearg, which terminates in the Inaccessible Pinnacle, embraces two summits of 947 and 992 metres respectively. MacLean is presumably referring to the outline these form.

50   Situated W and slightly S of Sgùrr Alasdair, Sgùrr Sgumain (947 metres) has three summits extending W: the East Buttress, the Coich Buttress and the West Buttress.

51   At this point the Aberdeen manuscript has four lines as the beginning of a new paragraph, of which the second is fragmentary. These are reproduced in Douglas Young's transcript in St Andrews:

> Gunnachan mòra a' chinne-daonna
> > air d' àrd-dhùin aosda
> annta cuifeannan baotha
> a' bualadh air arm-sgiathan laochraidh.[103]

Sgùrr Dubh an Dà Bheinn indicates two summits E of Sgùrr Alasdair of nearly the same height, 938 and 944 metres, of which the former is known as Sgùrr Dubh Mòr.

53   Hugh Cheape, in his study of the 'Traditional Origins of the Piping Dynasties', quotes Dr Samuel Johnson's account of his 1773 tour to the Hebrides, where he heard the Highland bagpipes played in Armadale, Dunvegan and Coll:

> Some of the chief families still entertain a piper, whose office was anciently hereditary. *Macrimmon* was piper to *MacLeod*, and *Rankin* to *Maclean of Col...* The tunes of the bagpipe are traditional. There has been in Sky, beyond all time of memory, a college of pipers, under the direction of *Macrimmon*, which is not quite extinct. There was another in Mull, superintended by Rankin, which expired about sixteen years ago. To these colleges, while the pipe retained its honour, the students of musick repaired for their education.[104]

Cheape believes that the treatment of the MacCrimmons in Angus Mackay's 1838 *A Collection of Ancient Piobaireachd or Highland Pipe Music* is 'full of story and incident in its opening sections and reads more as an exercise in storytelling than a history of piping'.[105] Alistair Keith Campsie takes energetic issue with Mackay in *The MacCrimmon Legend*. The traditional account, from which Campsie quotes extensively, would seem to lie at the basis of MacLean's references to the family:

> The most celebrated Pipers were the MacCrummens, who, under the liberal patronage of the Lairds of

MacLeod, became famous all over the Highlands; and their abilities were so well appreciated, that students from all quarters resorted to them, or were placed by their respective chiefs under those famous masters, whose residence consequently became dignified with the name of College... Their Oil-thigh or College was at Boreraig, eight miles north of Dunvegan castle, and they held the farm rent-free in virtue of their office, on which at present eighteen families reside, paying upwards of £100...

Donald Mor was succeeded by his son, Patrick Mor,

a diligent composer of Piobaireachd, of whom it is related that he was accompanied to Church one Sunday by eight sons who all, with one exception, died within twelve months, on which bereavement he composed a tune called Cumha na Cloinne, or Lament for the Children... His only surviving son Patrick Og succeeded. He was a composer of scarcely less merit than his father, and his pupils were considered the best Pipers of those days.[106]

Norman MacLeod, who was the first publicly to sustain that the family name pointed to an origin in the Italian city of Cremona, offers a more extended motivation for the 'Lament for the Children' which meant so much to MacLean (here quoted from Campsie in a translation supplied by John MacInnes):

No pipers in Scotland were as famous as the MacCrimmons of the Dun. For many a generation they were pipers to the chiefs of the MacLeods. The first of his name came with MacLeod from a town in Italy called Cremona; he was a harper, a renowned musician in his own day and generation. He took the name of his birthplace and those who had descended from him they called the MacCrimmons... This man's son, Patrick Mor, was as famous as his father. He composed more tunes of piobaireachd than any other man of whom we have record. One day he went to church with his eight sons by his side, young men as handsome as ever stood in shoe; but before the end of the year came he had laid seven of them in the churchyard of Kilmuir. That was when he composed the sad, poignant tune known as 'The Lament for the Children'. The son who survived, Patrick Og, was no less a piper than the others; he, too, composed many a melodious tune.[107]

Campsie gives an alternative background for 'Lament for the Children' from notes made by Donald MacDonald some time after 1806, between 12 and 20 years in advance of Mackay's treatment. The dates traditionally ascribed to the principal members of the MacCrimmon family are: born 1570 for Donald; ca.1595–1670 for Patrick Mor; and ca.1645–1730 for Patrick Og.[108] For two further tunes traditionally ascribed to the MacCrimmons, see note to V: 78–82.

57 For a recurrence of the term 'sàth-ghaol' and its possible implications, see note to VI: 40–41.

61 Barra lies SSW of South Uist in the Outer Hebrides. The island is roughly 8 miles by 5 in size:

its outline is exceedingly irregular, broken by headlands and inlets. The western coast includes two or three sandy bays, but elsewhere presents to the Atlantic a series of high rocky cliffs, torn with fissures and pierced with caves. The eastern coast also is both sandy and rocky, but includes several bays, which serve as good harbours.[109]

66 Grula is a tiny settlement just N of Allt an t-Slugain where the latter flows into the Eynort River. Braigh Brunal descends steeply into the west side of Loch Eynort. The two hills of Scarall (210 & 211 metres respectively) lie east of Glen Eynort, which is itself separated from Glen Brittle to the W by Beinn a' Bhràghad. Brae Eynort, Gruille and Brunnal were townships and farmsteads within the bounds of the Rhundunan/ Glenbrittle farm.[110] MacLean imagines someone forced into exile from a beloved homeland evoked in placenames which would be familiar only to a very restricted number of people. See note to I: 47ff. for the ship which left Glenbrittle for America in 1811.

86 MacLean's native island of Raasay, which affords striking views of the Cuillins, is separated from the E coast of Skye by the Sound of Raasay, and from Applecross, on the mainland, by the Inner Sound. The waters of the latter, reaching 138 fathoms, are unusually deep.

> The greater part of the surface... is barren and heathy, but on the strip of secondary rocks on the E side along the top of the cliffs the soil can be tilled to advantage, as well as in the flat portion about the mansion-house at the extreme SW of the island. There is but little wood, a considerable amount of natural wood and coppice that once existed having been almost entirely cut down for fuel in the wet seasons of 1836 and 1837, when the peats were too wet to burn.[111]

The small island of Rona lies half a mile NE of Raasay, with which it 'forms a ridge nearly in a line'.[112]

87   Soay is 'nearly bisected by two bays, indenting it on opposite sides. Its surface is low and broken... and its coast is bold and rocky, and generally presents to the surge perpendicular cliffs of 60 or 70 feet in height.' The parish of Strath in Skye bounds with Portree, Bracadale and Sleat. Landowner Alexander MacAlister of Strathaird is referred to at I: 212. Between 1841 and 1861 the population here fell from 3150 to 2664.[113]

97   In Christopher Marlowe's play *Doctor Faustus*, the clock has just struck eleven. Mephostophilis is to come for the hero's soul at midnight, and he pronounces the following lines:

> The devil will come, and Faustus must be damned.
> O I'll leap up to my God! Who pulls me down?
> See, see where Christ's blood streams in the firmament!
> One drop would save my soul, half a drop: ah my
>   Christ –[114]

MacLean makes further reference to this passage in l. 35 of '1939. Fuil' ('Unpublished Poems' 24): 'brat fuil Chrìosda air àird nan speuran'.[115]

98   Karl Liebknecht became an adherent of Marxism while still a student. He was elected to the Reichstag as a Social Democrat in 1912, and he and Rosa Luxemburg were among the founders of the Spartacus League late in 1914. Captured two days after the suppression of the January 1919 uprising in Berlin, they were tortured and murdered. German author Rudolf Leonhard (1889–1953), a fellow insurgent, initiated the *Gruppe 1925*, which included Berthold Brecht, Alfred Doblin and Kurt Tucholsky among its members. Interned from 1939 to 1944, he took up residence in East Berlin in 1950. MacDiarmid included a Scots version of his poem 'Der tote Liebknecht' ('The dead Liebknecht') in his collection *Penny Wheep* (1926).[116] This reference is one further instance of how often in MacLean's poetry a political affiliation goes hand in hand with a poetic and literary one.

102 What was to have been a widespread uprising of socialists against the Republican government of Spain in October 1934, provoked at least in part by the entry into the government of the right-wing CEDA (Confederación Española de Derechas Autónomas), had the most serious consequences in the Atlantic coast province of Asturias, whose miners were comparatively well-paid and particularly well-organised. Troops under Generals Goded and Franco were sent to crush the rebellion, as a result of which some 3000 miners were killed, and perhaps ten times that number arrested. Containing a strongly anticlerical element, the Asturian revolt radicalised positions on both right and left in the run-up to full-scale Civil War. In 'Dàin do Eimhir' IV MacLean laments 'am mèinnear Spàinnteach a' leum ri cruadal/ is 'anam mòrail dol sìos gun bhruaillean'.[117]

111–123 This passage, like ll. 164–171, 178–179 and 182–199, is omitted from C, presumably due to vehemence of expression in the first case, and the strongly topical nature of the references in the remainder.

152 In his 'projection' Douglas Young translates 'John Macpherson' (the 'Glendale martyr', for whom see notes to I: 59 & 199–200), probably after consultation with MacLean. Otherwise readers might be led to think of the MacMhuirich dynasty of classical Gaelic bards, of whom the last, Dòmhnall, was active around 1710.[118]

157 MacLean here quotes Alasdair Mac Mhaighstir Alasdair's song 'Òran Ailein', whose second stanza runs as follows:

> Ailein duinn, gabh sgoinn 's bi 'g èirigh;
> tionail do chlann, cuimhnich d' fheum orr':
> bidh Alba mhòr fo bhinn bhèistean
> mur a dìon a muinntir fhèin i.[119]

The original song is a coded composition aimed to generate

support for the Jacobite cause. MacLean incorporates its not so covert political activism to a very different context.

164   In the speaker's view, the Scottish press is a mouthpiece for the interests of industrialists, without room for the views or talents of dissident intellectuals and artists such as MacDiarmid. III: 51–52 indicate he takes an equally dim view of the press in France and Germany, Italy and England.

167   Shortly before the death of their father in June 1908, Sir James Lithgow, first baronet (1883–1952) and his younger brother Henry (1886–1948) entered into full partnership of the most significant cargo shipbuilders on Clydeside. Their Port Glasgow yard changed its name from Russell & Co. to Lithgows Ltd. in 1919, and in 1922 James became president of the National Shipbuilders' Confederation. In the 1930s, as chairman of National Shipbuilders' Security Ltd, he oversaw a reduction of capacity in the industry with consequent loss of jobs, in his view essential if the shipyards were to recover from wartime expansion.

> Between 1874 and 1952 the Lithgow family created an industrial empire unrivalled in Scotland's economic history. Little of consequence was achieved in Scotland's industrial economy between the 1920s and the 1940s that did not in significant measure owe something to the contribution, the drive, the energy, and the leadership of the Lithgows of Port Glasgow.[120]

181   Precisely what it was that, in the speakers' view, made the Polish leadership a laughing stock in all of Europe's eyes is hard to decide. In 1926 the short-lived democratic government was overthrown in a military coup led by Józef Piłsudski (1876–1935). MacLean might have in mind the generals left in charge after Piłsudski's death, the cession of Czech territory to Poland in the wake of the Munich agreement, or simply Poland's failure to oppose effective resistance to the dual invasion from Nazi Germany and Soviet Russia (not to mention a small Slovak contingent) on September 1st 1939. Two days earlier the mobilisation of Polish troops had been announced, then revoked under pressure from France. The government had assured the civil population that any attempted invasion could be repulsed without difficulty. MacLean's English rendering 'landowners' restricts the meaning of the original in such a fashion as to make clarification still harder.

195   The boggy area known as Mararaulin (for Douglas Young, 'Mararowlin') lies S of Coire an t-Seas(g)aich close to the N end of Glenbrittle. In Part III it becomes one of 'An Cuilithionn''s most potent symbols, representing the combined forces of bourgeois society and culture and western capitalism.

203   In his history of Soay, Reed writes that

> The MacAskills distinguished themselves in the clan battles of old, and much of the fighting took place in the district of Minginish. Indeed the last great clan fight on Skye was fought in the upper reaches of Glenbrittle but a short distance from the MacAskill stronghold at the Rhu. This was the battle of Ben Coolin and the year was 1601.[121]

Alexander Mackenzie offers more detailed coverage in his history of Clan Donald:

> At length, in the year 1601, while Ruairi MacLeod was absent seeking assistance from the Earl of Argyll against his enemies, the Macdonalds invaded MacLeod's lands in Skye in considerable numbers, wishing to force on a battle. The Macleods, under Alexander, the brother of their chief, took post on the shoulder of the Coolins (a very high and rugged mountain or ridge of hills in Skye), and did not decline the contest. After a fierce and obstinate battle, in which both parties fought with great bravery, the Macleods were overthrown. Their leader, with thirty of their choicest warriors fell into the hands of the victors...[122]

See also note to VII: 92.

206–215   The concluding paragraph is omitted in C.

207   The battle of Festubert was fought on the western front between May 15th and May 25th 1915. In the initial attack mainly Indian troops were involved, followed by the British 2nd and 7th divisions. The advance was renewed on the 18th by the Canadian division and the 51st Highland division. Gains of 1km were made at the cost of some 16,000 dead. A poem by MacLean entitled 'Festubert 16–17.V.1915' was published in 1993 by Portree High School in their volume

Skye 1992. The battle of Loos followed, on the same front, between September 25th and 28th, and marked the first use of poison gas on the part of the British forces. Territory gained could not be held due to problems with communications, supply and reserves. Casualties were in the region of 20,000. The Queen's Own Cameron Highlanders, whose traditional base was Inverness-shire, played a significant role in the combat.[123]

209 The war memorial in Somerled Square in Portree features a lion perched at the top of a hexagonal column of grey granite, making the lower parts of its anatomy clearly visible to the spectator below.

211 Reference is made to the opening day of the Battle of the Somme, July 16th 1916, on which more soldiers were killed than on any single previous day in the history of the British Army. Losses amounted to over 57,000. Beaumont-Hamel was a hamlet along the line of the offensive.

214 The much altered building of the Sligachan Hotel was erected in the 1830s and became a traditional basis from which climbers set out for the Cuillins[124] – hence the scornful reference, veined with class hostility, to those who merely survey the range while eating.

Part III

25–26 For the subsequent fate of these two lines see note to I: 265.

41 See VI: 149 for a further reference to the French Revolution of 1789 as ultimately a failure.

47–62 This attack on the newspaper press and the radio (what would today be called 'the media') takes up from II: 164ff. and, like that passage, is omitted in C.

69 MacLean confessed to Douglas Young, in a letter dated March 30th 1942, that

> I always hanker after a restrained, calm manner that would express depth and not fire, a manner that would belie an intensity of matter, something that would suggest or be in some way like the greatest of Mozart and of the MacCrimmons, and I look with disgust at some of my own too patent subjectivity... when I think

> what kind of poem I should ideally like to write, it
> would be one not like anything I know in Shakespeare,
> Blake, Yeats or Grieve [Hugh MacDiarmid] but rather
> like 'Cumha na Cloinne' [Lament for the Children] or
> 'Maol Donn' or one or two things I heard in Mozart...

And on June 15th 1943 he complained:

> What chance has any Gaelic poetry when 'Cumha na
> Cloinne', probably one of the greatest pieces of music in
> the world, and not hampered by language difficulties, is
> all but unknown in Scotland, even among Highlanders?

For Patrick Mor MacCrimmon, see note to II: 53, and for
'Maol Donn' V: 82. This and the following three lines are
omitted in C.

70   Of his reading while at school MacLean wrote to Young
(letter dated September 7th 1941) as follows:

> ... history and socialism were my main interests and I
> think there was much of this in my enthusiasm for
> Shelley. Keats I was more critical of, but liked
> 'Hyperion' immensely, also the Milton I read. I disliked
> Shakespeare except the great tragedies (and I disliked
> much even of them) but I consider the sonnets the
> greatest things in all English poetry.

Literary assessments are as it were filtered through the prism
of political engagement, and the same happens to an even
greater extent in 'An Cuilithionn'. If the bog of Mararaulin
represents bourgeois appropriation, then large areas of the
western cultural tradition have been rendered unusable for
the purposes of revolutionary change.

    MacLean's troubled and contradictory relationship to the
work of William Butler Yeats (1865–1939) was a blend of
identification and rejection. Having already told MacDiarmid
(letter dated December 20th 1936) that

> To me Yeats seems a man full of all sorts of misgivings
> and indecisions, making half-hearted attempts to make
> the best of a few worlds.

MacLean later expanded on his views to the same
correspondent (letter dated May 25th 1940):

I sometimes imagine that I could be a humble follower
of the School of Yeats, who essentially is a very mun-
dane poet compared with you. I am especially interested
in Yeats because I am certain a sense of inferiority is
one of the main dynamics of his poetry, though this
sense of inferiority frequently, as in his Anglo-Irish
ascendancy aristocratic sense, is an inferiority complex.
I don't think I have the complex but I have the
inferiority feeling quite clearly.[125]

He told Young some six months later (letter dated December
6th 1940) that

I now am come very much to doubt the depth of Yeats's
feelings. That's not what I mean. What I really mean is
that most of his finest poetry is just a specious
camouflage for his feelings. He had to erect the Anglo-
Irish aristocratic myth to cover his self-contempt. I even
doubt the depth of his feelings to Maud Gonne. After
all he did not become a revolutionary for her sake. He
just remained a crossed troubled aesthete.

For the youthful MacLean, at any rate at a rational level,
love attachments are also to be assessed in terms of their
usefulness to the revolutionary cause. Some kind of
reconciliation emerges from the late poem 'Aig Uaigh Yeats'
('At Yeats's Grave'), whose positioning in *O Choille gu
Bearradh* suggests that it may derive from the same visit to
the Republic which inspired MacLean's poem on Connolly's
bloodstained shirt. The revolutionary hero is referred to by
name ('na h-euchdan coire/ bu bhinn an cluais O Conghaile
's an cluasan a sheòrsa'[126]). The image of 'a' ghaisge 's a'
bhòidhche/ 's an croinn bratach troimh do chliathaich',[127]
addressed to Yeats, recalls an image the speaker had applied
to himself in 'Dàin do Eimhir' LIV,[128] and the poem's close
implies that Yeats's imperfections as a human (political?)
being need not interfere with our evaluation of his poetry:

ach tha leisgeal air do bhilean,
an leisgeal nach do mhill do bhàrdachd,
oir tha a leisgeal aig gach duine.[129]

For James Connolly in 'An Cuilithionn', see note to V: 179.

72   In a letter dated September 7th 1941, MacLean told
Douglas Young that

> By far the greatest intellectual stirring in my teens was
> my first reading of Shelley's *Prometheus [Unbound]* and
> for years Shelley was almost everything to me. His
> music intoxicated me (now I find it pretty thin).

Considering his alienation from the religion of the Free
Presbyterian Church, which he terms 'Secederism', in a
continuation written four days letter, he spoke of 'a sort of
anti-Secederism latent in my childhood' which was

> quasi-Promethean or Shelleyan... my Promethean view
> of Socialism is an inversion of the career of the 'saved'
> in the sense that it was a justification of the 'lost',
> 'damned' Promethean. I had to find a humanist, hence
> Promethean, substitute... in my teens my Socialism
> would have repudiated the 'class war' utterly. My later
> Communism or Socialism is probably a fortifying, or
> rather restatement, of the Promethean, non-class war,
> boyish socialism, in the light of my experiences of the
> actualities of life.

How far the poet had travelled from these youthful
enthusiasms by the time 'An Cuilithionn' was written
emerges in his assertion that 'Lenin, Stalin and Dimitroff [sic]
now mean more to me than Prometheus and Shelley did in
my teens' (letter to Douglas Young dated September 11th
1941). Yet certain lines at the close of Act I of the play
indicate how easily Shelley's hero could act as a prototype
for Lenin, Stalin and Dimitrov: 'I would fain/ Be what it is
my destiny to be,/ The saviour and the strength of suffering
man...' (ll. 814–816). A poem addressed to Shelley and dated
July 8th 1934 remained in manuscript during MacLean's
lifetime (see 'Unpublished Poems' 17).

MacLean devoted two prose essays[130] to the work of
Islay-born Uilleam MacDhunlèibhe (William Livingston
1808–1870). The phrasing of his conclusion is particularly
interesting when read in the context of 'An Cuilithionn':

> ... in a few poems his passionate contemplation of the
> actual state of the Highlands in his own day is
> crystallised in verse of noble and moving eloquence,

which I think just misses being great poetry because it is slightly rhetorical, but I suppose that is a failing which is inherent in the nature of all political poetry.[131]

In a letter dated January 23rd 1935, MacDiarmid writes

I am sending Livingston's poem, and will be very glad indeed if you can let me have as soon as possible translations of a couple of typical poems of his (or of good passages from his longer poems) – particularly poems or passages which are markedly political and bring out to the full the quality of his nationalism and his Anglophobia.[132]

MacLean looked back on the episode with some impatience in a letter to Douglas Young dated February 22nd 1941:

But seriously I have not been able to find anything in Livingston apart from 'Eirinn ag gul' and 'Fios thun a' Bhàird' that is very good even among 19th century Gaelic poems. Why the hell has Grieve to boost Livingston as a poet because of his political opinions? He never does that with Scots Lowland poets whom he knows at first hand.

85–92 These lines, like 95–96 and 105–114, are omitted from C: the description of the bog as both rising and dancing (at l. 105) is interesting with regard to an overall 'choreographic' reading of 'An Cuilithionn' (for which see the 'Introduction').

93–94 The notion of the cliff formation as a stallion being gelded is also found in a flippant epigram on a certain George MacLean, considered for inclusion in the 'Eisgeachd is mi-mhodh' section of the 1943 collection, but which remained in manuscript during the poet's lifetime (see 'Unpublished Poems' 6). The faint echo of 'Là Inbhir Lochaidh' (1645) by Iain Lom (c.1625-post 1707) at this point becomes explicit at ll. 141ff.

109 Sgùrr nan Gobhar ('the peak of the goats', 630 metres) is the Wmost outlier of the Cuillins, at a point not far from the mouth of Glenbrittle relatively distant from the bog itself.

125–128 MacLean here parodies a well-known comic song by John MacDougall (died 1875) whose refrain runs:

> Chuir iad an t-sùil à Pilot bàn,
> chuir iad an t-sùil à Pilot;
> chuir iad an t-sùil à Pilot bochd,
> gun fhios ciod an lochd a rinn e.[133]

The song tells how a poor dog got his eye put out, and Queen Victoria offered a guinea to pay for a gold one to replace it. Among his praises we learn that 'Policeman riamh cha robh aig na Goill/ cho math ris air faireadh na h-oidhche'.[134] The lines are omitted in C.

141ff. MacLean consciously echoes, and parodies, one of the earliest dated poems by Iain Lom, on the Battle of Inverlochy, fought in February 1645, which the poet witnessed in person. The first three stanzas are as follows, with added italics to emphasise the closeness in wording:

> *'N cuala sibhse* 'n tionndadh *duineil*
> thug an camp bha 'n cille Chuimein?
> *'S fada chaidh ainm air an iomairt,*
> *thug iad* as an naimhdean iomain.
>
> *Dhìrich mi moch madainn Dòmhnaich*
> *gu bràigh caisteil Inbhir-Lochaidh;*
> *chunnaic mi 'n t-arm dol an òrdugh,*
> *'s bha buaidh a' bhlàir le Clann Dòmhnaill.*
>
> *Dìreadh a mach glùn* Chùil Eachaidh,
> *dh'aithnich mi* oirbh *sùrd bhur* tapaidh;
> ged bha *mo dhùthaich 'na* lasair,
> *'s éirig air a' chùis* mar thachair.[135]

See Whyte 2005 for a discussion of MacLean's poignantly distorted echoing of earlier Gaelic poetry within the context of Modernist sensibilities. The first quatrain is omitted from C.

149 MacLean probably has in mind Coir' an Eich ('corrie of the horse'), a small "coire" immediately S of Coire a' Ghreadaidh from which it is separated by An Diallaid ('the saddle'). S in its turn lies Sgùrr nan Gobhar (see l. 109).

157–160 Omitted in C.

169ff. This passage which, despite the conditionals, risked being interpreted as a claim to outdo MacDiarmid, was carefully toned down in 1987, ll. 171 and 173 being turned into interrogatives ('an robh mi air beireachd air Mac-

Dhiarmaid... An robh mi air beireachd air MacDhòmh-
naill...'[136])

195   MacLean attempts to answer Young's scepticism about
this combination in his letter dated October 27th 1940:

> You mention that in the Cuillin I leave Lenin and Christ
> [...][137] and do not question what they would say to one
> another. Well, the point is that in 'The Cuillin' nothing
> is absolute. Christ and Lenin are not alone only almost
> random examples of great minds moved by the 'miseries
> of the world'. I am not at all interested in 'great minds'
> of the emotionless contemplative types [sic] especially
> the scientist. Christ and Lenin to me are only almost
> random examples of great minds realising emotionally
> as well as intellectually the 'miseries that will not let
> them rest'. For that matter there could be many others
> with them. As to what they would say to one another I
> am not concerned. I think final systems of philosophy
> are just play. No, it is not my early Secederism. It is
> quite a humanist conception of Christ that I had.

Lenin and Christ appear together again, separated only by a
line-break, at VII: 202–203.

200–211   Given that one theme of the 'Dàin do Eimhir' is
how love destabilises and undermines political commitment,
an overlap between the two texts is unexpected. Yet, along
with the reference to Donald MacCallum at I: 281, this
would seem to be a point where a traceable figure from the
poet's biography makes an appearance in the poem.
MacLean told Young (letter dated March 30th 1942) that

> 'The Cuillin' was started in Edinburgh in April or
> May 1939[,] was being rapidly written and had
> reached the line before 'Seo là eile' when a chance
> meeting with E[imhir] brought back the old passion
> and it was completely interrupted until it was restarted
> in Hawick in November 1939.

'Eimhir' here stands for A. M., the Scottish woman who
came to dominate the love cycle and whose initials were at
one point to appear at the head of MacLean's 1943
collection.[138] In a letter from the previous year (September
9th) he confided that

By far my greatest period was the last three months of
1939 when I saw her very often and when I was
exhilarated at what I thought was the beginning of the
suicide of European capitalism.

MacLean was teaching evacuated children in Hawick and
may have made frequent trips to Edinburgh to see this
woman. The optimism of these lines fits well with his
description of the period, and is counterposed by the darker-
hued return of the beloved at VII: 41–47.

Part IV

19   The first concentration camp established by the Nazis
was situated close to Dachau, some 12 miles north of
Munich, and acted as a model for the other camps
subsequently created. Some 32,000 inmates are estimated to
have died there from disease, malnutrition, maltreatment or
execution. A gas chamber was built but never used. It was
the scene of horrendous experiments on camp inmates, seven
doctors who operated in the camp receiving death sentences
at Nuremberg.
33–34   Douglas Sealy notes the reference to a song by
Norman Nicholson of Sgoirebreac which has the refrain ' 'S
gann gun dìrich mi chaoidh/ dh'ionnsaidh frithean a'
mhonaidh'.[139]
37–40   These lines are omitted from C.

Part V

1ff.   From the years immediately preceding the First World
War until the early 1930s, Clydeside could reasonably claim
to represent the hub of working-class political organisation
and resistance in the British Isles. Significant stages were a
strike at the Singer sewing machines factory in 1911, antiwar
agitation, rent strikes with accompanying measures to stall
evictions and, at the end of January 1919, a massive rally
attended by some 90,000 in George Square in Glasgow where
the Red Flag was displayed and the Riot Act read out
publicly. John Maclean (for whom see note to I: 260) was the

only theoretician of note which the movement produced, and its genuine revolutionary potential is still a matter of dispute.[140]

22 The leap envisaged is a considerable one, from Sgùrr na h-Uamha (736 metres, located S of Sgùrr nan Gillean) S and E across the Sligachan River and Loch an Athain to Blaven (located S of Garbh-bheinn in the parish of Strath); then W across Loch na Creitheach and Loch Coruisk to Garsven ('the echoing mountain', 895 metres), the point furthest SE of the Cuillins, at which they end.

23 Douglas Young glosses 'gàmag' as a 'long bound in running full-speed'.

35–146 The first of two extended lyrical episodes which play a fundamental role in the progress and mode of the poem as drafted in 1939. Of the 14 stanzas given here 9 survived in the 1987 C version,[141] while the second lyric (see note to VII: 212–323) was cut in its entirety. Young notes in his St Andrews copy that 'these lyrics try to reproduce a pibroch movement', a vague enough designation, given that both Mac Mhaighstir Alasdair and Duncan Ban Macintyre attempted to provide an equivalent to the extended pibroch forms of 'ceòl mòr', a species of theme and variations, in long poems. A more useful reference could be to the vocal music or 'port-à-beul', without instrumental accompaniment, imitative of pipe music but designed as an accompaniment to dancing. The crucial characteristic of both this and the episode in VII is movement. In the fourteenth stanza the Cuillin are spoken of as in turn an eagle, a lion and a thunderbolt. MacLean adopts and masters with aplomb a stanza of the utmost technical complexity, belied by its concision and apparent spontaneity. The structure of rhymes is maintained consistently. Even those with no Gaelic can trace it in the spellings:

Eich mhòir gh*ao*laich,
na muinne chr*ao*bhaich,
chual' thusa f*ao*chadh
a' Ch*ao*gaich ch*ai*s.
Eich mhòir nan t*onn*,
a'mharcachd sh*onn*,
chual' thu f*onn*
Maol D*onn* nan g*ath*. (ll. 75–82)

78, 82   See note to II: 53–54 for the traditions associated
with the MacCrimmon family of pipers. Campsie quotes
Mackay as follows concerning the tune referred to in l. 78:

> Donald Mor had a brother, who lived in Glenelg, part
> of MacLeod's estate, who was known by the name of
> Patrick *Caog*, on account of a squint or defect in one of
> his eyes. This young man had a quarrel with his foster
> brother, a native of Kintail. Sometime after the dispute,
> while he was in the act of washing his face, in a burn
> or rivulet adjoining his dwelling, the Kintail man came
> behind him, and treacherously with his dirk gave him a
> mortal blow.
>
> This being made known to Donald Mor at Dunvegan,
> he prepared to revenge the untimely death of his
> brother, and taking his Pipes up to MacLeod's room, he
> threw them on the bed. MacLeod surprised, demanded
> to know what had occurred. In a few words he related
> to him the affair, when the laird pacified the enraged
> piper, and promised him, on condition of his remaining
> at home, to see justice done before the expiration of
> twelve months.
>
> MacLeod thought that his wrathful Piper would
> forget the cruel murder by that time, and allow his ire to
> abate; but such was not the case, for once the
> termination of twelve months, he set out himself for
> Glenelg, without informing anyone of his intention; and
> finding on his arrival there, that the murderer of his
> brother had gone to Kintail, he pursued his journey
> thither.
>
> The offender having been apprised of his arrival,
> concealed himself in the house of a friend; and the
> inhabitants of the village not choosing to deliver him
> up, MacCrummen was so enraged, that he resolved to
> set their houses on fire, – and burned eighteen of their
> houses, which caused the loss of several lives. Donald
> then made his escape to Lord Rea's country, where he
> remained for some time under the protection of Donald
> Doughal MacKay, afterwards Lord Rea, with whom
> he had been formerly acquainted.[142]

Campsie adds that before escaping, the piper was said to
have played his new tune to the shrieking villagers. A

competing account is found in the Gesto collection, where a different tune is quoted with the title 'Lassan Phadrig Chiegch', translated as

> Lassas alias the Flame of Phadrig Chiegh. Played by him at a time he, with his Party, set fire to many houses in Kintail, in consequence of a Quarrell between the MacKenzies and the MacKays of Lord Reay.[143]

Campsie lists 'MacCrimmon's Sweetheart' with the Gaelic title 'Vuail Doan', while Mackay refers to it as 'Cumha Mhuil Duin – supposed to be a lament for Muil Duin, son of Conol, King of Cantyre'. In the Campbell *canntaireachd*, transcribed towards the end of the 18th or the beginning of the 19th centuries, containing 169 tunes and now deposited in the National Library of Scotland, the title is 'Voal Daon'. The 'Lament for the Children' does not appear in this collection, while the previous item is referred to there as 'MacCeich's Flame of Wrath or Flash of Temper'.[144] The tune 'Maol Donn' is cited in MacLean's 'nocturne' poem, XXXV in the 'Dàin do Eimhir'.

97   According to Douglas Young, Donald MacCallum (see note to I: 275) is intended here, though not explicitly named until l. 103.

105   This line originally read 'is Steuart-Glennie'. The name occurs in a song by Màiri Mhòr entitled 'Fàistneachd agus Beannachd do na Gàidheil' and is referred by Meek to a London lawyer, a member of the Highland Land Law Reform Association who was very active in support of the crofters.[145]

147   This pivotal line harks back to the lament of IV (see ll. 1, 57 ff.) which had seemed to nullify the prophecy which closes III ('èiridh latha air a' Chuilithinn') ('day will rise on the Cuillin'). The lament returns at l. 163, to be immediately followed by a renewed turn for the better at l. 165. From this point on an upwards, freeing motion increasingly dominates the poem, becoming definitive at VII: 192–193 ('A dh'aindeoin chithear trianaid Cuilithinn/ ag èirigh thar taobh eile duilghe') ('Nevertheless, the Cuillin is seen/ rising on the far side of agony').

177   In C 'baothaireachd Shasainn' becomes 'uachdarain Shasainn' ('the folly of England', 'the rulers of England').

179 Edinburgh-born James Connolly (1868–1916) was among the founders of the Irish Socialist Republican Party and lived in New York from 1903 to 1910, where he helped set up the International Workers of the World,. He took over from James Larkin as head of the Irish National Transport and General Workers' Union at the outbreak of World War I, expressing resolute opposition to involvement in the war. Like John Maclean an ardent proponent of Marxism – the two are paired at V: 179ff. and again at VII: 204 – he was executed by a British firing squad after taking part in the uprising in Dublin in Easter 1916. MacLean wrote a poem inspired by the sight of Connolly's bloodstained shirt, exhibited in the National Museum of Ireland.[146] See 'Unpublished Poems' 8 for two further quatrains on Connolly which remained in manuscript during the poet's lifetime.

187–202 MacDiarmid's long poem *A Drunk Man Looks at the Thistle* (1926) draws into its onward progress texts in translation from a series of poets such as the Russian Alexander Blok (1880–1921, see note to VI: 179), Rudolf Leonhard (see note to II: 98) and Else Lasker-Schüler (1876–1945). In a deft homage to his declared model, MacLean inserts at this point a Gaelic translation of 'If there are bounds to any man' from MacDiarmid's collection *Second Hymn to Lenin and other poems* (1935).[147] It is not hard to see what made MacLean's choice so apt. MacDiarmid's text refers to 'the eternal hills', stating that 'All Earth's high peaks are naked stone', and its vision of a humanity capable of practically endless self-improvement is appropriate to the political optimism with which MacLean's poem concludes. In the Aberdeen ms only its first three stanzas are translated. In the Edinburgh typescripts, here viewed as belonging to stage B in the elaboration of 'An Cuilithionn', the fourth and last stanza has been added. This is also how the passage appears in C:[148]

Mullach an t-saoghail a' chlach lom;
cur dheth is èiginn neach
na ghabhas, agus sin gach eile,
mus bi an àird 'na bheachd.

Edinb NLS ms 29558 f62 gives a slightly different version of the second line: 'is èiginn neach cur dheth'. In MacDiarmid's original, this stanza reads:

All Earth's high peaks are naked stone
    and so must men forego
all they can shed – and that's all else
    proportionate heights to show.

Part VI

1ff. As MacLean's poem enters on its penultimate section he introduces a new mode, dramatic monologue, in two highly effective passages which give voice to the personages adumbrated at I: 182–189. The narrative of the Gesto girl is compelling, a powerful symbol which can be said to possess both ethical and, in the broader sense, historical validity. It nonetheless does not correspond to fact, given that what was known as the Slave Ship voyaged no further than Donaghadee in Northern Ireland. For a further instance which may be looked on as forming part of the background to this figure, see note to I: 47ff.

14–18 These four lines, where those held responsible for the episode of the Slave Ship are named, were omitted from C. Norman Macleod of Unish in Berneray, tacksman to MacLeod of Dunvegan, connived with the owners of *The William*, from Donaghadee in County Down, Ulster, to force about a hundred people on board at Loch Bracadale in Skye and Finsbay in Harris in spring 1739. Some of the 96 prisoners in the hold escaped when the ship docked at Donaghadee for repairs, but were rounded up in a brutal fashion. Rumours of what was going on led to them being freed and brought before the magistrates. None were however able to return home. Warrants were issued for the arrest of both Macleod of Unish and the ship's captain, William Davison, without either being apprehended. The whole affair provoked considerable embarrassment for Alexander MacDonald of Sleat and Norman MacLeod of Dunvegan, though no proof of effective connivance on their part was found.[149]

40–41 'Cumha do Shir Tormod Mac Leoid' ('Lament for Sir Norman MacLeod'), the elegy composed by Màiri Nighean Alasdair Ruaidh (c.1615-c.1707) on a MacLeod chief whose death shortly preceded the birth of his son in 1706, begins with the following lines:

Mo chràdhghal bochd
mar a thà mi nochd
is mi gun tàmh gun fhois gun sunnd.

In the notes to his edition, however, J. Carmichael Watson
offers an alternative text, taken down by Frances Tolmie in
Ebost, Skye in 1861, which MacLean would appear to refer
to here:

Mo shàthghal goirt
mar atà mi nochd
is mi gun tàmh gun fhois gun sunnd.[150]

MacLean deftly exploits the phonetic linkage between
'sàth-ghal' and 'sàth-ghaol' in making a transition to three-
line stanzas, where concern for the fate of the chief and
his family yields to concern for deprived people throughout
the world ('dàl nam bochd'). It is interesting to find the
wording of the original elegy recurring in 'Dàin do Eimhir'
XV, a suggestion that it had sustained resonances for the
poet: ' 's chan e goirteas mo shàth-ghal/ mi bhith fàgte gun
m' eòl'.[151]

75–89   The *Annie Jane* set sail from Liverpool in the middle
of August 1853 for Montreal in Quebec, carrying some 450
passengers and about 1110 tons of railway lines on board.
She lost her mainmast in a terrible gale on September 15th,
after which the ship drifted northwards and broke up in the
sound between Vatersay and Barra in the early hours of
September 29th. A memorial now marks the point where the
bodies of 348 victims were buried.[152]

90–185   Organising his review of the muse of History in
her different manifestations cost MacLean some effort. As
first arranged in the Aberdeen manuscript, the order was:
Skye – Spain – Germany – China – Scotland – England –
France – Italy – India – Ireland – Greece – the world. Lewis,
Harris, Mull and the Hebrides were then inserted on the
facing, blank page, and the new order indicated by numbers
in blue pencil. In C a further Clio, of Inverness, is introduced
after the Hebrides, and Scotland becomes the Lowlands,
while the position of Germany is shifted from immediately
before France to between India and China.

102–103   Willie Orr gives the following account of the
incident referred to here, with its precedents:

In 1872 the Cuallin grazings on the mainland of Lewis of the Bernera crofters were taken to form an addition to Scaliscro forest and the crofters were given alternative grazings at Earshader... Two years later, in March 1874, the factor announced that they were to lose these grazings and confine their stock to Bernera. The crofters protested vehemently and the landlord served all fifty-six with notices of eviction; in attempting to deliver these the sheriff's officer was deforced and the factor, in his capacity of procurator fiscal, had some of the crofters arrested. Three hundred to four hundred crofters went in a body to Stornoway Castle to protest and, after the trial in July when a verdict of 'not proven' was returned, the sheriff removed the factor from his legal office and the grazing remained in the hands of the people.[153]

105 On November 22nd 1897 about two hundred crofters and cottars marched into Lady Matheson's deer forest at Park in Lewis, with the proclaimed intent of slaughtering as many deer as they were able. In December 1882 the proprietor had rejected a second petition in which local fishermen from three townships had asked for the lease of the Park sheep farm because of what she considered its threatening tone. The land in question had earlier in the century been cleared of twenty-eight townships so as to be given over to sheep. The crofters involved made no attempt to avoid legal prosecution for their action, which was seen as an opportunity to inform public opinion of the abuses associated with the institution of deer forests. At a trial held on January 16th 1898 all six defendants were acquitted.[154]

108–109 The background to these lines is effectively summarised by James Hunter:

In the 1820s and 1830s... the fertile machair lands on the Atlantic coast of Harris – lands which had been occupied from time immemorial – were completely cleared and the evicted population settled on the island's eastern shores. This was so bleak and stony a district that, as a Harris crofter observed bitterly, 'beasts could not live' in it. Among the rocks on which they were thus forced to set up home, the newly arrived inhabitants of the eastern part of Harris painstakingly constructed the lazybeds or *feannagan* which are still to be seen there and which alone could provide a depth of soil sufficient to raise a crop... Such harvests could not support a population used to living on the hugely more productive lands to the west, however, and many Harris people, 'reduced to extreme distress by being crowded into places incapable of affording them subsistence', were duly forced to emigrate.[155]

124 In 1845 and 1846 the blight *Phytophthora infestans*, which is thought to have arrived from South America, led to massive failure of the Irish potato crop, on which large segments of the population were dependent for their sustenance. Between 1841 and 1851, the overall population of Ireland dropped from just over eight million to six and a half, in consequence of disease, starvation and emigration.

128 Patrick Henry Pearse (1879–1916) was, like Connolly, executed for taking part in the Easter Rising in Dublin of 1916, when he was proclaimed first president of the provisional republican government. An enthusiastic supporter of the Irish language, he was editor of the Gaelic League's weekly newspaper from 1903 to 1909, and in 1914 published a collection of his own poems in the language.

129 Wolfe Tone (1763–1798) was in October 1791 among the founders of the mainly Protestant Society of United Irishmen, committed to universal suffrage and to Catholic emancipation. An attempt to invade Ireland with French forces failed in December 1796, when a storm dispersed the fleet. A second attempt in May 1798 led to Tone's capture, trial and a death sentence.

Lord Edward Fitzgerald (1763–1798), like Tone a member of the Society of United Irishmen, helped plan a revolt against English rule set for May 23rd, 1798, but was arrested four days earlier, dying in prison of a wound received while he was being apprehended.

Robert Emmet (1778–1803), also one of the United Irishmen, was one of a small band intent on attacking Dublin Castle during a chaotic and confused uprising in July 1803. His contingent killed the Lord Chief Justice and his nephew, after which Emmet went into hiding in the Wicklow Hills. He was captured, put on trial and executed in autumn of that year.

132   Walter or Wat Tyler headed the Peasants' Revolt in England of 1381. The confiscation of all church properties was among the demands made. He was beheaded in London in June 1381.

John Ball, a Lollard priest sympathetic to the doctrines of John Wycliffe, and said to have been excommunicated for his radical views, was freed from prison by Kentish rebels at the time of the revolt, and preached a celebrated sermon to the insurgents at Blackheath. He was hung, drawn and quartered on July 15th 1381, in the presence of Richard II.

Robert Ket or Kett was involved in a revolt in Norfolk, England in 1549, fired by opposition to enclosures. The rebels were defeated by John Dudley, Earl of Warwick, and Ket and his brother executed in December of that year.

134–135   George Gordon Lord Byron (1788–1824) took his seat in the House of Lords on reaching his majority in 1809 and delivered his first speech, in support of rioting Nottinghamshire weavers, in February 1812. This rueful backward glance at the inheritance of the French Revolution in *Childe Harold's Pilgrimage*, written at a time when the subsequent restoration of Napoleon's opponents appeared unshakeable, expresses the poet's undisguised commitment to the revolutionary cause, even when it seemed doomed to failure:

> What deep wounds ever closed without a scar?
> The heart's bleed longest, and but heal to wear
> That which disfigures it; and they who war
> With their own hopes, and have been vanquish'd, bear
> Silence, but not submission: in his lair
> Fix'd Passion holds his breath, until the hour
> Which shall atone for years; none need despair:
> It came, it cometh, and will come, – the power
> To punish or forgive – in *one* we shall be slower. (III,
>   lxxxiii)

Byron and Percy Bysshe Shelley (1792–1822) met in Geneva in May 1816, in Venice in August 1818, and were both in Pisa during the latter part of 1821. For Shelley, see further note to III: 72.

137   Animated by his radical sympathies, the black bass-baritone singer and actor Paul Robeson (1898–1976) toured Republican Spain at the time of the Civil War, made repeated visits to coal-mining regions of Wales in the 1930s, and visited the Soviet Union in 1934. Robeson drew explicit parallels between abuses of the local population in the colonies of the European powers and discrimination against black people in the United States. His passport was revoked from 1950 to 1958 and for lengthy periods he was under surveillance by both the British and the United States secret services.

149 The French Revolution which MacLean's muse interestingly classifies as a failure, is commonly regarded as marking the start of modern political radicalism expressed on a national scale. Our terms 'left-wing' and 'right-wing' are derived from the seating arrangements of the deputies in the Estates General of 1789, where Montagnards and Jacobins tended to take their places to the left of the presidential chair. The term 'ideology' is considered to have been invented in 1796 by French writer Antoine-Louis-Claude (1754–1836).

150–151 After France's defeat in the Franco-Prussian War of 1870–71, and the collapse of the Empire of Napoleon III (1852–1870), a victory by revolutionary candidates in elections organised on March 26th 1871 by the central committee of the National Guard in Paris led to the setting up of a revolutionary government. The attempt was brutally crushed by troops representing the Versailles government during a 'week of blood' at the end of May involving some 20,000 casualties. Karl Marx published a passionate address in favour of the revolutionaries, which won him European notoriety as a revolutionary ideologue.

152–155 Leader of a revolt against Rome in 73–71 BC, initially involving escaped gladiators, Spartacus could at one point call upon forces numbering 90,000. The revolt was, however, unsuccessful and the general entrusted with suppressing it, Marcus Licinius Crassus, crucified some 6,000 prisoners along the Appian Way. Apart from its symbolic quality, the name would have had multiple resonances for MacLean. Lewis Grassic Gibbon (pseudonym of James Leslie Mitchell, 1901–1935), closely associated with Hugh MacDiarmid at certain points in his career, published his novel *Spartacus* in 1933. The uprising in Germany between 5th and 12th January 1921, suppressed by the social democratic government, was known as the 'Spartacus revolt'; and the Spartacus League, opposed to participation in the

First World War and committed to revolutionary rather than parliamentary methods, counted Karl Liebknecht and Rosa Luxemburg among its founders. It became the German Communist Party in December 1918.

158 Giacomo Matteotti (1885–1924), secretary general of the Italian socialist party, was kidnapped and murdered by six fascist "squadristi" on June 10th 1924. Opposition deputies staged a walk-out from parliament in protest. The eventual outcome was that Mussolini dispensed with a parliament and instituted totalitarian rule. In January 1925 he publicly assumed responsibility for the murder. His challenge to anyone to prosecute him for it evoked no response.

160 An ultraroyalist in politics, Ioannis Metaxas (1871–1941) opposed the Greek plans to conquer western Anatolia which led to catastrophe in 1921–22. After the restoration of the monarchy in 1935, King George II, fearing the advance of communism, appointed Metaxas premier. The following year he established an authoritarian dictatorship. In October 1940 he refused Mussolini's demands to occupy strategic sites in Greece, organising successful opposition to the Italian invasion, but did not live to see the onslaught by German troops in April 1941.

165 Mahatma Gandhi (1869–1948) won an international reputation for his defence of Indian rights in South Africa. By 1921 he was India's most outstanding political figure, committed to non-violent resistance, to unity between Hindus and Muslims and to the ending of discrimination against India's 'untouchables'. Jawaharlal Nehru (1889–1964) was India's first prime minister, holding office from 1947 until his death in 1964. He met Gandhi in 1916. In 1929, when the Congress Party Gandhi had welded into an effective political force made complete independence from Britain its goal, Nehru was elected its president. He visited Europe and the Soviet Union in 1926–27 and was familiar with Marxist thought, though never a slavish adherent. Nehru suffered a total of nine terms of imprisonment between 1921 and 1945.

170 Edgar Snow described the crossing of the Long River as 'the most critical single incident of the Long March' in his *Red Star Over China* (first published in 1938). An iron-chain suspension bridge known as the Liu Ting Chiao or 'bridge fixed by Liu' represented the communist forces' only hope of escape from encirclement. The bridge

was built centuries ago, and in the manner of all bridges
of the deep rivers of western China. Sixteen heavy iron
chains, with a span of some 100 yards or more, were
stretched across the river, their ends imbedded on each
side under great piles of cemented rock, beneath the
stone bridgeheads. Thick boards lashed over the chains
made the road of the bridge, but upon their arrival the
Reds found that half this wooden flooring had been
removed, and before them only the bare iron chains
swung to a point midway in the stream.[156]

The communist forces succeeded in crossing, using only the
chains, despite being exposed to enemy machine-gun fire
from the opposite bank.

175   Given the company he keeps here, Greek philosopher
Plato (428 or 427–348 or 347 BC), pupil of Socrates and
master of Aristotle, presumably concerns MacLean primarily
as a political thinker and author of the *Republic* (ca.380
BC), a dialogue in which Socrates sets out from the question
of the nature of justice to describe the organisation of an
ideal city state.

Swiss-born Jean-Jacques Rousseau (1712–1778) was,
alongside Denis Diderot, at the centre of the group of
intellectuals responsible for the *Encyclopédie*. Renowned as a
novelist and composer, his political thinking influenced both
Marx and Lenin. He saw mankind as alienated from an
original state of savage blessedness by the emergence of
private property, the social contract needed to protect that,
and the inequalities between individuals and classes which
resulted.

176   A fluent English speaker renowned in his own day as
a poet and writer of tragedies, Voltaire (pseudonym of
François-Marie Arouet) (1694–1778) argued that progress
would in time ensure the happiness of all human individuals
and looked to the enlightened despot to enact this process –
an anticipation, under very different circumstances, of
MacDiarmid's attitude to Lenin and of MacLean's to Stalin.
His correspondences with Frederick the Great of Prussia and
with Catherine, Empress of Russia are emblematic of hopes
subsequently entertained by many writers and intellectuals of
a privileged dialogue with similar figures.

Marie-Jean-Antoine-Nicolas   de   Caritat,   Marquis   de

Condorcet (1743–1794) had philosopher and mathematician Jean le Rond d'Alembert as his mentor and took an active part in the preparation of the *Encyclopédie*. He was a friend of Voltaire, of whom he published a biography in 1789. Elected to the Legislative Assembly, he drew up a scheme for state education whose recommendations were largely adopted in the course of time. Steadfast hostility to Christianity and a determined belief in the ultimate perfectibility of human society characterised his thought.

A vociferous opponent of widespread electoral corruption and supporter of the 1832 Reform Bill, political journalist William Cobbett (1763–1835) was, however, no friend to the French Revolution, his support for radical measures never dispelling an underlying conservatism and attachment to the values of the English countryside. In the course of an adventurous life he twice took refuge in the United States to escape the consequences of the courageous stances he assumed on a range of social issues.

178 In these lines MacLean also summarises a tradition of political and social idealism in which the individual genius necessarily has a place (cf. the references to Einstein in Part VII). The reputation as a master of visual art of Leonardo da Vinci (1452–1519) is based on barely 17 surviving paintings. In addition he was a military engineer and a prolific inventor, writing in a reverse script which requires a mirror to be read.

The shift of focus from France to Germany before concentrating on Russia is hardly surprising, given the primacy of German-language texts in the development of political and philosophical thinking throughout the 19th century. Faithful to his chosen brand of leftism, MacLean shows no interest whatsoever in the theories of Freud. If the result is something of a hotch-potch, setting Voltaire's faith in progress alongside Schopenhauer's pessimism, the Frenchman's interest in sophisticated social organisation (countered by his subsequent retreat to Ferney and the urge to *cultiver son jardin*) alongside the German's glorification of music and the individual, perhaps this should be laid to the Gaelic poet's credit – symptomatic of MacLean's intellectual voracity, the openness to ideas of one who never actively engaged in communist militancy and never became a party member.

Arthur Schopenhauer (1788–1860) reacted against Hegel's

idealism, strongly influenced not only by Immanuel Kant but by the teachings of the Indian *Upanishads*. His mother formed part of Goethe's circle in Weimar. In its second half, his major work *The World as Will and Idea* (1819) seeks a means of gaining liberation from the operation of the individual will. Johann Gottlieb Fichte (1762–1814) is regarded as a founder of German Idealism, his works constituting a crucial link between Kant and Hegel. An important element in his thinking is that the freedom of the invididual will naturally be limited by his or her awareness of the freedom and rights of other individuals.

179 Unlike so many of his contemporaries, Russian symbolist poet Alexander Blok (1880–1921) could be represented during the Soviet period as having adopted a basically favourable attitude towards the Bolshevik revolution, notwithstanding the ambivalent close of his major poem 'The Twelve', where Bolshevik soldiers are envisaged as enjoying Christ's protection.[157] Blok, who gave clear signs of disillusionment and increasing desperation as his death approached, forms along with Gaelic poet William Ross and W. B. Yeats a trio of poets unhappy in love cited at the close of 'Dàin do Eimhir' XX. It is almost certain that Blok came to MacLean's attention thanks to MacDiarmid's highly evocative translation into Scots (from an English version) of the Russian poet's 'Neznakomka', 'The Stranger', early on in his long poem *A Drunk Man Looks at the Thistle* (1926).[158]

The name of German philosopher Friedrich Nietzsche (1844–1900) is perhaps unintentionally highlighted by its placing at the end of the list and of a verse paragraph. Was the motivation the uneasy rhyme achieved with 'Fichte'? Nietzsche's critique of Christianity, and his delineation of the Nihilism which emerged as the former yielded inevitably to secular thought, were tragically open to abuse and misinterpretation. His positing of the 'superman' as one willing to embrace the possibility of 'eternal recurrence', with the renewal of suffering that entails, is veined with inherent paradox.

The supposed reader of all these texts, the muse of world history ('Clio an t-saoghail'), has just announced 'chan fhaca mi mòran faochaidh' ('I have not seen much respite'). Yet she is the one who, some thirty lines later, will affirm that history is ultimately directed towards a positive end: 'Thèid a' chuibhle mun cuairt/ is tionnda'idh gu buaidh an càs' ('The wheel will go round and the distress will turn to triumph'). If we read 'An Cuilithionn' as a political tract, expressions of ambivalence must inevitably be seen as defects; if we read it as poetry, however, these can only add to its strength.

183 The Winter Palace in the city then known as Petrograd was occupied by Bolshevik forces on the night of November 6th to 7th (Western calendar) 1917. Largely taken up by a military hospital, the Palace was also the seat of the Provisional Government which had replaced the Tsar's autocracy in the wake of the February revolution, but which had a formidable rival in the Petrograd Soviet of Workers' and Soldiers' Deputies. The event became a milestone in Soviet historiography, a focus of considerable subsequent mythification. It would appear that in reality the takeover did not meet with significant resistance.

186–187 A near quotation of the opening lines of 'Smeòrach Chlann Dòmhnaill' by the North Uist poet John MacCodrum (1693–1779), much of whose work has survived 'thanks to the diligence and enthusiasm of William Matheson, who collected from a still flourishing oral tradition in the 1930s'.[159] Matheson's edition of MacCodrum's songs appeared in 1938. The lines in question are 'Smeòrach mis' air ùrlar Phaibil/ Crùbadh ann an dùsal cadail' ('A mavis I on Paible's flat, huddled in a drowse of sleep').[160] By far the best known of MacCodrum's songs, it is generally assumed to have been an imitation of Mac Mhaighstir Alasdair's 'Smeòrach Chlann Raghnaill', but Matheson suggests the reverse may have been the case, as the latter may well have heard 'Smeòrach Chlann Dòmhnaill' 'from the lips of the composer during the encounter which they are known to have had at Tigharry some time after 1755'.[161] In a letter dated July 27th 1934, MacLean proposes making a version of this poem as a basis for a translation by MacDiarmid, who accepts the proposal in his reply dated August 9th.[162] MacDiarmid was, however, clearly already acquainted with it, given the imitation offered in *To Circumjack Cencrastus* (1930):

> I am the mavis o' Pabal
>   back on the tap o' the hill,

my voice and things still wantin'
  a wee thing in strength and skill.
I am the mavis o' Pabal, lang
I've lain wi' my heid on my breist...[163]

188–189   MacLean here quotes the alternative two opening
lines of a lament for Iain Garbh of Raasay as sung by his
uncle Alasdair MacLean. The better known version begins
''S mi 'nam shuidh air an tulaich/ 's mi ri feitheamh na
fàire'.[164]

200   The interest in Copernicanism of Italian philosopher
and astronomer Galileo Galilei first attracted the attention of
the Inquisition in 1613. In 1615 heliocentric views of the solar
system were pronounced heretical. Galileo was instructed to
neither pursue nor defend them. It was however not until
1633 that he was summoned to answer charges of heresy in
Rome, forced to abjure formally, and condemned to life
imprisonment. His closing years were spent in a villa above
Florence. In l. 201 MacLean gives a Gaelic version of the
astronomer's famed riposte: 'Eppur si muove.'

215ff.   MacLean echoes here the opening of the second
stanza from 'Oran do Mhac Leòid Dhùn Bheagain/ A Song
to MacLeod of Dunvegan' by An Clarsair Dall[165] (Roderick
Morison, the 'Blind Harper') (c.1656–1713/4): 'Chaidh a'
chuibhle mun cuairt,/ grad thionndadh gu fuachd am blàths''
('The wheel (of fortune) has come full circle, warmth has
suddenly turned cold.') Eight lines further on, at l. 223, his
reference is to the fourth stanza of the same song: 'Chaidh
Mac-talla as an Dùn/ an am sgarachdainn dùinn ri 'r triath'
('Echo deserted the Castle at the time we separated from our
lord'). Replacing 'Echo' ('mac-talla') by Clio, the muse of
history, neatly integrates the reference into the ongoing
discourse of Part VI.

A note in John Mackenzie's *Sar-Obair* gives the traditional
setting for this song, which was interpreted as emblematic of
the termination of a style of artistic patronage with a
centuries long pedigree:

> John Breac McLeod was one of the last chieftains that
> had in his retinue a bard, a harper, a piper, and a fool, –
> all of them excellently and liberally provided for. After
> his death, Dunvegan Castle was neglected by his son
> Roderick, and the services of these functionaries dis-

pensed with to make room for grooms, gamekeepers, factors, dogs and the various *et ceteras* of a fashionable English establishment.[166]

While Morison's editor, William Matheson, is sceptical in this regard, MacLean is likely to have viewed these verses through the generally accepted prism. He proposes translating 'Òran Mòr MhicLeòid' in the letter to MacDiarmid dated July 27th 1934 already referred to, subsequently informing his correspondent that

> Eight verses of this poem have never been published. I have never seen them. I believe they are in the National Library. The attack on Roderick evidently becomes so scurrilous that the polite ears of Gaelic editors cannot bear it.[167]

247–258 These three quatrains, with their direct reference at l. 251 to the hammer and sickle, insignia of communist revolution, are omitted in C.

267–270 No longer a direct translation from MacDiarmid, these lines nonetheless constitute a reprise of the conclusion of V. The step referred to at 270 has to be Dimitrov's, though the replacement in C of 'a shàir Dimitrov' by 'A shàrchuraidh' ('Greatest of heroes') makes the allusion less specific.

Part VII

2 'Dàin do Eimhir' XXV also refers to the myth of Prometheus who, having made mankind the gift of fire, suffered eternal punishment from Zeus, being exposed on the mountains of the Caucasus, where an eagle fed on his liver. The legend inspired a play (perhaps a trilogy or even a tetralogy) by Aeschylus (525 or 524–456 or 455 BC). The dating, even the authorship of *Prometheus Bound* continue however to be matter for dispute. Both it and what is known about its lost sequel offer the background to Shelley's *Prometheus Unbound*, whose atmosphere and radical, utopian tendencies are effectively summed up in the following comments:

Given Shelley's ethics and his theory of knowledge (epistemology), it seems likely that he believed that when human beings viewed the universe correctly, it would appear to be beneficent rather than hostile... whereas Acts I and III deal primarily with conditions in the human world – with the psychology of tyranny (Act I) and of freedom (Act III) – the other two acts explore the metaphysical implications of human bondage – how a slave psychology distorts the human view of the universe... Finally, as Prometheus in his opening speech had described his situation in relation to past events, so Demogorgon, addressing the spirits of all creatures in the Universe, summarizes the present joy and tells how to recapture freedom, should it be lost again.[168]

For the importance of Shelley's play to the adolescent MacLean, see note to III: 72.

22 Roger Casement (1864–1916) came of Ulster Protestant stock and became internationally famous for his denunciation of cruelty to native workers in the Congo (1904) and in Peru (1912). His attempts to secure German support for the planned Easter Rising failed and, put ashore in Ireland by a German submarine, he was arrested on April 24th and condemned to death for treason. The authenticity of the Casement diaries, which contain detailed descriptions of homosexual activities, was long contested.

25–26 Douglas Young notes a reference to *Prometheus Unbound* I 91–92: 'But never bowed our snowy crest/ As at the voice of thy unrest', where the First Voice recalls the moment at which Prometheus cursed Jupiter. But note ll. 38–40 from the same act:

and the Earthquake-fiends are charged
To wrench the rivets from my quivering wounds
When the rocks split and close again behind...

41–47 This reference to the beloved, who becomes a vulture to the speaker's Prometheus, is very different in tone from her earlier appearance at III: 200–210, and may be indicative of a darkening in the poet's relations with the Scottish woman he referred to as 'Eimhir'.

67   Nadezhda Konstantinova Krupskaya (1869–1939) joined Lenin in his Siberian exile in 1898, the year of their marriage. Acting as his personal secretary, she lived with him in several European cities and, after the Bolshevik Revolution, was active in the People's Commissariat for Education. One version of her death has it that she was poisoned on Stalin's orders.

68ff.   These were the first lines to be cancelled from the text of 'An Cuilithionn'. Their championing of MacDiarmid against the giants of London-based modernism (both of North American origin), not merely on a literary basis, but in terms of class and political affiliation, is characteristic of the attitudes of many writers associated with the Scottish Renaissance Movement which MacDiarmid founded in the early 1920s.

The latter's relations with Thomas Stearns Eliot (1888–1965) were generally cordial in nature. Eliot tends to be seen as subsisting on the margins of the Bloomsbury group which numbered Virginia Woolf, Lytton Strachey, E. M. Forster, the economist Maynard Keynes and the painter Duncan Grant among its exponents. MacLean may wish to evoke the aura of class privilege and sexual non-conformism which suffused the group, whose members tended to be politically disengaged and, in many cases, made a specific commitment to pacifism and non-violent resistance. At Pound's suggestion, Eliot cut *The Waste Land* (1922) by almost half, in an episode not lacking analogies with composer Frances George Scott's less drastic, apparently largely structural intervention in MacDiarmid's work on *A Drunk Man Looks at the Thistle*.

Eliot separated formally from his wife on returning from the United States in 1933. Since 1925, he had been working in London for the publishing firm Faber & Gwyer, later Faber & Faber. Ezra Pound moved to Paris in 1921, and to Italy in 1924. His fascination with Douglas's theories of Social Credit would have found favour with MacDiarmid at at least one stage in the latter's development. During the Second World War, Pound became notorious for his anti-Semitism and, in consequence of a series of radio broadcasts made from Italy between 1941 and 1943, faced charges of treason in the United States after the conclusion of the war.

The official lunch following a ceremony on July 12th

1939, at which Pound received an honorary doctorate from his *alma mater* in the United States, Hamilton College, deteriorated into a shambles when the honorary guest challenged the anti-fascist opinions being expressed. There is, however, no record of the poet receiving actual blows.[169] The wording of MacLean's reference indicates that he may have an untraced Italian incident in mind.

It may be appropriate to read in l. 75 a direct reference to the poems inspired in MacDiarmid by the seascapes of Shetland, where he had been living, on the island of Whalsay, since May 1933, not least 'On a Raised Beach'.[170]

78 Were it not for a footnote in the Edinburgh typescript of MacLean's English translation, a reference here to the serpent which is a pervasive symbol of MacDiarmid's *To Circumjack Cencrastus* could easily escape the reader's attention.[171] The poet linked the snake to a serpentine path known as 'the Curly Snake' close to his birthplace of Langholm. In a letter of February 1939 to Helen Cruickshank he explained that:

> Cencrastus... is a Gaelic (or Scottish) version of the idea common to Indian and other mythologies that underlying Creation there is a great snake – and that its movements form the pattern of history... my poem... identifies it with the evolution of human thought – the principle of change and the main factor in the revolutionary development of human consciousness... In so far as it is a specifically Scottish poem, and concerned in particular to glorify the Gaelic element in our heritage (which I believe underlies our Scottish life and history in much the same way that consciousness underlies and informs the whole world of man) the doctrine it is filled with [concerns] World Consciousness which I believe to be the great function and destiny of Man...[172]

While these lines highlight obvious points of contact with MacLean's approach in 'An Cuilithionn', the notion here of the serpent being lifted out of the sea may be a confused reminiscence of a passage in six-line stanzas close to the end of MacDiarmid's poem where, however, serpent and sea are counterposed and contrasted.[173]

92 A similar footnote to that referred to above indicates that this is a 'parody of verse celebrating Battle of Cuillin in 1600'.[174]

100 Although a French writer named François-Vincent Toussaint (1715–1792) contributed to the earlier volumes of the French *Encyclopédie*, it is more likely that MacLean has in mind Toussaint Louverture (c.1743–1803), son of a slave, leader of the independence movement in Haiti at the time of the French Revolution and a firm opponent of slavery. This line in its original form began with Lucretius, not Toussaint.

Canonised by the Catholic church, English humanist Thomas More (1478–1535) makes an odd choice for MacLean's pantheon in 'An Cuilithionn'. Dutch humanist Erasmus wrote *In Praise of Folly* while a guest of More's in London. The latter's *Utopia* 'describes a pagan and communist city-state in which the institutions and policies are entirely governed by reason'[175] and was first published in Leuven in the Low Countries in 1516. More's refusal to condone Henry VIII's repudiation of papal supremacy led to his trial and execution.

109 Influenced in his writings by Fichte, Proudhon and Bakunin, Gustav Landauer (1870–1919) translated Wilde, Shaw and Whitman into German, and opposed his country's involvement in the First World War on anarchist and pacifist grounds. He was a member of the government of the Soviet Republic proclaimed in Bavaria in April 1919 but resigned when the German Communist Party assumed control. Arrested the following month, he was murdered brutally by members of the Freikorps.

Having been imprisoned towards the end of the First World War for encouraging munitions workers to go on strike, Kurt Eisner (1867–1919), like Landauer of Jewish origin, master-minded a socialist uprising which toppled the Wittenbach monarchy in Bavaria in November 1918. His assassination in February 1919 was instrumental in provoking the short-lived experiment with a Soviet-style regime there.

Experiences in the trenches on the western front made a convinced pacifist of Ernst Toller (1893–1939), son of a Jewish grain merchant. Both Max Weber and Thomas Mann spoke in his favour during the trial which followed his participation in the Bavarian uprising. While serving the prison sentence that resulted, Toller produced a series of plays which established his reputation as a writer. The Nazis denounced him on achieving power, and he emigrated to the United States. Having helped organise support for the Republican side during the Spanish Civil War, he committed suicide in a New York hotel room.

110–129 Only eight lines from this paragraph survive in C; **132–143** and **150–159** are cut entirely there, so also the double mentions of Einstein and Dimitrov.

115 Scottish political reformer Thomas Muir (1765–1799) read out an address from the United Irishmen at a meeting of Scottish reform societies held in Edinburgh in December 1792. Though a moderate rather than a revolutionary, and opposed to violence, he was arrested for sedition. Freed on bail, he travelled to France and was prevented from returning to attend his trial by the outbreak of war with Britain. Transported to Botany Bay, Muir managed to escape, found his way back to France and died there in mysterious circumstances.

118 Donald MacLeod (c.1814–1857) was himself a victim of the clearances in Sutherland. which he denounced in a series of letters to the *Edinburgh Weekly Chronicle* in 1840–41. A stonemason by trade, he emigrated to Canada. where his letters and pamphlets were published as *Gloomy Memories* in Toronto in 1857. The chosen title is an ironic parody of the book in which Harriet Beecher Stowe, authoress of *Uncle Tom's Cabin*, described her visit to the area.[176]

132 Albert Einstein (1879–1955) published two articles on his theory of relativity as early as 1905, but it was his work on the photoelectric effect that gained him a Nobel Prize in 1921. He resigned from the Prussian Academy when Hitler came to power and moved to the United States, where he supported the research which led to the manufacture of the atom bomb without becoming directly involved.

200–211 This passage, which performs an important function as both summing up (celebrated pipe tunes, cultural and political heroes, the serpent from MacDiarmid's poem and the stallion from MacLean's own) and anticipation ('a' màrsail air mullach soilleir... a' coiseachd air an àirde luim'), disappeared in C, where a direct cut is made to l. 324.

202 Despite indications he may have been dead by 54 BC, almost nothing is known of the life of Latin poet Lucretius Carus. His principal, indeed his only surviving work, *De* *rerum natura* ('On the Nature of Things') is an elaboration of Epicurean philosophy, basically atheistic and materialist in nature. He looked upon belief in the gods or in life after death as forms of superstition.

Ludwig van Beethoven (1770–1827) is, alongside Patrick Mor MacCrimmon, a principal focus of the "concert poem", 'Dàin do Eimhir' XXIII, written after MacLean had heard Beethoven's *Eighth Symphony*, played by the Reid Symphony Orchestra, with Adrian Boult as conductor, at the Usher Hall in Edinbugh on Saturday December 9th 1939. Earlier in his life, Beethoven's radical sympathies had led him to take Napoleon Bonaparte as inspiration for his *Third Symphony*. When Napoleon assumed the title of Emperor, however, the planned dedication was jettisoned.

212–323   This outstanding lyrical outburst is omitted in C, thus profoundly transforming the tone and balance of the poem as a whole, not merely of its conclusion. While the verse form is substantially the same as that deployed at V: 35–146, the extensive use of syntactical parallelism, and of nouns paired in compounds, gives an impression of greater speed, rendering the twin stresses in each line more forceful, even overwhelming. The lyric is presented in quatrains rather than as eight-line stanzas. Conceptually the discourse is pushed towards the bounds of comprehension, not least through the persistent use of the vocative. The mountain range is identified with the Slave Ship at ll. 268ff., transformed into a more hopeful symbol of the progress of the masses of humanity as a whole, while at l. 296 it combines with the other dominant positive symbol of the poem, the 'Àigeach' or stallion. Given that by the time C was published MacLean would appear to have accepted that his poetry must perforce appear in double form, with facing English translation, it is not impossible that the difficulty of rendering this passage satisfactorily into another language played a part in its deletion. Young's solution is hardly happier in his 'projection', where the passage is grouped in octaves. The opening is quoted:

> Coolin of Skye,
> mountains of ire,
> savage and wild,
>   your outcry thrilling.

Coolin of stone,
peaks unthrowable,
mountains of sportiveness,
    your roar goes shrilling.

Coolin of the skyline,
sharp belt of the high peaks,
Coolin of mightiness,
    fine end of dull yearning.
Summit-circuit
of the human spirit,
danger-precipitous,
    your hope's pith burning.[177]

There can be no doubt that in terms of sheer poetic achieve-ment this passage represents the most significant addition to MacLean's poetic *corpus* achieved with the publication of 'An Cuilithionn' as originally drafted.

284, 288, 292 It is tempting to emend these lines to the vocative form 'A Chuilithinn', but the reading given here is reproduced in the Edinburgh typescripts and not corrected there (with the exception of l. 288, absent, see below).

285–288 These four lines are to be found only in the Aberdeen hand-written copy of the poem. The English trans-lation is editorial. A possible explanation of their dis-appearance is that the person who made a typed copy of the Gaelic text (probably Jessie Kosmarova, *née* Scott[178]), who would appear to have been ignorant of the language, made a slip. Her eye may simply have jumped from 'luaineach' at l. 286 to 'bhuadhan' at l. 290. As both quatrains use the 'ua' rhyme, such a slip could have occurred all the more easily, subsequently escaping the poet's attention.

328ff. Concerning the haunted, dream-like conclusion to his poem, MacLean told Young (letter dated March 30th 1942) that

> 'Cò seo' to the end was composed in bed in Raasay in the early hours of January 1st 1940. I had a bad throat and went to bed, I think, immediately the New Year was in. I think the 'Cuillin' was finished apart from that before December 20th 1939.

Something of the same atmosphere can be detected in 'Na Samhlaidhean' and 'Coin is Madaidhean-Allaidh' ('The

Ghosts' and 'Dogs and Wolves', 'Dàin do Eimhir' XXVIII
and XXIX), written down in the early hours of Wednesday
December 20th. With respect to the latter two items,
MacLean claimed to have 'composed them simultaneously in
a troubled sleep', and not to have 'changed one word from
that first writing down'.[179] At a point when discussion of the
1943 volume *Dàin do Eimhir agus Dàin Eile* was in the early
stages, MacLean recommended this passage for inclusion,
adding that George Campbell Hay ('Deòrsa') considered it to
be 'the very best thing in' 'An Cuilithionn', adding 'I myself
also do' (letter dated November 9th 1941). The enthusiastic,
yet considered accolade which Young offered for the whole
poem, in a letter dated June 26th 1940, must have been very
welcome to MacLean, not least given the noteworthy diver-
gence in the political views of the two men:

> This is very great poetry. In literature, apart from
> Aeschylus' *Prometheus*, Sophokles' *Oidoipous at
> Kolonos*, and one or two passages of Dante and Goethe,
> I cannot think of any sustained flight on a similar scale
> which keeps on a plane of such intensity and ardour.
> But the comparison is rather with music, with one of the
> great symphonies or quartets of Beethoven.

Ever the Greek scholar and philologist, Young noted

> at the end, by the way, a very good use of the
> Sophoklean quiet close.[180]

Endnotes

1. Groom 1894: VI, 355 s.v. 'Skye'. In preparing this commentary,
careful use was made of online resources such as the *Oxford Dictionary of
National Biography*, the *Encyclopedia Britannica* and *Wikipedia*.
Information not explicitly footnoted should be regarded as having been
culled from these sources.
2. Ross & Hendry 1986: 211–222, here 218ff.
3. 'One day and I on Sgurr a' Ghreadaidh,/ standing on the high
notched knife-edge,/ looking down on the Corrie of Loneliness/ through
the surging mists around me,/ in a breaking of the drift/ there glittered a
flash of gold on the wings/ of an eagle passing below,/ along the flanking
walls:/ above the glory of all bird-life to me/ the gold gleam of the Skye
bird'.
4. In her edition of Iain Lom's poems, Annie M. Mackenzie quotes

an elegy by Angus MacDonald of Glencoe which has however no obvious connection with MacLean's 'Dedication'. See Mackenzie 1964: xxxi.

5. See ms 29559 ff105–123.

6. See Bold 1988 and Wilson 2010.

7. MacLean 1985: 12.

8. Wilson 2010: 180–181, 184.

9. Referred to frequently in the course of this commentary, these letters may be consulted in National Library of Scotland Accession 6419 Box 38b.

10. Nicolson 1979: 27.

11. For Thomson, 'it seems likely that he was throwing in his lot with his clan and political allies rather than expressing a religious conversion', see Thomson 1996: 9.

12. Thomson 1996: 33 and 1983: 185. See also Black 1986.

13. 'And I must stay where I may,/ a Skyeman by the side of great Mary'.

14. Heights are quoted from Sillar & Meyler 1973: 196.

15. Forbes 1923: 326.

16. Throughout the commentary, when reference is made to lines from the 'earrann' being discussed, these are preceded by 'l.' or 'll.' (indicating 'line' or 'lines'). A reference to lines from a different 'earrann' is preceded by a Roman numeral immediately followed by a colon.

17. Bold 1988: 349, 355. For the poem itself see MacDiarmid 1978: 2, 1186–1193.

18. The link lies in the resilient, impenetrable, slab-like quality of the verse, which MacDiarmid obtains by very different means from MacLean, injecting specialist vocabulary into his lines with which almost none of his readers are likely to be familiar. MacLean's approach, in terms of the Gaelic tradition, is no less innovative. See MacDiarmid 1978: 1, 422–433.

19. For a convincing explanation of how Màiri may have been framed, which respects the available facts and reconciles them with her innocence, see Meek 1998: 24.

20. Meek 1998: 106–112.

21. For this and subsequent descriptions see Humble 1986: 5–7. He glosses these peaks respectively as 'the red peak', 'Mackenzie's peak', the 'peak of Charles' and 'the stack peak'. The meanings given by Dwelly for 'sgùman' include 'bag formed by gathering up the four corners of a square of cloth, and often used as a strainer', 'lock of hair on the forehead, especially of sheep' and 'stack of corn'.

22. This spelling, with capital 'D', is used throughout the commentary in referring to the family of landowners and clan chiefs in Skye. Where another source is quoted, the spelling of the original has been reproduced.

23. Tentatively to be identified with Louise Hugon, who married Sir Thomas Coats Glen Glen-Coats, 2nd Baronet, on April 5th 1935. Her husband's mother, the previous Lady Glen-Coats, had died in 1910. See http://www.thepeerage.com (consulted June 8th 2010).

24. Wilson 2010: 169, 170–172, 175.

25. Wilson 2010: 186.
26. See National Library of Scotland ms 29561, where these lines are numbered 55–58.
27. Information from the poet's daughter Ishbel.
28. Nicolson 1930: 383–384.
29. Reed: 24–25, 29–31.
30. Hunter 2000: 88–89.
31. MacPhail 1989: 25.
32. Cameron 1912: 53–54. For a modern account, as balanced as it is judicious, readers are referred to MacPhail 1998: 52–62.
33. For a modern account, readers are referred to MacPhail 1989: 36–52.
34. MacPhail 1989: 37.
35. Forbes 1923: 27, 184. 191.
36. Groom 1894: VI, 362 s.v. 'Sleat'.
37. MacLean gives Donald Archie MacDonald a detailed explanation or 'sloinneadh' of his own relationship to the people cleared from Sgoirebreac in the conversation already mentioned . See Ross and Hendy 1986: 214.
38. See the note on Scorrybreck House at http://www.scotlandsplaces. gov.uk (consulted October 18th 2010).
39. 'The children, women and big men/ of Sgoirebreac in a fank in Braes,/ poverty and hardship their pain.// And the green lush pastures/ of Sgoirebreac without efficacy for them.'
40. Quoted in Nicolson 1930: 384.
41. Eagle: 106, 107. Note that MacKenzie's birth date is elsewhere given as 1856 (http://www.sligachan.co.uk/sligachan-history.php, consulted October 18th 2010).
42. Eagle 1991: 120–121, see also Brown 2005.
43. Thomson 1983: 265.
44. Maclean 1985: 107–108.
45. MacFarlane 1925: 261.
46. Letter dated February 27th 1938, see Wilson 2010: 171.
47. Thomson 1977: 225, 228.
48. 'The Castle on Fire': 'Though Dunvegan was "nearly" burnt/ there was no "nearly" about the burning of the houses/ MacLeod set fire to so as to keep/ Dunvegan haughty upon its rocks' (editor's translation). See MacLean 1943: 94.
49. 'how can this thought keep alive', 'remain alive', 'how can the essence of this thought resist/ on the slippery roads of the world?' (editor's translation)
50. 'resist', 'keep'; the final version of the lines is translated 'how will this love keep its hold/ on the icy rock of the world' in MacLean 1999: 69.
51. Forbes 1923: 159.
52. 'On the same subject': 'Where are the Lewismen who can put out/ the bitter fumes of this noble dwelling?/ The ocean next to Barra put paid to them/ beyond the Kyle of Vatersay' (editor's translation). See MacLean 1943: 94.
53. Thomson 1977: 231, Thomson 1983: 170.
54. Help in identifying the participants in this diabolical ceilidh was

offered by John MacInnes, who believes MacLean to have 'demonised' the Dunvegan MacLeods, and added that it was not unusual for incoming tenants to speak favourably of the landowners. Dymock considers these figures one by one in 'Appendix III' of her thesis. Many notorious clearers would have been familiar to the poet from oral tradition, which naturally conveys truth of a different order from that of either a judicial investigation or an academic study.

55. MacPhail 1989: 53.
56. MacPhail 1989: 80.
57. MacPhail 1989: 56.
58. MacPhail 1989: 26.
59. Reed: 87.
60. Reed: 77.
61. MacPhail 1989: 28.
62. Meek 1998: 171–174.
63. Nicolson 1930: 387.
64. Vol. 1: 25. Consulted online October 18th 2010 at the Lochaber College site, http://www.highland-elibrary.com, where a downloadable pdf version of Vol. 1 is available.
65. Vol. 1: 219.
66. Vol. 1: 343. A 'lippie' is '¼ of a SCOTS PECK, varying in weight according to district and commodity, *now usu* =1¾ lbs for goods sold by weight and used *esp* for oats, barley, and potatoes'. See *Concise Scots Dictionary* s.v. 'lippie'.
67. Vol. 1: 80.
68. Vol. 1: 256.
69. Vol. 1: 22, 280, 452–453.
70. MacPhail 1989: 26–27.
71. Sharpe 1977: 61–63.
72. MacLeod 2002: 100.
73. MacLean 1943: 94. 'To Mr Neville Chamberlain': 'Generations will remember your face,/ the betrayal of the Czechs and of the Spaniards/ portrayed in your ugly snout' (editor's translation). In Aberdeen ms 2864 an earlier version is preserved: 'Ruigidh do chliù-sa na h-àirdean,/ daorsa Abyssinia, nan Teacach, nan Spàinteach/ air a dhealbh nad aodann grànda.' ('Your fame will reach the heights,/ the slavery of Abyssinia, of the Czechs and of the Spaniards/ portrayed in your ugly face' (editor's translation)).
74. Stier et al. 1973: 84.
75. Nicolson 1930: 385–386.
76. Richards 2008: 303–305.
77. 'in one was never seen there/ the intellect of Lenin and the red side of Christ'.
78. 'cast a cloud/ over poverty and a bitter wound/ and over the world of Lenin's intellect,/ over his patience and his anger.'
79. The dedicatee of the 'First Hymn to Lenin', Prince Dimitry Mirsky, returned to the Soviet Union in 1932, was arrested in June 1937, arrived in Magadan at the start of November, and was dead by the following January (see Smith 2000). For the three 'hymns', dating from 1931, 1932 and 1957 respectively, see MacDiarmid 1978: 1, 297–299, 321–328 and 2:

893–901. The passage quoted can be found at 1, 298. MacDiarmid's most noteworthy contribution to the cult of Lenin is probably the four-line poem 'The Skeleton of the Future (At Lenin's Tomb)' (1, 386).

80. Letter dated September 7th 1941.

81. 'Glasgow,/ where Maclean's grave is green'.

82. 'a red fresh rose'.

83. 'the red rose of Clyde pouring/ in its great mighty flood of anger/ when Maclean raised a standard'.

84. 'a pillar on the heights'.

85. 'I heard the laughter of the stars, the pealing laughter of sun and moon, the muffled laughter of the universe encircling the bareness and expansiveness of the year. Laughter, peals of laughter, from blue summits in the skies, belly-laughter of the brutes mocking you, my fellow creature.' MacLean 1943: 94, with the poet's English version from NLS ms 29557 f72r.

86. 'the high head of our story... the battle-post of the poor', MacLean 1999: 46–47.

87. MacDiarmid 1978: 1, 604–605.

88. 'I was in Leipzig with full desire/ when Dimitrov stood before the court'.

89. 'alone/ making the human spirit/ leap out of its shell, unhusked,/ to stop the breath of the world'.

90. 'until the whole Red Army together/ comes battle-marching across Europe,/ that song of wretchedness will seep/ into my ears and my heart.'

91. 'Who will cast out the dung for us/ unless Stalin descends from the heights?'

92. MacLean 1999: 63.

93. 'as strong as Dimitrov, as wise as Stalin' (editor's translation).

94. Meek 1998: 204–208.

95. MacPhail 1989: 27–36.

96. Brown 1893:204.

97. Meek 1998: 179–183.

98. Meek 1995: 322.

99. Mackenzie 1907: 430–431.

100. MacKillop 1998 s.v. Goll mac Morna.

101. MacKillop 1998 s.v. Cùchulainn.

102. Groom 1894: VII, 355.

103. 'The great guns of mankind/ [...] on your old high castle/ with foolish idiots in them/ beating on their heroes' military shields' (editor's translation).

104. Cheape 2009: 100.

105. Cheape 2009: 99.

106. Campsie 1980: 47–48, 66–67.

107. Campsie 1980: 68.

108. Campsie 1980: 81. 73.

109. Groom I: 131.

110. Reed: 81.

111. Groom VI: 234.

112. Groom VI: 256.

113. Groom VI: 366, 408.
114. Scene 13, ll. 70–74. See Gill 1989: 91.
115. 'the banner of Christ's blood high in the skies' (editor's translation).
116. MacDiarmid 1978: I, 57. MacDiarmid, like MacLean, uses the spelling 'Leonhardt'. In the Aberdeen ms of 'An Cuilithionn' the name is 'Reinhardt', presumably a slip of memory on MacLean's part.
117. 'the Spanish miner leaping in the face of horror/ and his great spirit going down untroubled'.
118. See Thomson 1983: 185–186
119. 'Brown-haired Allan, rouse and gird thee,/ raise thy clan, think of thy need; if Alba's folk do not defend her,/ she'll be 'neath a brutal breed.' See Macdonald & Macdonald 1924: 190–191.
120. *Oxford Dictionary of National Biography* (online version) s.v. Lithgow family.
121. Reed: 23.
122. Mackenzie 1881: 202–203.
123. See further Watson 1925 and Bewsher 1921.
124. See http://www.sligachan.co.uk/sligachan-history,php, consulted October 18th 2010.
125. Wilson 2010: 162, 185.
126. 'the generous deeds/ that were sweet in the ears of Connolly/ and in the ears of his kind'
127. 'courage and beauty/ ...their flagpoles through your side'
128. 'ged tha bior glas an dòlais/ tro chliabh m' òg-mhaidne sàthte' ('though the grey stake of misfortune is/ thrust through the breast of my young morning').
129. 'but there is an excuse on your lips,/ the excuse that did not spoil your poetry,/ for every man has his excuse'. MacLean 1999: 260–261
130. MacLean 1985: 134–155, 156–161.
131. MacLean 1985: 155.
132. Wilson 2010: 125.
133. 'They put out fair-haired Pilot's eye,/ they put out Pilot's eye,/ they put our poor Pilot's eye,/ without him doing anything to deserve it' (editor's translation). See Cameron 1932: 220–221, where we read (217) that the author 'was the son of Rev. Duncan MacLucas, who was for many years a Baptist minister in Tiree. He lived at Balephuil' and 'composed many songs'.
134. 'The Lowlanders never had a policeman/ who was as good at keeping watch by night'.
135. 'Have you heard of the heroic countermarch made by the army that was at Kilcumin? Far has gone the fame of their play – they drove their enemies before them.// Early on Sunday morning I climbed the brae above the castle of Inverlochy. I saw the army arraying for battle, and victory on the field was with Clan Donald.// When you were ascending the spur of Culachy I perceived in you the enthusiasm your bravery inspired; although my country was in flames what has happened is compensation.' Mackenzie 1964: 20–21.
136. 'would I have caught up with MacDiarmid... Would I have caught up with MacDonald' MacLean 1999: 90–91.

137. At this point comes an indecipherable word.

138. 'And as to the business of putting "Do A. M." I think you had better leave it out' (letter to Young dated November 9th 1941).

139. 'Rarely do I ever ascend/ to the heath land on the high moor'. See Ross & Hendry 1986: 67 and Sinclair 1879: 491ff.

140. See http://sites.scran.ac.uk/redclyde/redclyde/index.html, also MacLean 1983, Kenefict & McIvor 1996.

141. The stanzas omitted were 1, 2, 4, 10 and 11 from the 1939 sequence.

142. Quoted in Campsie 1980: 84–85.

143. Quoted in Campsie 1980: 85.

144. Campsie 1980: 179–180.

145. Meek 1998: 223.

146. 'Ard-Mhusaeum na h-Eireann' ('The National Museum of Ireland'), MacLean 1999: 258–261.

147. See MacDiarmid 1978: 1, 555.

148. See MacLean 1999: 104–105.

149. See two articles on the affair by Norrie Maclennan in the *West Highland Free Press*, 12th and 19th May 1989.

150. Watson 1965: 96, 141. The first passage is translated as follows on p. 97: 'Sad and heart-sore my weeping, for I find myself tonight without rest, without peace, without cheer'.

151. 'and my abundant weeping is so bitter/ not because I no longer know myself' (editor's translation), see MacLean 2002: 50–51.

152. http://www.isleofbarra.com/for-visitors/vatersay/the-annie-jane.html (consulted June 8th 2010).

153. Orr 1982: 121–122.

154. Orr 1982: 135–139, see also MacPhail 1989: 202–206.

155. Hunter 2000: 88.

156. See http://afe.easia.columbia.edu/china/modern/long_stu.htm (consulted June 4th 2010).

157. For an account of the poem, including its mysterious and enigmatic close, see Pyman II: 287–291 where the author observes, in a footnote, that 'There have been at least a dozen more or less unsuccessful attempts to translate "The Twelve" into English. I have no reason to think any effort of mine would improve upon the better of these'. Sydney Goodsir Smith, a close friend of MacLean's, offers a translation into Scots in his volume *Figs and Thistles* (1959, see Smith 1975: 109–119.)

158. MacDiarmid 1978: 1, 88–89.

159. Thomson 1994: 161.

160. Matheson 1938: 44–45.

161. Matheson 1938: 240.

162. Wilson 2010: 119.

163. MacDiarmid 1978: 1, 191.

164. See MacLeod 2002: 250 and MacLean 1976: 386.

165. Matheson 1970: 58–72.

166. Mackenzie 1907: 103.

167. Letter dated January 13th 1936. Wilson 2010: 150.

168. Reiman & Fraistat 2002: 203–204.

169. Carter 1988: 563–565.

170. MacDiarmid 1978: 1, 422–433.

171. National Library of Scotland ms 29559 f98.

172. Quoted in Bold 1988: 251.

173. See MacDiarmid 1978: 1, 289–291.

174. National Library of Scotland ms 29559 f28. The date of the battle was in fact 1601 (see note to II: 203).

175. *Encyclopedia Britannica* online s.v. Sir Thomas More.

176. See further Richards 2008: 281–283.

177. See National Library of Scotland ms 29561 p. 61.

178. In a letter to MacLean dated December 25th 1939 (National Library of Scotland ms 29501 ff7–9), George Davie, returning a typescript of the English translation of 'An Cuilithionn', as yet incomplete, states that 'Jessie would like to see the Gaelic original and no doubt could be brought sometime next week or thereabouts to type that too.' A note added (very likely by Derick Thomson) in ballpoint pen to Young's bound copy of the poem in St Andrews states that the English version was typed from a partial copy made by Jessie Scott, later Kosmarova, of a literal translation by MacLean.

179. See Whyte 2006 for a sober evaluation of the latter statement in light of the Aberdeen ms copies of these poems.

180. See National Library of Scotland ms 29540 for this letter.

TEXTUAL COMMENTARY

The Gaelic text of this edition is based on a ms copy in MacLean's own hand in Aberdeen University Library Special Collections ms 2864. Spelling, punctuation and paragraph division are editorial. Careful attention was paid to practice in the A and B versions of the poem. Every attempt was however made to achieve consistency and clarity, in the interests of easier reading on the part of a contemporary audience. The resulting text is the responsibility of the editor, rather than deriving from the poet himself, who never prepared this version of the text for publication. The recommendations of GOC regarding Gaelic spelling have been followed, but not slavishly (for example, retention of initial apostrophe in the prepositional possessive forms ' 'na', ' 'nam', ' 'nan'). MacLean's practice (not entirely consistent) of using an '-ia-' spelling to indicate the 'split', diphthongal pronunciation of words such as 'briag' ('breug') has been respected and, where appropriate, extended.

MacLean's own English translation is sourced from Edinb NLS ms 29559 as follows:

Dedication, Parts I to III (ff1–17)
Part IV (ff47–48)
Part V (ff18–22)
Part VI 1–89 (ff54–55)
Part VI 90–270, Part VII 1–67, 78–157 (ff23–29)
Part VII 68–77 (f98, set out as prose)
Part VII 158–159 (f100v)
Part VII 160–193 (f63)
Part VII 194–211 (f101r & v)
Part VII 212–303 (ff30–31, but translation of 285–288 is editorial)
Part VII 304–363 (f102r & v, f103r)

This English translation reflects an early stage of version B. Where adjustments were necessary to bring it into line with the A version in Aberdeen, note was where possible taken of the translation in Douglas Young's copy at St Andrews.

(1) deleted readings from Abdn ms 2864 (A-text)

(the variants below are to be considered as superseded by the text of the current edition)

Earrann I

2 an àigh dhiubh] as fheàrr dhiubh
16 gun glac mi] gu ruig
180 thàinig] so all subsequent mss; Abdn has 'tha'

Earrann II

51 see note in 'Commentary' for four incomplete lines inserted here
75 òr-laist' ceann mo luaidhe] fuilt na h-ighne ruaidhe
77 tlàman] corrected from ms 'tlàthan'
149 's i] a tha

Earrann III

16 le do] ann do
137 brùidhte] breòite
188 ceòl] sùrd
191 treuntas is aighear] treuntas, bròn is
195 Lenin is taobh] Lenin no taobh
198 àit'] àite
204 leat] leatsa
205 chridhe 'na lasadh caoire] chridhe-sa gu laomadh

Earrann IV

3 àird' a thèid an dìreadh] àirde an dìreadh
36 air am] far am
41 Cha dèan mi gleachd no carachd] Rinn mi gleachd is carachd
44 le iomairt luasgan] a thuigsinn luasgan
45 'nam] ann mo
46 'nam] ann mo

Earrann V

8 ceangal] snaidhm
14 spiorad] eanchainn

Earrann VI

  82 nan gath] nam blas
100 sianail] siaradh [?]
105 Mac a' Phearsain] Steuart-Glennie
191 ma] ged
185 Boilseabhach] an t-sluaigh

Earrann VII

  38 bàirr] bàrra
100 Toussaint] Lucretius

(2) variant readings from Edinburgh ms 29558 (B-text)

The readings below may be read as progressive, i.e. they supersede one another proceeding from left to right. But it is important to remember that B represents a fluid state of the text. Not all the modifications indicated below were in fact subsumed into the C or 1989 version of the poem.

Dedication

  2 nam biodh] nan robh
  8 dàin] B1 theann
10 nam biodh] nan robh
11 an] ar

Earrann I

  2 an àigh] as fheàrr
 15 gu ruig] gun glac e
 45 breugach] mhilis
 81 Sgoirebreac is] an Eilein agus
 83 fiachan an uasail] malairt nan uasal
 96 crodh agus faingean] chrodh agus fhaingean
 99–102] to be replaced by 'nach dèan luaidh air eachdraidh neo-ghlan/a bheir diomb dar maithean mòra'
127 Nic Ualraig-Friseal] an dream bu chlise
134 dè ruigeas sgreamh san] cà ruig sgreamh an
135 nach e] ge b' e

136 nan triathan] thriathan
143 Gun tubhairt e nach ruiginn] Tha fhios 'm fhìn nach
ruig mi
145 a'm fhìn] agam
146 aigesan 'na theangaidh chiùigich] dòigheil anns an
teangaidh ghiùigich
159 tarsainn] ri taobh
162 air mo chùlaibh] an iar 's an iar-thuath
163 am beachd mo shùilean] 'na bòidhiche shianta
168 rùin] rùin-sa
209 morairean] na morairean
216 an Camshronach] bha fear eile
223 Tòrr Mòr] Fear a' Choire
243 b' e i] b' e
264 piantan] pianta
267 chlaoidheadh] chlaoidhteadh

Earrann II

48 a thoir deifir do na speuran] anns an deifir bh' air na
speuran
64 an] na h –
75 cancelled version 'mar chuachan fuilt na h-ighne
ruaidhe', with typed below 'mar chiabhan òr-laist ceann mo
luaidhe'
101 ràinig gal saoghail a' bhròin] lìon an saoghal le gal
bròin
102 tuiteam] mar thuiteam
107 le sagart, ministear is strìopaich] agus leis gach
buidheann strìopach
118 nam fùidse] glas an spùillidh
127 meallan] mill
151 a chionn] chionn
164 clo-bhualadh] gob labhar
175 fo mhaoineas bùirdeasach 'nan] air an claoidheadh
fon aon
183 bùirdeasachd] 'a' bhùirdeasachd' then 'luchd a' mhaoin'
184 i] iad
212 bhios sibh beò] thig sibh às
214 an Sligeachan] gu greadhnach
215 faicinn] amharc

Earrann III

14 mìltean] mìle
21 sgriosail] mhòr
39] ort fhèin, a Mhararabhlainn] oirbh, a bhoglaichean sanntach
44 mòr-roinn] magh mòr
47 mòinteach] boglaichean [?]
70 gu leòr] an còrr
90 a' bhùirdeasachd] an Roinn-Eòrpa
91 a Dhia] mo sgreamh
94 spothadh] mhilleadh
97 bùirdeasach] uachdaran
128 dhearbh] rinn
134 iad] iad fhèin
142 bùirdeasaich] ar maithean mòra
147 a' Bhùirdeasachd] 'n t-arm ùr
156 is fhùidsean] 's am fùidsean
160 clamaidh na Bùirdeasaich] 's ann a chlamas iad
183 chunnacas] chunnaic mi
189 gaisgeachd] gaisge
200 'na mo chridhe] ann am spiorad
204 leat a thaobh] leatsa 'thaobh
205 lasadh] lasair

Earrann IV

11 ghràdhach] an àrdain
16 is] air
17 aon] 'n aon
31 san] fon
51 bho] one typescript has 'air' corrected in pencil to 'bho'

In the B typescript, the order of ll.37–40 and 41–44 is reversed with respect to A.

Earrann V

28 's dh'fhàg e e 'na] a stamp e mar
30 bùirdeasachd] uachdaranachd
30 fùidse] fùidsean
34 Mararabhlainn] a' bhoglach
37 an uchd] uchd an

  50 bheucail] bheucach
  60 stàileann] stailinn [sic]
  84 chual' thu an] chual thusa
 132 dallabhrat] 'n dallabhrat
 146 le feirg] 's air leirg
 178 cur a bochdan] a' cur bhochdan

Earrann VI

   8 leathar den] creachadh air a'
   9 an clàr m' aodainn] 'nam aodann
  42 tha] a tha
  63 uallach] uachdrach
  67 uachdrach] uallach
  81 ar] na
  86 leam fhìn agus] leamsa 's le
  87 giall] bial
 105 Fiadhach] faghaid
 107 a'm] agam
 114 ceòl mòr] pìob mhòr
 121 togail] a' togail
 129 Fitzgerald] Mac Gerailt
148–151 In one of the ms 29558 typescripts, the 'Clio na Frainge' lines precede those about Germany. This is also the case in Douglas Young's St Andrews copy.
 177 is] agus
 178 in two typescripts 'Hume' is inserted in pen before 'Fichte'
 181 *passage*] m'aiseag
 211 spiorad] aigne
 216 is tionnda'idh] on one sheet corrected in pen to 'a' tionndadh'
 225 bu fhalbhach] a b' fhalbhach
 244 is] 's à
 249 eucail] fo eucail
 250 an] anns an

Earrann VII

   8 a ghrùdhain] 'ghrùdhain
  16 nach] 's nach
  54 làidir] coimhich

88 Lenin 's e] còmhlan a bh'
89 sgurra nach robh idir ìseal] geur chreag sgurrachan stritheil
94 a' chinne-] cinne-
99 a thug] 's am
106 ag] a' sìor
114 is comann] 's Càisg bhiothbhuan
115 an t-slèibhe] nan slèibhtean
117 am bàs] sa bhàs
119 air a'] a'
129 dìon] dìonta
139 buaidhe] buaidh
143 bog] beag
147 inntinn] eanchainn
150 cian, mòr] cian ciar
153 a' spàirn] an spàirn
167 onfhaidh] a h-onfhaidh
169 àmhghar] ànradh
181 a'] ga
194 A dh'aindeoin chithear trianaid Chuilithinn] Neo-ar-thaing chithear an Cuilithionn
207 losgadh] lasadh
219 cruaidh gàirich] cruaidh-ghàireach
241 rùisgte] rùiste
257 meall] mhill
299 an] tha t'
301 sgaoilidh] sgaoilte
311 threòirmhoir] threòraich
341 spioraid] 'n spioraid
343 rùisgte] rùiste

(3) passages marked for deletion in NLS Edinb ms 29558

f4 I 43–46
f7 I 99–102
f8 I 133–146 (squiggly line)
f33 II 156–181
f35 II 206–215 pencil bracketing only
f38 II 156–181
f47 III 70–72
f49 III 129–136
f50 III 157–160

f56 V 59–66
f58 V 107–114
f61 V 171–178
f73 VI 251–258
f77 III 26
f77 III 28–32 with question mark
f78 III 85–92
f79 III 105–114
f80 III 157–160
f84 V 25–42
f85 V 59–66
f86 V 107–114
f86 V 115–122 with question mark
f125 VII 50–55
f128 VII 220–223, 228–239
f129 VII 276–283
f130 VII 284, 289–295 (285–288 missing here, so cut continuous)
f130 VII 308–319

(4) further variants from occasional publication of extracts

II: 1–110 were printed in *17 Poems for 6d* (see MacLean & Garioch 1940) with these variants:

14 nochd mi] nochdadh
48 thoir] thoirt
65 a] don
74 'na] 'nan
76 chuachan] chiabhan

VII: 160–199, 324–363 appeared in *Gairm* 72 (Autumn 1970) under the title 'Crìoch dàin fhada a stadadh gu h-obann anns an Dùbhlachd 1939', with the following variants:

167 onfhaidh] a h-onfhaidh
168 thar àmhghar buan] os cionn truaighe bhuan
176 misneachd] treuntais
181 ànradh] truaighe a'] ga
182 ànradh buan] truaighe bhuan
183 t-ànradh] truaighe
184 t-ànradh] truaighe

185 t-ànradh goirt, mairbhteach, fada] truaighe ghoirt
mhairbhteach fhada
188 gach mìle bliadhna] linntean na
189 searbha an] an
194 A dh'aindeoin chithear trianaid Cuilithinn] Neòr-thaing
chithear an Cuilithionn
195 ag] 's e 'g
329 tha] seo ag
340 spioraid] 'n spioraid
342 a'] 's e
351 a'] 's e
352 'chinne] chinnidh
360 eu-dòchais] euceartas

Two extracts were included in MacLean, Sorley, George
Campbell Hay, William Neill, Stuart MacGregor *Four Points
of a Saltire* (Edinburgh, Reprographia 1970), with the
following variants:

I: 1–38

1 Sgùrr Alasdair an sgùrr as] An Sgurra Biorach sgurra 's
2 Sgùrr] Sgurra sgùrr an àigh] sgurra 's fheàrr
15 righinn-ghàirdean] gaoirdean righinn
16 gu ruig] gun glac e
20 an crios-onfhaidh] crios an onfhaidh
28 thar] air
34 Fhionn-] Fhionna-

VI: 1–89

8 leathar den] creachadh air a'
9 an clàr m' aodainn] 'nam aodann
42 tha] a tha nochd] 'n nochd
59 An] 'S an
61 nam monadh riabhach] a' mhonaidh riabhaich
63 uallach] uachdrach
67 uachdrach] uallach
81 ar] na
85 leam fhìn agus] liomsa 's le
87 giall] bial

(5) Comparison of A and C texts of the poem

The following table details the correspondences between the 1939 A and 1989 C versions of 'An Cuilithionn'.

A text	C text
[Coisrigeadh]	
1–12	1–12
Earrann I	
1–42	1–42
47–64	43–60
115–126	61–72
152–167	73–88
170–246	91–167
255–264	169–178
267–298	179–210
Earrann II	
1–110	1–110
124–160	111–147
162–163	148–149
172–177	150–155
180–181	156–157
200–205	162–167
Earrann III	
3–5	3–5
8–22	6–20
27–46	23–42
63–68	43–48
73–84	49–60
93–94	61–62
97–104	63–70
115–124	71–80
129–132	81–84
137–140	85–88
145–156	89–100
161–218	101–158

Earrann IV

1–36	1–36
45–48	37–40
41–44	41–44
49–64	45–60

Earrann V

1–34	1–34
51–58	35–42
67–104	43–80
123–146	83–106
147–153	107–113
155–202	115–162

Earrann VI

1–13	1–13
18–99	14–95
100–107	98–105
110–111	106–107
108–109	108–109
112–115	110–113
116–143	122–149
148–167	150–169
144–147	170–173
168–197	174–203
203–246	206–249
259–270	250–261

Earrann VII

1–36	1–36
39–67	37–65
78–87	66–75
92–109	78–95
112–115	96–99
118–119	100–101
122–123	102–103
130–131	104–105
144–149	106–111
160–199	112–151
324–363	152–191

Glossary of Placenames, Persons, Historical Events and Abstract Concepts mentioned in 'An Cuilithionn'

Citations are given as a Roman numeral indicating the 'Part' or 'Earrann' of the poem ('Ded' indicates the opening 'Dedication') followed by a colon and line number(s).

Adharc an Sgùrr Dheirg II: 46
Aeschylus VII: 2
Afraga III: 44
Africa, see Afraga
Àigeach, an t- II: 113, III: 94, 154, V: 12, 29, 43, 67, 83, 107, VII: 211, 296
Àird Mhòr I: 179, II: 72
Àisia, an III: 4
Alasdair Roy, see Alasdair Ruadh
Alasdair Ruadh I: 223
Alba I: 64, 294, 298, II: 157, 173, III: 42, 120, 131, IV: 11, V: 131, 143, 171, 181, VII: 164
Ameireaga II: 65, III: 4, 43, VI: 96
America, see Ameireaga
Annie Jane VI: 78, 94
Ar-a-mach Frangach, an t- III: 40, VI: 149
Ardmore, see Àird Mhòr
Arm Dearg, an t- I: 285, III: 24
Asia, see an Àisia
Asturaidhich, na h- II: 102, 125
Asturians, the, see na h-Asturaidhich

Ball, John VI: 132
Ballingall I: 221
Barcelona, see Barsalòna
Bhàrdachd, a' II: 166
Baron, the, see am Morair
Barra, see Barraigh
Barraigh II: 61, VI: 79
Barsalòna I: 251, VI: 140
Batal a' Bhràighe VI: 182

Clio of Greece, see Clio na Grèige
Clio of Harris, see Clio na Hearadh
Clio of the Hebrides, see Clio Innse Gall
Clio of India, see Clio nan Innsean
Clio of Ireland, see Clio na h-Èireann
Clio of Italy, see Clio na h-Eadailte
Clio of Lewis, see Clio Leòdhais
Clio of Mull, see Clio Mhuile
Clio of Scotland, see Clio na h-Albann
Clio of Skye, see a' Chlio Sgitheanach
Clio of Spain, see a' Chlio Spàinnteach
Clio of the world, see Clio an t-saoghail
Cluaidh II: 164, V: 5, VI: 119
Clyde, see Cluaidh
Cobbett VI: 177
Coire a' Mhadaidh I: 32
Coire an t-Seasgaich I: 85
Coire 'n Uaigneis I: 154
Coir' Each III: 149
Coire Lagain I: 31
Commune, la (the) VI: 150, VII: 112
Condorcet VI: 177
Connollach, an (Connollaigh) V: 179, VI: 128, VII: 22, 101,
    114, 205
Connolly, James, see an Connollach
Corran, an VI: 251
Corrie Each, see Coir' Each
Corrie of Loneliness, the, see Coire 'n Uaigneis
Crìosda II: 97, 163, III: 195, VII: 19, 23–24, 86, 186, 204
Cù Chulainn II: 37
Cuan Siar, an III: 164
Cuibhle na h-Eachdraidh VI: 213, 215
Cuchulainn, see Cù Chulainn
Cumha na Cloinne VII: 200

Dachau IV: 19
Dalaich I: 59, III: 115
the Dale men, see Dalaich
Desperate Battle, the, see an Cath Gailbheach
Dia II: 187, III: 17
Dimitrov, George I: 261, VI: 204, 247, 261, VII: 29, 37, 90,
    120, 141, 157

Inbhir Nis I: 148
India, see na h-Innsean
Innsean, na h- III: 43, 119, V: 171
Inverness, see Inbhir Nis
Ireland, see Èirinn
Italy, see an Eadailt
Iupiter VII: 13

Judgement, the, see am Breitheanas
Jupiter, see Iupiter

Kennedy-Fraser, see NicUalraig-Fhriseal
Kett, Robert VI: 133
Krupskaya VI: 67
Kyle Vatersay, see Caolas Bhatarsaigh

Lament for the Children, see Cumha na Cloinne
Land of MacLeod, see Dùth' MhicLeòid
Landauer VII: 110
Leipzig VI: 203, 247
Lenin I: 260, III: 195, V: 185, VI: 179, VII: 66, 76, 88, 100,
    205
Leningrad VI: 183
Leòdaich III: 148
Leonardo VI: 178
Leonhard II: 98
Liebknecht II: 98, V: 183, VI: 147, VII: 101, 100
Litchù (Lithgow) II: 167
Lithgow, see Litchù
Livingston, see MacDhunlèibhe
London, see Lunnainn
Long nan Daoine I: 177, VI: 2, 181, VII: 268
Loos II: 207
Lords, House of see *Lòrds*, na
Lòrds, na VI: 135
Lucretius VII: 204
Lunnainn I: 170, 253, IV: 23, VI: 241

MacÀidh I: 224
MacAlasdair na h-Àirde I: 212
MacAlister of Aird, see MacAlasdair na h-Àirde
MacCallum, Donald see MacCaluim, Dòmhnall

Pound, Ezra VII: 70
Prague, see Pràtha
Pràtha I: 254

Raasay, see Ratharsair
Rainy, see Rèanaidh
Ratharsair II: 86
Red Army, the, see an t-Arm Dearg
Rèanaidh I: 224
Revival, the, see an Dùsgadh
Robeson, Paul VI: 137
Ròimh, an I: 248, II: 178, III: 51
Rome, see an Ròimh
Rona, see Rònaigh
Rònaigh II: 86
Rousseau VI: 176
Rubha 'n Dùnain I: 48, 215, II: 76
Ruisia III: 119, V: 185
Russia, see Ruisia

St Congan's, see Cille Chòmhghain
Sasann I: 172, II: 174, III: 52, 123, 133, V: 177
Scarral, see Sgarral
Schopenhauer VI: 178
Scorrybreck, see Sgoirebreac
Scotland, see Alba
Sealtainn VII: 74
Seangaidh I: 252
Seasgach Corrie, see Coire an t-Seasgaich
Seton Gòrdan, I: 100
Seton Gordon, see Seton Gòrdan
Sgarral II: 66
Sgitheanach I: 98, 168, II: 139, III: 129, 137
Sgoirebreac I: 81
Sguman, see Sròin an Sgumain
Sgùrr a' Ghreadaidh I: 152, 206, V: 16
Sgùrr Alasdair I: 1, 269
Sgùrr an Fheadain I: 88, V: 25
Sgùrr an Sgumain I: 214, II: 50
Sgùrr Dearg II: 46, III: 84
Sgùrr Dubh an Dà Bheinn II: 51
Sgùrr na Banachdaich I: 202

Sgùrr na h-Uamha V: 22

Sgùrr nan Gillean I: 2, 6, 218, II: 134, IV: 51, V: 19, VI: 264

Sgùrr nan Gobhar III: 109

Sgùrr Thuilm I: 175

Shakespeare III: 70

Shanghai, see Seangaidh

Shelley III: 72, VI: 134, VII: 25

Shetland, see Sealtainn

Ship, the Great Ship, the Slave Ship, the Ship of the People, see Long nan Daoine

Shlaopain, Loch I: 53

Sickle, the see an Corran

Sìne, an t- III: 44, 120, V: 171

Skye, see an t-Eilean

Skyeman, see Sgitheanach

Slapin, Loch, see Shlaopain, Loch

Sleat, see Slèite

Slèite I: 75, 121, II: 85, 120, VI: 15

Sligachan, see Sligeachan

Sligeachan II: 214

Soay, see Sòdhaigh

Sòdhaigh II: 87

Soitheach Mòr, an (Soitheach nan Daoine) faic Long nan Daoine

Son of Cuillin, see MacCuilithinn

Spain, see an Spàinn

Spàinn, an I: 247, 290, II: 94, 177, III: 46, IV: 13, V: 173, VII: 103

Spartacus VII: 20, 187

Srath, an I: 257, II: 87

Srath Shuardail II: 72, VI: 94

Sròin an Sgumain I: 87

Stàilin I: 265, III: 26

Stalin, see Stàilin

Stallion, the, see an t-Àigeach (also an Eist)

Steòrnabhagh VI: 103

Stornoway, see Steòrnabhagh

Strath, see an Srath

Strath Swordale, see Srath Shuardail

Suidhisnis VI: 98

Suishnis, see Suidhisnis

English versions of the unpublished, incomplete and fragmentary poems

1.
Duncan

Your progress through people's homes
provoked uproar, big Duncan;
you left delight in many a house,
set many a roomful laughing.

Your progress through people's homes
provoked uproar, big Duncan;
you left conversation in many a house,
tall tales, drinking and laughter.

2.
**To the Pope who offered thanks to God
for the fall of Barcelona**

Deceitful pious whore of a bitch
who carries Christ's tiara,
around this time last year you were wallowing
in children's blood and in your holiness.

3.
'Honoured MacDonald'

Honoured MacDonald
who has every man's affection
because of your kindness and your eloquence,
your honest wisdom and your patience,
you have no need of my feeble words,
for you have many kinds of protection,
even a far from foolish armour
against shrill flattery in English.

Unpublished, incomplete and fragmentary poems

1.
Donnchadh

A Dhonnchaidh mhòir, bu ràbhartach
bha t' fhalbh air feadh nam fàrdaichean;
is iomadh taigh san d' fhàg thu spòrs,
is iomadh seòmar ghàirich thu.

A Dhonnchaidh mhòir, bu ràbhartach
bha t' fhalbh air feadh nam fàrdaichean,
's iomadh taigh san d' fhàg thu glòir
is ròlaist òil is gàireachdaich.

2.
Don Phàp a thug buidheachas do Dhia airson tuiteam Bharsalòna

A ghalla shiùrsaich shlìom, dhiadhaidh,
's tu giùlan tiara Chrìosda,
mun àm seo 'n-uiridh bha thu blianadh
am fuil naoidhean 's nad dhiadhachd.

3.
'A Dhòmhnallaich urramaich'

A Dhòmhnallaich urramaich
dha bheil spèis nan uile fear:
do choibhneas is do dheasachd beòil,
do ghliocas còir 's do fhulangas:
cha ruig thu leas mo bhriathran breòit'
's tu còmhdaichte air iomadh dòigh,
eadhon le armachd nach eil baoth
ro Bheurla chaoil an t-sliomaire.

4.
To Mr Alasdair Mackenzie
at the Gaelic Society of Inverness dinner
17.III.67

Alasdair, generous hero,
whom have you left in London or Edinburgh?
You left thousands and hundreds,
but which of them can match you?

Honest Alasdair Mackenzie,
mouth that speaks only truth,
an honest heart without ill-will,
many place their trust in you.

We know you cannot be corrupted
by the skilful adulation of the wealthy   10
nor by the branching snares of England
or the Gaels who speak shrill English –

know you will continue to be as you are –
that is the best you can do for us –
though every possible honour were paid you,
honour from Lowlanders and Highlanders.

We know the delight which you take
in your people and your heritage,
that pride in a deer's antlers does not inspire you
but rather the day's talk in Inverness.   20

5.
The Powers That Be

Murdering thousands each day,
godly Franco, the spindrift will come
that will choke your heart and lungs.

Blessing the murderers for eternity,
you with him, godly Pope,
your black sail will be torn by a drift.

4.
Do Mhaighstir Alasdair MacCoinnich
aig Dinneir Comann Gàidhlig Inbhir Nis
17.III.67

Alasdair, a sheòid na fèile,
cò dh'fhàg thu 'n Lunnainn no 'n Dùn Èideann?
Dh'fhàg thu na mìltean is na ceudan;
cò dh'fhàg thu dhed leithid ann?

Alasdair MhicCoinnich dhìrich,
bial a dh'innse na fìrinn,
cridhe ceart a tha gun mhìorun,
tha earbsa mòrain air do thì-sa.

Tha fhios againn nach tèid do shaobhadh
le brosgal seòlta na maoine,   10
no ribeachan Shasainn, 's iad cho craobhach,
no Gàidheil na Beurla caoile;

nach bi thus' ach mar a tha thu –
agus sin an nì as fheàrr leinn –
ged bheirte dhut gach aon bhàrr dhiubh,
urram nan Gall is nan Gàidheal.

Tha fhios againn gu bheil t' ùidh-sa
'na do dhaoine 's 'na do dhùthchas,
nach uabhar Chabar Fèidh do dhùrachd
ach an dòigh bh' aig Clach na Cùdainn.   20

5.
Na Cumhachdan a Tha

A' mort nam mìltean gach latha,
a Fhranco dhiadhaidh, thig an cathadh
a thachdas do chridhe 's do sgamhan.

'S tu beannachadh nam mort gu sìorraidh,
thusa còmh' ris, a Phàip dhiadhaidh,
sracar do sheòl dubh le siaban.

And you, Archbishop of England,
with your smooth, ready fawning,
History will shite on you foully.

And you, ministers of Scotland,   10
the smoke will check this course
that your sleek, good-going tongues have.

6.
'Venerable George MacLean'

Venerable George MacLean,
that day we were on Neist Point,
why didn't you geld the stallion with your teeth
or with the edge of your devilish tongue?

7.
Snuffling

Snuffling around the rose of nobility,
you plucked the occasion to act basely,
to be deceitful, lying, corrupt,
but you saw the red rose of nobility.

Chipping at the rock of nobility,
you found the precious gem.
You placed it around your lovely neck
mounted in reddish gold;
but when it acquired your body's warmth
it was spoiled in no time at all   10
and seeped away, leaving behind streaks
which showed how base and worthless you are.

8.
James Connolly

When the pale day dawned in 1916,
weak and dazed, with tormenting wounds,
tightly bound to the chair you would be executed in,
having cast your soul from you before God's Son,

Agus thusa, Àrd-easbaig Shasainn,
led shliomaireachd mhìn ealamh,
cacaidh an Eachdraidh ort gu sgreamhaidh.

Is sibhse, mhinistearan Albann,   10
bacaidh an toit am falbh seo
th' aig bhur teanganna slìoma falbhach.

6.
'A Sheòrais MhicGhill-Eathain fhiachail'

A Sheòrais MhicGhill-Eathain fhiachail,
latha dhuinn air an Eist Fhiadhaich,
carson nach do spoth thu e le t' fhiaclan
no le faobhar na teangaidh diabhlaidh?

7.
Snòtachadh

A' snòtachadh air ròs na h-uaisle,
spìon thu an cothrom a bhith suarach,
a bhith cealgach, briagach, truaillidh,
ach chunnaic thu ròs dearg na h-uaisle.

A' piocadh ann an creig na h-uaisle,
fhuair thu 'n neamhnaid a bha luachmhor.
Chuir thu i mud amhaich àlainn
anns an òr-bhuidh' air a càradh;
ach nuair ghabh i blàths do cholainn
cha b' fhada gus an deach i dholaidh   10
's gun shruth i às, a' fàgail strìochan
a nochd gur suarach thu 's nach b' fhiach thu.

8.
Seamus Ó Conghaile

Aig bànadh an là ghil am bliadhna nan Sia-Deug,
tràighte, faoin-lag, cràdhte, fo chreuchdaibh,
ceangailte gu dlùth ri cathair nam pian dhut-
seadh, tilgeil t' anam an làthair Mhic Dhè uat,

if anyone could have told you on that morning
that men and woman today throughout your land
would be poverty-stricken and naked, with no aspiration
beyond misery and deprivation, living as beggars.

9.
Tailor's Dummy

Would you rather have me neat and trim,
a tailor's dummy as regards my dress,
sleek, handsome, foolish, spotless,
than what I am, a firebrand of the understanding,
offering you beyond your grasp
the mind of Scotland and Ireland's poets?

Why was I born a poet
to give your beauty immortality
if this tale is true that you would prefer
a mindless dummy in a tailor's window?   10

10.
'Is the world going to wake up anywhere'

Is the world going to wake up anywhere
if it doesn't happen in France?
Was the great awakening in Russia
nothing more than a brief watchfulness
after which people were buried
in a narrow, constricting creed?
What sort of awakening was there in China?
Is the flesh of the Viet Cong
the best flesh for sacrificing?

There were so many of them, so many of them   10
at the Meuse and at the Sambre,
their great hearts beating
at the gates of iron
which would open on the land of their longing
on the bright islands of their promises
manured with the substance of their blood.

nan abradh neach riut madainn an là ud
gum biodh daoine an-dràsta air feadh do thìre
bhiodh bochd is nochd; gun an dùil ri aon rud
ach an-shògh is call, is iad beò an dèirce.

9.
Cumadh Tàilleir

Am b' fheàrr leat mi nan robh mi gleusta,
'nam chumadh tàilleir a thaobh èididh,
slìom, eireachdail, baoth, glè-ghlan,
na mar a tha mi 'nam chaoir cèille,
a' toirt dhut os cionn do cheudfàth
aigne bàird Albann 's Èireann?

Carson a rugadh 'nam bhàrd mi
a chur biothbhuantachd air t' àilleachd
ma tha an sgeul seo fìor gur fheàrr leat
balbhan cèille 'n uinneag tàilleir?   10

10.
'Am bi dùsgadh anns an t-saoghal'

Am bi dùsgadh anns an t-saoghal
mura tig e às an Fhraing?
An robh dùsgadh mòr na Ruis
ach 'na chaithris airson greis
gus an tiodhlaicteadh an duine
ann an creud chruaidh chumhaing?
Dè an dùsgadh bha san t-Sìn?
An e feòil Viet Cong
an fheòil as fheàrr gu ìobairt?

Na bh' ann dhiubh, na bh' ann dhiubh   10
mun a' Mheuse, mun t-Sambre,
a' bualadh len cridheachan mòra
anns na geatachan iarainn
a dh'fhosgladh gu tìr na h-iargain,
gu eilean sorcha a' gheallaidh
mathaichte le brìgh am fala.

No other human nation
is like France
which produced great thousands of martyrs   20
who pursued their cause.
Here is no continuing city,
yet that's no reason why it should be filthy,
harsh, haughty, restricted,
with no God but Mammon
and the bankers of Zurich.
Money is the father of whores.

"Great Scotland will be ruled by beasts"
in the ear of the man who slept so deeply
but in Charles Stewart's head   30
there were beasts and many a whore,
perhaps as many of them in his head
as in that of the Butcher
and in Fair Colla,
in the head that ploughed the beach
so as to keep the shellfish
from the poor creatures of the world.

Every army has had two faces
since they stood by the Meuse;
Thermidore and the Directoire
and Bonaparte, with his many faces,   40
murdered those courageous French soldiers
who had the valour of angels.
Where can their like be found now
if not with Mao,
crying as they did that the world
was vast and free for mankind?

Christianity has thousands of martyrs
but never in one year had it
this great generation which rose at the Meuse
in the French armies;   50
humanity has since
had only one nation.
France was the nation of the world
even though Bonaparte led it astray,
it is the nation of mankind.

Chan eil dùthaich aig an duine
coltach ris an Fhraing
a ghin na mìltean mòra mhartar
a' dol air adhart len agairt.   20
Chan eil an seo baile mhaireas –
'n e sin reusan a bhith salach,
e bhith borb uaibhreach caol,
gun Dhia aige ach Mamon
agus bancairean Zhurich?
'S e 'n t-airgead athair nan siùrsach.

"Bidh Alba mhòr fo bhinn bhèistean"
an cluais fear a' chadail mhòir
ach bha na bèistean 's iomadh siùrsach
ann an ceann Theàrlaich Stiùbhairt –   30
dh'fhaodadh gu robh uiread dhiubhsan
'na cheann 's a bha 'n ceann a' Bhùidseir
agus na bha 'n Colla Bàn
'na cheann a' treabhadh na tràghad
fiach an cumadh e a' mhaorach
o chreutairean bochda 'n t-saoghail.

Cha robh arm gun dà aodann
ann bhon sheas iad air a' Mheuse;
mharbh *Thermidore* 's an *Directoire*
agus Bonaparte le iomadh aodann   40
saighdearan curanta na Frainge
san robh treuntas nan ainglean.
Càit a-nis a bheil an leithid
mura h-eil iad aig Mao,
's iad ag èigheach gu robh 'n saoghal
farsaing saor don chinne-daonna?

Tha mìltean mhartar aig Crìosdachd
ach cha robh aice an aon bliadhna
am pòr mòr seo a dh'èirich mun Mheuse
ann an armailtean na Frainge;   50
cha robh aig a' chinne-daonna
ach aon dùthaich on uair sin.
B' e 'n Fhraing dùthaich an t-saoghail
ged chuir Bonaparte i iomrall,
's i dùthaich a' chinne-daonna.

11.
The Pair

There were two Murrays in Portree,
two of a different sort,
she was distinguished for her beauty
while he had verbal diarrhoea.

12.
My love in the plundered garden

The defensive wall was broken,
each dry tree cut down,
your dry body abused
while the gunners who loved you
slept deep and unaware –
the gunners who could have defended you,
as stalwart as you ever saw,
who could have kept violence from your body,
far from you, buried in the ground.

13.
To the Rev. Thomas M. Murchison
at the Gaelic Society of Inverness dinner
14.IV.61

Twists and eddies in the current
passing through Kylerhea as the tide turns
and the slopes of Glenelg
basking in the sun they stretch in.

The old strength with the old beauty
sets the sea tossing in the Sound of Sleat
and the battlements of our Island
are sculpted in the blue-green exultation of the skies.

Knoydart, Glenelg and Lochalsh
and the great miracle of Kintail   10
in a struggle that is no struggle against the Island,
an eternal, unspoken dialogue.

11.
Dithis

Bha dà Mhoireach am Port Ruigh'dh,
dithis a bh' air caochladh brìgh,
bha an tè brèagha sgiamhach
agus am fear brèagha bialach.

12.
Mo ghaol san lios chreachte

Briste 'm balla-dìon,
geàrrte tioram gach craobh,
màbte tioram do chom
agus gunnairean do ghaoil
sa chadal aineolach throm –
na gunnairean a bhiodh gud dhìon,
bu trèine chunna tu riamh,
a thilleadh ainneart bhod chom,
fada bhuat 's an talamh trom.

13.
Don Urramach Tòmas MacCalmain
aig Dinneir Comann Gaidhlig Inbhir Nis
14.IV.61

Càir is cuartagan an t-srutha
tigh'nn tro Chaol Reatha leis an lìonadh
agus leathadan Ghlinn Eilge
sìnte ris a' ghrèin gam blianadh.

Tha 'n seann neart 'na sheann àilleachd
a' luasgadh clàr na Linne Slèitich,
agus baidealan ar n-Eilein
geàrrt' an luathghair ghuirm nan speuran.

Cnòideart, Gleann Eilge 's Loch Aillse
agus mìorbhail mhor Chinn t-Sàile
san t-strì gun strì ris an Eilean,
an còmhradh suthainn gun chànan.

10

History's breezes blow
on the deeps with time's mildness,
no matter how much bitterness was involved
at times of warping or confusion.

Donald Murchison's rock is at peace,
his loyalty wreathed in the warmth of story
and, fragrant in the narration,
the name of the man from Auchtertyre.   20

No ebb but is followed by a full –
part of the secret of the seasons –
but our ebbing will not return
if Time's current sweeps away our language.

You understood so well, Murchison,
that it would be a mistake to move with Kylerhea,
that following the current of the world
does not prove a man, or a ship's, worth.

You were young when you won your people's praise,
toiling without rest at a pilot oar,   30
and at your most effective
your input was no small one.

Your way was not the Lochaber man's –
sitting on the cargo quaffing wine –
you concentrated all your strength on the task,
and the distant shelter was not Kyleakin.

Others weakened but you did not,
nor did you doze off, Murchison:
you trained both body and mind
on the ocean from your perch.   40

You are a look-out for your people:
you made your gift to the Gaels
and kept your eye on the windward side,
watching for a menace from any direction.

Kylerhea offers an appropriate image
for your life, Murchison:
you pointed the slim prow of oakwood
strong and steadfast against the waves.

Agus tha oiteagan na h-eachdraidh
le tlàths na tìme air na cuantan,
ge b' e bha annta de shearbhachd
an àm dèabhaidh, no de bhruaillean.

Suaimhneach carragh Dhòmhnaill MhicCalmain:
suainte 'm blàths an sgeòil a dhìlse,
agus cùbhraidh anns an aithris
ainm an fhir bha 'n Uachdar Thìre.   20

Cha tig aon tràigh gun a lìonadh –
's e sin roinn diamhaireachd nan tràthan –
ach oirnne thig an tràigh gun tilleadh
ma sguabas sruth na Tìm ar cànan.

'S math a thuig thusa, MhicCalmain,
nach mithich falbh le Caol Reatha,
nach ann a' dol le sruth an t-saoghail
a dhearbhar daoine no soitheach.

'S òg a fhuair thu cliù do dhaoine,
ag iomairt gun fhaochadh ràmh bràghad: 30
agus air àirde a' choimeis
cha b' e do chothachadh bu tàire.

Cha b' e do ghnìomh-sa gnìomh an Abraich –
'g òl gucagan fìon air a fàradh –
ach cumail rithe le do dhian-neart,
's a' chairidh cian – cha b' i Caol Àcainn.

Ge b' e lagaich, cha do lagaich
's cha do chaidil thus', MhicCalmain:
mhothaich thu an corp 's an spiorad
air do spiris ris an fhairge.   40

'S tu fear-faire do chinnidh:
thug thu do ghibhtean do na Gàidheil,
chùm thu do shùil air an fhuaradh
a' feitheamh fuathais gach àirde.

Is math an samhladh Caol Reatha
air do bheatha-sa, Mhic Calmain:
chùm thu ceann caol a daraich
gu treun daingeann ris an fhairge.

14.
On top of a lorry, at night, next to an artillery piece

Night of loss, what makes you so at peace there in the sky?
I will not lean on you, cannon, nor will you push me away.
Neither that star up there nor a kiss shows the path
to your body, where sleeps the essential hostility of the gun.
Your mouth is constantly calling out a flood-warning
to heartbeats and to the stone. You throw your husky
    bellow
amidst men's fear, in stuttering baptisms
when you are far away, a shepherd of fire and powder.
Now your chill touches my fevered brow:
put me to sleep on my own with no banner to cover me   10
speckled with the itching of your [...] red lament.
Why are you so mild, spring wind?

15a.
'The worst thing wasn't the adultery'

The worst thing wasn't the adultery
or your smooth, rich bourgeois man
but the deadly, unerring bullet
in the back of the heroic Lowlander.

15b.
'The worst thing wasn't the adultery'

The worst thing wasn't the adultery
or the rich, effeminate bourgeois
but the deadly, treacherous bullet
in the back of another man during the battle.

16.
'I see the dogs approaching'

I see the dogs approaching,
passing by me and howling,
the slender insatiable dogs
on the savage hunt.

14.
Air mullach làraidh, air an oidhche, ri taobh gunna-mhòir

Carson a tha thu cho suaimhneach san speur, oidhche challa?
Cha leig mi mo thaic ort, a chanain, ach cha phut thu bhuat mi.
Cha sheall an reul ud shuas no pòg an ceum
gu do cholainn, far an caidil smior-fhuath a' ghunna.
Tha do bhial a-ghnàth a' gairm na tuile
don bhuille chridhe 's don chloich. Tilgidh tu do bheuc [?]
   tùchain
am measg eagal nan daoine, ann am baistidhean gagach
nuair a tha thu fad' às nad chìobair teine is fùdair.
A-nis tha t' fhuachd ri mo bhathais theinntidh
agus cuir a chadal mi leam fhìn gun sgàil brataich   10
a tha breac le tachas do ghuib lasrachail [?] dheirg.
Carson a tha thu cho tlàth, a ghaoth an earraich?

15a.
'Cha b' e 'n t-adhaltranas bu mhiosa' (an ciad tionndadh)

Cha b' e 'n t-adhaltranas bu mhiosa
no do bhùirdeasach slìom beairteach
ach am peilear nimheil seòlta
chuireadh an cùl a' Ghoill ghaisgeil.

15b.
'Cha b' e 'n t-adhaltranas bu mhiosa' (an darna tionndadh)

Cha b' e 'n t-adhaltranas bu mhiosa
no 'm bùirdeasach boireann beairteach
ach am peilear nimheil foille
chaidh 'n druim fir eile sa bhatal.

16.
'Chì mi na coin a' tighinn'

Chì mi na coin a' tighinn,
a' gabhail seachad orm le sianail,
na coin chaola neo-shàsaicht'
air an lorg iargalt.

Where will the impetuous rush of hounds
come to a halt on reaching peace
in the distant halls
where their longing can be stilled?

Satisfaction beneath white tables,
torn flesh and juicy bones   10
for dogs that have been flogged
by musical notes.

Will they ever lie down
unless released from the leash of days
which ties the mountains in
a tight knot?

17.
Shelley 8.VII.34

One hundred and twelve years since
the Italian sea poured over your head,
you, foremost among English poets
and closest of all to us!
One hundred and twelve years since
the elements rushed to cover your flesh,
since they set a seal on profundity of love
and on cold, corrupt animosity.
You are dead, but alive though dead,   10
inspire me with your purpose –
even if I were to get a share of that knowledge,
the coal which set your eyes alight!

18.
For Sir Lachlan MacLean of Duart
on the 80th anniversary of the
restoration of the castle

Five years after Culloden
the secret information that reached London
about the state and spirit of every clan
was that the Clan MacLean was rash and proud,

Cà bheil an deann-ruith mhadadh
a' dol a sgur le ruigheachd sìthe
anns na tallachan cèine
chasgas an ìota?

Riarachadh fo bhùird gheala,
feòil riaslaichte is cnàmhan sòghmhor'   10
aig coin is iad gan grèidheadh
fo na puing cheòlmhor'.

An dèan iad laighe gu dìlinn
mur saorar iad bho iall nan làithean
tha cearlachadh nam beanntan
le teanntachd [...] ?

17.
Shelley 8.VII.34

Ciad is dusan bliadhna on thaom
cuan Eadailteach thar do chinn,
o thusa, 'phrìomh de bhàird na Beurla
as dlùithe a thaobhas rinn!
Ciad is dusan bliadhna on bhàrc
na dùilean thar do chrè,
bhon chuir iad seul air doimhneachd gràidh
's air gamhlas fuar nam breun.
Is thusa marbh, ach beò ge marbh,   10
o deachd mi le do rùn –
ged gheibhinn roinn den eòlas ud,
an èibheall loisg do shùil!

18.
Do Shir Lachlainn MacGill-Eain Dhubhaird
air ochdadhach ceann-bliadhna ath-thogail
a' chaisteil

Còig bliadhna às dèidh Chùil Lodair
's e 'n t-iomradh dìomhair a ràinig Lunnainn
mu chor 's mu spiorad gach cinnidh
gu robh Clann Ghill-Eain bras is uaibhreach,

with no great prudence of their worldly state,
with a boast that they never turned their backs
on enemies even ten times their number,
the Spartans of the North.

Duart Castle was then
a ruin with broken walls,   10
and its lord in exile, as was his father,
its company scattered,
with no gathering of the host in Aros,
except what was in the mouths of seanchaidhs
about the deeds of Lachlan Mor and Hector Roy;
where Donald Glas's body fell,
and what MacLean of Boreray said on Leac an Lì.

Duart Castle a ruin
for more than two hundred years,
and Mull going under sheep,   20
bracken, rushes and heather.
The MacLean chiefs unfortunate
in the eyes of the big world,
but fortunate in the fame of generations:
that they never cleared tenantry from Mull,
from Morvern or from Tiree,
or from Iona,
or from any other place.

Duart Castle restored
by a generous and brave chief,   30
as was his grandson after him
from what I heard
from a brave Skyeman who was with him
in the last great war,
and from many another mouth.

Therefore the Castle of Duart
is young in its eighty years
and stainless from the generations
of three hundred years,
scoured from every blemish   40
left on any old building.

gun ro-chùram mun staid saoghail
le bòst nach do chuir iad riamh an cùl
air nàimhdean deich uairean cho lìonmhor,
Spartanaich na h-Àirde Tuath.

Bha Caisteal Dhubhaird an uair sin
'na làraich de bhallachan briste,   10
is a thriath air fògradh, mar bha athair,
a' chuideachd a bha ann air sgaoileadh
's gun chruinneachadh sluaigh ann an Àros,
ach na bha 'm briathran nan seanchaidh
mu ghnìomhan Lachlainn Mhòir is Eachainn Ruaidh,
far na thuit corp Dhòmhnaill Ghlais
is dè thuirt Fear Bhoraraigh air Leac an Lì.

Caisteal Dhubhaird 'na làraich
còrr is da cheud bliadhna,
agus Muile dol fo chaoraich,   20
fo fhraineach, luachair is fraoch.
Cinn-cinnidh Chloinn Ghill-Eain mì-shealbhach
ann am beachd an t-saoghail mhòir,
ach fortanach ann an cliù nan linntean:
nach do thog iad tuath à Muile
no as a' Mhorbhairne no à Tiridhe
no à Ì Chaluim Chille
no à àite sam bith eile.

Caisteal Dhubhaird air ath-thogail
le ceann-cinnidh còir treun,   30
mar a bha ogha às a dheaghaidh,
a rèir na chuala mise
o Sgitheanach treun a bha cuide ris
sa chogadh mhòr mu dheireadh,
agus o iomadh beul eile.

Uime sin tha Caisteal Dhubhaird
òg 'na cheithir fichead bliadhna,
agus gun smal o na linntean;
fad nan trì cheud bliadhna
air a sgùradh o gach smal   40
a dh'fhàgar air seann togail sam bith.

19.
'Making a laughing-stock of my gifts'

Making a laughing-stock of my gifts,
worshipping a woman who is lying and base
as if she were an idol –
that is what besmirched my reason.

20.
'What did you get, my heart'

What did you get, my heart,
for your sole noble action?
In return for your toil and diligence
you yourself got wretchedness,
bitter sorrow and laming,
shame and confusion.
You suffered sufficiently, my heart,
for your sole noble action.

21.
1793–94

The hope of humanity,
blue and white and red
above the army at the two rivers,
the army of the Sambre and the Meuse
possessed of a doughtiness beyond words,
the heart of humanity
in the army of France.

How could any living being
possessed of love and reason
not catch its breath in contemplating them?   10
Not Robespierre or Carnot
or even Danton himself,
but the hundreds, the thousands
of young French men and women
who gave their doughtiness as a sacrifice
to the cause of love for humanity,

19.
'Cùis-bhùrta dhèanamh de mo bhuadhan'

Cùis-bhùrta dhèanamh de mo bhuadhan,
toirt iodhal-adhraidh do thè
a tha briagach agus suarach –
sin an gànrachadh dom chèill.

20.
'Dè a fhuair thusa, 'chridhe'

Dè a fhuair thusa, 'chridhe,
air lorg d' aon ghnìomh uasail?
Aig do spàirn is do dhìcheall
fhuair thu fhèin an truaighe
agus mulad searbh is siachadh
agus tàmailt 's buaireadh.
Rinneadh gu leòr riutsa, 'chridhe,
air lorg t' aon ghnìomh uasail.

21.
1793–94

Dòchas a' chinne-daonna,
'n gorm 's an geal 's an dearg
os cionn arm an dà abhainn,
armailt an t-Sambre is a' Mheuse
san robh treuntas thar cainnte
agus cridhe 'chinne-daonna
ann an arm na Frainge.

Ciamar as urrainn do chreutair
anns a bheil an gràdh 's an reusan
bhith gun stad analach fa chomhair?   10
Chan e Robespierre no Carnot
no eadhon Danton fhèin
ach na ceudan, na mìltean
de dh'òigridh na Frainge
a thug an treuntas 'na ìobairt
do dh'adhbhar gaol a' chinne-daonna,

who defended mankind's worth
in the struggle where they gave their blood,
in the long contention at which they laboured
and in their inconceivable valour.   20

There were so many of them, fighting for us,
for every living being
which breathes a human breath.
A soldier's job is not
killing, but being killed.
The sacrifice of France coincided
with the interests of mankind as a whole.

Nothing comparable emerged at Culloden,
and two faces were shown along the Somme,
two faces at Verdun: 30
but the army at the Sambre and the Meuse
showed only one face,
the face of fellow-feeling and freedom
which Thermidor could not soil,
nor could Robespierre with his broken jaw
or even the Directoire,
dishonest and mendacious as that was.

Where can it be found once more,
the one face deserving of love?
Does Mao's Red Guard possess it,   40
or else Palach in Prague?
Recently there were only one or two
Palachs to be had in Bohemia
while a dozen in France
gave voice to their doubt.

Where are the masses
for the sake of the great world [...]

22.
Duncan and Goering, a delightful combination

Duncan and Goering, a delightful combination:
one murders poets, the other murders songs.

a thubhairt gur fhiach an duine
ann an agartas am fala
le argamaid fhada an saothrach
agus an curantais do-smaointinn.   20

Na bh' ann dhiubh, air ar taobh-ne,
air taobh gach creutair
sa bheil anail an duine.
Chan e obair an t-saighdeir
marbhadh, ach e bhith marbh.
Cho-aontaich ìobairt na Frainge
ri rùn a' chinne gu lèir.

Cha tubhairt Cùil Lodair dad a b' fhiach,
's bha dà aodann air an t-Somme
agus dà aodann air Verdun: 30
ach cha robh ach aon aodann
an arm an t-Sambre 's a' Mheuse,
aodann a' choibhneis is na saorsa
nach do shalaich *Thermidor*
no Robespierre 's a pheirceall briste
no eadhon an *Directoire*
ge bu phlamach i is briagach.

Cò às a-rithist an t-aodann
singilte dan dligheach gaol?
A bheil e air Geàrd Dearg Mhao   40
no air Palach ann am Praha?
Cha robh ach Palach no a dhà
ann am Bohemia an-dràst'
agus dusan anns an Fhraing
a' cur teagamh 'na chainnt.

Càit a bheil am mòr-shluagh
air sgàth an t-saoghail mhòir [...]

22.
'Donnchadh is Goering, coinneamh an àigh'

Donnchadh is Goering, coinneamh an àigh:
murtair nam bàrd is murtair nan dàn.

23.
The Drowned Man

The mother

Leave the door open,
he is going to come tonight.
Put more peats on the fire.
Cut, keep cutting more bread.

(The sisters move their heads, looking at her and at each
other)

The mother

I hear the noise of a beloved footstep
within my heart. He is coming.
Give me needle and thread
and the suit he left.

The sea

Absolutely, absolutely in vain.
He will never be awakened.
He will become a...
for all eternity.

24.
1939. Blood

Blood on the snow and gore on the streets,
lungs getting burned and bodies violently beaten,
skulls getting broken and ribs shattered,
gore on the doorposts and blood on the keystones.

Children's feet are racing along the pavement,
lament in the cities and wailing in the glens,
lies and blasphemies dancing together:
you asked for all of that, chose it, preferred it.

You took it all because that is what you wanted,
rather than a loss you did not suffer, or the choice of heroes;
you rejected Lenin as you rejected Christ,
your gods were perversion, blindness and greed.

23.
Am fear bàthte

A' mhàthair

Fàgaibh an doras fosgailte –
's ann a-nochd a thig e.
Cuiribh barrachd connaidh air an teine.
Gearraibh, gearraibh an còrr arain.

(Na peathraichean a' gluasad an cinn ga coimhead 's gan
coimhead fhèin)

A' mhàthair

Cluinneam fuaim cheum annsa
a-staigh 'nam chridhe. Thig e.
Thoiribh dhomh snàth is snàthad
agus an deise dh'fhàg e.

A' mhuir

Gu tur, gu tur gun fheum.
Cha dhùisgear gu bràth e.
Theid e 'na [illegible]
fad na sìorraidheachd.

24.
1939. Fuil

Fuil air an t-sneachd' agus gaorr air na sràidean,
sgamhan ga losgadh is colann ga stràcadh,
claigeann ga bhristeadh is broilleach ga phrannadh,
gaorr air an ursann is fuil air na bannan.

Casan nan naoidhean 'nan ràs air a' chabhsair,
gal anns na bailtean is gaoir anns na gleanntan,
a' bhreug is an toibheum cuideachd a' dannsa:
dh'iarr sibh iad uile, ur roghainn 's ur n-annsachd.

Ghabh sibh iad uile, oir b' iad a b' fheàrr leibh
na call nach robh agaibh, na roghainn nan sàr-fhear;   10
dhiùlt sibh Lenin mar dhiùlt sibh Crìosda,
a' chlaoine, an doille 's an sannt ur diathan.

Your ears opened to a noise that was always there;
you closed your eyes as corruption swelled,
you ate, drank and praised lies,
you kissed them, fed them and tried nothing more.

What did you care for the path of justice,
Blake, Liebknecht, Maclean, Macpherson?
What did you care for the sacrifice in Spain,
Jesus Hernandez and Lorca, noble victims?   20

You preferred Lithgow and Smith;
you got your fill from Thyssen and Krupp;
your greatness came from Rockefeller, Carnegie,
Morgan, Chamberlain and Vickers.

Cajole your Duke, Sutherland remnants
and, Lochaber people, your Locheil,
and, Londoners, your numerous earls
and, Frenchmen, your hundreds of families.

Gore on the streets and blood on the pavements,
a brain being split, that gets your favour;   30
consumption, fever, poverty and frailty
and now the other face of glory.

Your children will pluck from your cheeks
unhealthy roses of the tree of horror:
a banner with Christ's blood high in the skies
and your blood congealing on the claws of rottenness.

You defended wealth and you will get chlorine,
mustard and phosgene to your heart's content,
and when alleviation comes
you will receive the freedom that you got before.   40

You will get the freedom to be plundered
and to be deceived with multiple defilement:
Elstree, the press and the B.B.C. –
they will not leave you in want of anything.

Won't you be the tractable, well set up ones
cutting many a throat
of wretched, misguided Germans
who were deceived in the same fashion!

Dh'fhosgail ur cluasan don fhuaim a bha daonnan;
dhùin ur sùilean 's an truailleachd air laomadh,
dh'ith sibh iad, dh'òl sibh iad, mhol sibh na breugan,
phòg sibh iad, bhiadh sibh iad 's an còrr cha do dh'fheuch sibh.

Dè b' fhiach leibhse slighe na còrach,
Blake, Liebknecht, MacGill-Eain, am Muireach?
Dè b' fhiach leibhse ìobairt Spàinnteach,
Ìosa Hernandez, Lorca sàr-mhairbh? 20

B' fhearr leibhse Litchù 's Mac a' Ghobhainn;
bho Thyssen 's bho Krupp fhuair sibh na dh'fhoghain;
bho Rockefeller, Carnegie 's Morgan,
bho Chamberlain 's Vickers ur mòrachd.

Slìobaibh ur Diùc, a Chataich iarmaid,
agus, Abraich, bhur Loch Iall-se,
agus, a Lunnainnich, ur n-iomadh iarla,
's, a Fhrangaich, ur teaghlaichean, ciad dhiubh.

Gaorr air na sràidean 's fuil air a' chabhsair,
eanchainn ga spealtadh, siud ur n-annsachd; 30
an èitig, an fhiabhrais, a' bhochdainn 's a' bhreòiteachd
agus a-nis ceann eile na glòire.

Ròsan euslainneach craobh an uabhais
buainidh ur clann bheag às bhur gruaidhean:
brat fuil Chrìosda air àird nan speuran
's ur fuil-se tiugh an ìne na breunaid.

Dhìon sibh maoineas 's gheibh sibh *chlorine*,
mustard is *phosgene* mar a dh'fhòghnas,
agus an uair a thig am faochadh,
mar fhuair sibh roimhe i, gheibh sibh saorsa. 40

Gheibh sibh saorsa bhith air ur spùilleadh
agus air ur mealladh le iomadh trùilleach:
Elstree, am pàipear 's am B.B.C. –
cha leig iadsan èis oirbh a thaobh nì.

Nach sibhse a bhios soitheamh, dòigheil
is sibh a' gearradh iomadh sgòrnan
aig Gearmailtich bhochda, mhì-sheòlta
a mhealladh air an aon t-seòl ud!

You'll be contented under the midden
enjoying your eternity of glory,   50
Your children frail orphans
on your high carved memorials their sustenance!

Blood on the snow, blood on the meadow,
blood on the shelter, blood to the windward,
Germany's blood, France's blood,
Britain's blood, all blood shed despite you.

25.
Knightsbridge, Libya, June 1942

Though I am today against the breast of battle,
not here my load and trial:
not Rommel's guns and tanks,
but that my darling is depraved and a liar.

What can the rest matter, since you showed
you deserve neither my pride nor my anguish,
since your baseness put to shame
the pride that was in my poems?

26.
Myself and a male hoodie-crow on a Portree street

He wore me down completely
with lying flattery and bragging,
so that the Cuillin trembled
and the Storr's prick softened.

27.
'You ruined everything there was'

You ruined everything there was,
ruined the moon above Blaven,
the blue islands of the western headland,
ruined the "big music" and poetry.

Nach sibh bhios sona 's sibh fon òtrach
a' mealtainn sìorraidheachd bhur glòire,   50
ur clann 'nan dilleachdain bhreòite;
ur cuilbh shnaidhte àrda lòn dhaibh!

Fuil air an t-sneachda, fuil air a' chluaineig,
fuil air an fhasgadh, fuil air an fhuaradh;
fuil na Gearmailt, fuil na Frainge,
fuil Bhreatainn, fuil uile gun taing dhiubh.

25.
Knightsbridge, Libia, June 1942

Ged tha mi 'n-diugh ri uchd a' bhatail,
chan ann an seo mo shac 's mo dhiachainn;
cha ghunnachan 's cha thancan Roimeil,
ach mo ghaol bhith coirbte briagach.

Dè 's fhiach an còrr on dhearbh thu
nach b' fhiach thu m' uaill is m' àmhghar
's on mhaslaich thu led shuarachas
an t-uabhar bha 'nam dhàintean?

26.
Mi fhìn agus feannag fhireann air sràid am Port Rìgh

Ghànraich e mo chàil gu h-iomlan
le sodal, breugan agus bòst,
gun tàinig clisgeadh air a' Chuilithionn
is bogadaich air Bod an Stòirr.

27.
'Mhill thu h-uile nì a bh' ann'

Mhill thu h-uile nì a bh' ann
mhill thu 'ghealach os cionn Blàbheinn,
eileanan gorma an rois shiair,
mhill thu an ceòl mòr 's a' bhàrdachd.

28.
'My feet broken at Alamein'

My feet broken at Alamein
and my heart pierced with a needle,
my love and my share were taken from me,
I am left with nothing now.

29.
Naked Girl

The girl reached a flowing brightness;
she took off her clothes and stood naked,
her white-skinned outline silhouetted in the bright sun,
the rays flattering her thighs,
her firm, round, jewel-like breasts,
her slim, delicate, comely belly
and the shapeliness of her buttocks.

30.
To my lying love

Truth comes at a high price,
saying you are perverted and worthless,
but, my love, I won't concur.
Though you are more lying than a landlord,
cold-hearted and shallow,
replete with pointless vanity,
fond of money and possessions,
your face is shapely and inspiring
and your head a marvel of red and gold.

31.
My Country

Scotland itself is my country,
Skye is my island
and Raasay of the MacLeods;
Portree and Osgaig are my towns,

28.
'Mo chasan brist' aig Alamein'

Mo chasan brist' aig Alamein
's mo chridhe gonte le bior,
thugadh bhuam mo ghaol 's mo chuibhreann,
chan eil dad agam a-nis.

29.
Nighean Nochd

Ràinig an nighean soilleireachd shrùlach;
chuir i dhith is sheas i rùiste,
a cumadh cneas-bhàn geàrrt' sa ghrèin ghil,
sodalaich nan gath ra slèistean,
ra cìochan daingne cruinne leugach,
ra broinn sheang mhìn àlainn
agus ri cuimeireachd a màsan.

30.
Do mo luaidh breugach

'S ann a thig an fhìrinn dhaor
ag ràdh gur tu an t-suarag chlaon,
ach cha chan mise sin, a ghaoil.
Ged 's tu as briagaiche na maor,
's tu fuar-chridheach agus staoin,
loma-lan de fhearas mhòir bhaoith,
dèidheil air airgead is maoin,
tha t' aodann eireachdail is còir
's do cheann 'na annas ruadh den òr.

31.
Mo Dhùthaich

'S e Alba fhèin mo dhùthaich,
m' eilean an t-Eilean Sgitheanach
agus Ratharsair nan Leòdach;
mo bhailtean Port Rìgh is Òsgaig,

Achnahanaid and Ollach;
and the village above all other villages
is blue-green Clachan over there –
and blue-green Clachan in Lochalsh.

My other country is Ireland
and after it, France;   10
but Mull and Uist
are tucked into the depths of my heart.
"Since the company scattered
which was in Mull of the hills" –
I, too, am of the company
that has not and will not come to this side.

32.
'That breaking means a double breaking'

That breaking means a double breaking,
your own and the breaking
the centuries wrought upon your kindred,
the disease that became part of us.
I realised the day we said goodbye
on Diurinish Point to the strong man
who combined the precious spirit
inherited from the Vikings and from the Gaels –
that our people would not again have
the share which once was theirs.   10

33.
'I thought she suffered from an infirmity'

I thought she suffered from an infirmity,
from a blemish
that reduced me to a state as painful
as the wounding of Heloise.

But in fact she was distressed
with a different kind of need;
she got my support thanks to lies
but then it proved superfluous, and she left.

Ach na h-Anaid is an t-Òlach;
agus an clachan thar gach clachain,
an Clachan gorm ud thall –
agus Clachan gorm Loch Aills'.

Mo dhùthaich eile Èirinn
's à deaghaidh-se an Fhraing;   10
ach tha Muile agus Uibhist
am falach an doimhne mo chridhe.
"On a sgaoileadh a' chuideachd
a bha 'm Muile nam beann" –
tha mise cuideachd dhen cuideachd
nach tàinig 's nach tig a-nall.

32.
' 'S e bhith briste leis an dà bhristeadh'

'S e bhith briste leis an dà bhristeadh,
do bhristeadh fhèin agus am bristeadh
a thug na linntean air do chuideachd,
'n èitig a thàrmaich air ar siubhal.
Thuig mi an latha dh'fhàg sinn
an Sròn Dhiùrainis am fear làidir
an robh còmhla an spiorad daor
sìnte on Lochlannach 's on Ghàidheal
nach biodh an cuibhreann a-rithist
mar a bha i do ar cinneadh.   10

33.
'Shaoil mi i bhith fo èislean'

Shaoil mi i bhith fo èislean
agus sin le gaoid
a dh'fhàg mo staid cho geur dhomh
ri lèireadh Heloise.

Thàrla dhi bhith 'n èiginn
air sheòrs' eile dìth;
ghabh i taic rium le breugan
ach dh'fhalbh a feum is i.

34.
Greeting to Kennedy-Fraser

Greeting to Kennedy-Fraser,
gentlewoman without fault;
she castrated our potent muse
and put sugar on the mutilation.

35.
At Ebb-Tide

A frequent topic on communion days:
there is no substance in the flesh,
here we have no continuing city.
The text for preaching was unequivocal.

For your sake, beautiful wretch,
I would have thrown my own flesh away;
I was going anyway to a war
where it was easy to get killed.

36.
'You, Sorley, are the laughing-stock'

You, Sorley, are the laughing-stock
more than any man or animal,
given that your balls
tripped up your intelligence.

37.
'Woman who was fond of a playboy'

Woman who was fond of a playboy
and his gelded, glossy money
and who misled my kindness
when I thought her life was ruined.

Woman who deceived me with lies
after her clandestine adultery
when I thought her body would not stoop
to adultery, either blatant or hidden.

34.
Soraidh le NicUalraig-Fhriseal

Soraidh le NicUalraig-Fhriseal,
bean uasal ise gun chron;
spoth i ar Ceòlraidh lùthmhor
's chuir i siucar air an lot.

35.
Aig muir-tràigh

'S tric a chualas latha ceiste:
chan eil tairbhe san fheòil,
chan eil an seo baile mhaireas.
Bha an ceann-teagaisg gun sgleò.

Air do sgàth-sa, thruaghain bhòidhich,
thilginn m' fheòil fhìn air falbh;
bha mi dol co-dhiù a chogadh
far am b' fhurasta bhith marbh.

36.
' 'S tusa, Shomhairle, 'chùis-bhùrta'

'S tusa, Shomhairle, 'chuis-bhùrta
thar gach duine 's ainmhidh
a chionn gun do chuir do mhagairle
a' bhacag air t' eanchainn.

37.
'Tè lem bu mhiann an gille-mirein'

Tè lem bu mhiann an gille-mirein
agus airgead spothte slìom
's a thug an car às mo choibhneas
nuair shaoil mi a beatha bhith a dhìth.

Tè a mheall mi le briagan
an dèidh a h-adhaltranais sa chùil,
's mi smaoineachadh gu robh a colann
seach adhaltranas follaiseach no 'n cùil.

Woman who told the foolish lie
about me since she thought   10
Rommel's soldiers would put
a muzzle on my mouth under the earth.

Woman who told the base lie
about another man in the fighting
so that her playboy could be
wordy and drawling as was his habit.

38.
Russia. Autumn 1941

The columns of the red fir trees
rise steep with barbed tips on the moorlands;
between them is the covering of joy,
a gentle rocking of grey-green wheat.

The people have a different church,
one made ready with no need of embroidery,
the church of man and land,
of hearts, of principles, of stars.

39.
'Famine lies beyond the horizon'

Famine lies beyond the horizon,   1
its heel on the sun's face,
grey smoke choking,
cold rising from the ground
and falling out of the sky,
crushing, sweeping away.

Famine lies beyond the horizon:
to south and east and west
the repulsive, pitiful images,
the child with twisted backbone,   10
its paunch of a belly swollen like a bag,
its chest mere skin and bones.

Tè a dh'innis briag na h-òinsich
mum dheaghaidh fhìn agus i 'n dùil   10
gun cuireadh saighdearan Roimeil
glas-ghuib air mo bhial san ùir.

Tè a dh'innis a' bhriag shuarach
mu fhear eile bha san spàirn
a chum gum biodh a gille-mirein
bialach, sgleogach mar a ghnàths.

38.
Ruisia. As t-fhoghar 1941

Tha cuilbh de an ghiuthas ruadh
sna h-aonaichean colg-stuadhach, casa;
eatarra tha brat an àigh,
maoth-luasganaich na criothnachd glaise.

Tha eaglais eile aig an t-sluagh,
eaglais ghrèidhte gun fheum grèiseadh,
eaglais an duine 's an fhuinn,
nan cridheachan, nan conn, nan reultan.

39.
'Tha 'ghort air cùl na fàire'

Tha 'ghort air cùl na fàire   1
's am bonn air aghaidh na grèine,
an toit liath a' tachdadh,
's am fuachd ag èirigh às an talamh
's a' tuiteam às an iarmailt,
a' dinneadh is a' sguabadh.

Tha 'ghort air cùl na fàire:
a deas is an ear 's an iar
na h-ìomhaighean sgreataidh agus truagh.
an leanabh le chnàimh-droma lùbte,   10
a mhaodal 'na balg leis an at
's a chliabh 'na chraiceann cnàmhach.

Famine lies beyond each horizon,
carcasses of cattle growing warm
on the bare grasslands,
the girl who should have been beautiful
repellent in the harshness of her fate.

40.
The Silver Button

(There is a tradition in Raasay that the last MacLeod chief
could give only a silver button off his coat to one of the
men who ferried him to Applecross when he was leaving
Raasay.)

Their plight is to my flesh and bones
a white-hot iron.

The fields empty under sheep
from the Raised Beach of Eyre to Meall Damh,
from Screapadal to Fearns,
from Rubha na Lice to Rubha Mhanais.

The children, women and big men
of Raasay among the rocks of Rona.
Children, women and men
on whom Rainy brought destruction.   10

The children, women and big men
of Sgoirebreac in a fank in Braes,
poverty and hardship their pain.

And the green lush pastures
of Sgoirebreac without efficacy for them.

Rainy and the MacDonald lords
spoiled the big men of my kind.

Children and women and good men
from the green glens of MacLeod's Due
turned to bracken in Brae Eynort   20
and gone to the sea-wrack
from Rubha 'n Dunain to Dunvegan.

Tha 'ghort air cùl gach fàire,
closaichean a' chruidh gam blianadh
air a' mhachair luim,
an nighean bu chòir a bhith bòidheach
sgreataidh le an-iochd a càis.

40.
Am Putan Airgid

(Tha bial-aithris ann an Ratharsair nach b' urrainn an triath
mu dheireadh de Chloinn Mhic Ghille-Chaluim ach putan
airgid dhe 'chòta a thoirt do fhear dhe na fir a dh'aisig e don
Chomraich 's e fàgail Ratharsair.)

Tha 'n càradh-san rim fheòil 's rim chnàmhan
'na iarann teinntidh geal.

Na raointean falamh fo chaoraich
o fhaoilinn Aoighre gu Meall Damh,
o Sgreapadal gu Baile na Feàrnaibh,
o Rubha na Lice gu Rubha Mhànais.

Clann is mnathan is fir mhòra
Ratharsair measg chreagan Rònaigh.
Clann is mnathan agus fir
air an tug Rèanaidh an sgrios.   10

Clann is mnathan is fir mhòra
Sgoirebreac am faing sa Bhràighe,
a' bhochdainn 's an t-anacothrom gan cràdhadh.

Agus raointean gorma brìoghmhor
Sgoirebreac gun dad brìgh dhaibh.

Rèanaidh is Morairean Chloinn Dòmhnaill
a mhill fir mhòra mo sheòrsa.

Clann is mnathan agus seòid
o ghlinn ghorma Dhùis MhicLeòid
air dhol 'nam fraineach am Braigh Aoineart   20
agus air a dhol don tiùrradh
o Rubha 'n Dùnain gu Dùn Bheagain.

Norman and other Norman,
John Norman and another Norman,
they got flattery enough;
their pin is in the bone and blood of the MacLeods.

He who was nearest to me
 among the chiefs of the MacLeods
left a silver button in his estate
as he took the stealthy ferry   30
to Applecross, his moonlight flitting.

Mac Gille-Chaluim did not clear
one man of the Clan MacLeod
nor one man of the Clan MacLean,
of the Clan MacSwan or Clan MacNicol,
of the Clan Mac Gill-Iosa
or of the Clan Mac Gill-Other.

He took the night ferry
leaving the silver button.
Not so the seed of Norman   40
nor the barons of Sleat.

My kinsman left no stain of filth
in the forehead of the Seed of Torquil of the Sun.

Poor John Mac Gille-Chaluim went
and left the debts. Small their disgrace
to the disgrace of the chiefs that stayed.
Their staying was a branding-iron
on Trotternish and Minginish,
on Bracadale and Sleat.

I prefer the Seed of Torquil of the Sun.   50

41.
Stalin

They keep saying you were
unscrupulous, ruthless,
out of your mind with lust for power,

Tarmad agus Tarmad eile,
Iain Tarmad 's Tarmad eile,
mheal iadsan sodal gu leòr;
tha 'm bior an cnàimh 's am fuil Shìol Leòid.

Dh'fhàg am fear bu dlùithe dhòmhsa
de chinn-chinnidh nan Leòdach
putan airgid 'na oighreachd
's e gabhail aiseag na foille   30
don Chomraich, imrich na h-oidhche.

Cha do thog Mac Ghille-Chaluim
fear sam bith de Chloinn MhicLeòid
no fear sam bith de Chloinn Ghill-Eain,
de Chloinn MhicSuain no Chloinn MhicNeacail
no de Chloinn Mhic Ghill-Ìosa
no de Chloinn Mhic Ghill-Eile.

Ghabh esan aiseag na h-oidhche,
a' fàgail a' phutain airgid.
Cha b' ionann sin do Shìol Tharmaid   40
no do Mhorairean Shlèite.

Cha d' fhàg mo charaid-sa smal brèine
am bathais Shìol Thorcaill na Grèine.

Dh'fhalbh Iain bochd Mac Ghille-Chaluim
's dh'fhàg e na fiachan. Bu bheag am masladh
seach masladh nan triath a dh'fhuirich;
bha 'm fiachan-san 'nan iarainn-losgaidh
air Tròndairnis 's air Minginis,
air Bracadal agus air Slèite.

'S fhearr leamsa Sìol Thorcaill na Grèine.   50

41.
Stàilin

Tha iad ag ràdha gu robh thu
cealgach, an-iochdmhor,
às do rian le miann na cumhachd,

that you caused millions to die
in a famine which could have been avoided
which you yourself inflicted on them.

But others say
your understanding
surpassed all other men's,
that your capacities were inexpressible,   10
that you saw coming
the crazed army of the Nazis
and Europe in its entirety
subjugated by capital,
with Christ's mask
on some of their banners;
that you murdered now
in the interests of tomorrow and the day after tomorrow,
that you preferred famine and death
affecting thousands and millions   20
for one, two, three or four years,
for five, six, seven, eight, nine or ten,
rather than see the future
in the hands of Wotan and Krupp,
of Rosenberg and Nietzsche
and their pitiless, inhuman creed;
that you saw both past and future,
that freedom could only mean
the understanding of necessity.

42.
'The mountains are speechless'

The mountains are speechless
if what they say cannot be understood,
and the many-voiced ocean is silent,
if no-one knows its language.

For all the voices that may emerge from lips
between Sutherland and the Mull
no point in being close to it
if their Gaelic is not heard.

gun do leig thu bàs le milleanan
le gort a ghabhadh seachnadh,
a thug thu fhèin orra.

Ach their càch
gu robh do thuigse
thar tuigse gach aoin eile,
gu robh do chomas do-labhairt,   10
gum faca tu tighinn
arm caothaich nan Nàsach,
's an Roinn-Eòrpa gu lèir
fo chumhachdan Mhamoin,
le aghaidh-choimhich Chrìosda
air cuid dem brataichean;
gun do mhurt thu an-dràsta
air sgàth màireach 's an-earar,
gum b' fheàrr leat a' ghort 's am bàs
aig mìltean is milleanan   20
airson bliadhna, no dhà, no trì, no ceithir,
no còig, no sia, no seachd, ochd, naodh, deich,
na gum biodh an tìm ri teachd
aig Bhòtan 's aig Krupp,
aig Rosenberg 's Nietzsche
's aig an creideamh an-iochdmhor mì-dhaonda;
gum faca tu na bha 's na bhitheadh,
nach robh an t-saorsa
ach an tuigse na b' fheudar.

42.
'Tha na beanntan gun bhruidhinn'

Tha na beanntan gun bhruidhinn
mura tuigear an glòir,
's an cuan iolaghuthach sàmhach,
ma tha 'chànain gun eòl.

Air gach guth thig o bhilean
eadar Cataibh 's a' Mhaoil,
mur èistear ri 'Ghàidhlig,
chan eil fàth bhith ri thaobh.

Ben Nevis has no voice
other than Donald of the Songs',   10
and Ben Doran is struck dumb
if Duncan Ban is dead.

Finlarig and Taymouth
are heaps of stone and mortar
to eyes which failed to see the flame
raised by love's revenge.

Ben Cruachan is merely a big lump,
voiceless, ignorant,
if the outlaw does not elude
pursuit on its hillside.   20

The Moriston river is dry, coming
through the glen without a burble
if the din made by Donald Donn's
boots cannot be heard.

And the warbling of Rùsgaich
is merely pointless birdsong
if that music does not pierce
the flesh when heard.

Sheep are reposing
on a hundred summits as high   30
as that speckled, beloved castle,
joyous Dun of the MacLeods.

The wind scours Culloden
with a chill, piercing blast –
the whitened corpses would have turned black
were it not for John Roy's lament.

Every custom and delight
our people had since the beginning
is dumb in a castle prison,
locked up in a fortress.   40

Blind folk are searching for them
and the key has been lost:
if Gaelic disappears
there can never be release.

Chan eil guth aig Beinn Nibheis
ach le Dòmhnall nan Dàn   10
's tha Beinn Dòbhrain 'na balbhan
ma dh'eug Donnchadh Bàn.

Tha Fionn-Lairig is Bealach
'nan torran cloiche is aoil
dhan t-sùil nach fhaca an lasair
a thog dìoghaltas a' ghaoil.

Chan eil an Cruachan ach meall mòr
gun ghuth is gun fhios
mura tàrr am fear fuadain
às an ruaig air a shlios.   20

Tha Moireasdan tioram,
tighinn gun ghlug tro na glinn,
mura cualas a' chaismeachd
a bh' aig bròg Dhòmhnaill Dhuinn.

'S chan eil ceileireadh Rùsgaich
ach 'na fhaoineas guth eòin
mura cluinnear a thorman
'na shitheadh san fheòil.

Tha na caoraich 'nan laighe
air ceud mullach cho àrd   30
ris an dùn sin breac gaolach,
Dùn Leòdach an àigh.

Tha 'ghaoth sguabadh Chùil Lodair
le sgal craingidh fuar
's na cuirp ghlè-gheal air dubhadh
mur b' e tuireadh Iain Ruaidh.

Tha gach gnàths agus annas
bh' air ar cinneadh o thùs
am balbh-phrìosan a' chaisteil
agus glaist' anns an dùn.   40

'S e 'n dall tha gan sireadh
's an iuchair air chall;
ma chaillear a' Ghàidhlig
chan fhuasglar am bann.

What matters it should another sun rise
over summit and ocean?
If it is not a Gaelic sun,
its aspect is indifferent to us.

43.
'I offered you my love and my poems'

I offered you my love and my poems.
Oh, girl, what did you want?
You told me you were mutilated,
that your body was dry and wretched.
What the devil did you want?
Was it the poems you were after?
Was it the shadow of love,
mist scattering
in the sun,
in the sun of poems?   10
You returned, cavalry of my love,
putting them all to flight,
they showed you their shining swords...

44.
'Pride caused you to stay'

The bombardier and the captain ran off
and crept down into a hollow
while the pride of Clan MacLean sustained
another man, his body filled with resistance.

He thought about the brae of Mull
and the meadows around Loch na Keal,
and somehow that lessened
the awfulness of his situation.

When the bullets came in a hail,
bubbling up in the bare sand,
he remembered Inverkeithing –   10
there was inflexible valour in his spine.

Dè ma dh'èireas grian eile
air creachainn no cuan
's nach i grian na Gàidhlig,
's coingeis dhuinne a tuar.

43.
'Thairg mi mo ghaol 's mo dhàin dhut'

Thairg mi mo ghaol 's mo dhàin dhut.
O nighean, dè bha bhuat?
Thuirt thu rium gu robh thu màbte,
gu robh do cholainn tioram truagh.
Dè 'n diabhal a bha bhuat?
An e na dàin a bha thu 'g iarraidh?
An e faileas a' ghaoil,
an ceò a' sgaoileadh
anns a' ghrèin,
ann an grèin nan dàn?   10
Thill thu, eachraidh mo ghaoil,
chuir thu ruaig orra gu lèir,
sheall iad dhut an claidhnean lainnir [...]

44.
'Thug an t-àrdan ort fuireach'

Theich am bombardair 's an caiptean   1
agus liùg iad ann an sloc,
is chum àrdan Chloinn Ghill-Eain
fear eile, 's an cruadal 'na chorp.

Smaoinich e air Bràighe Mhuile
's air lèanagan mu Loch nan Ceall
agus thainig seòrsa taisidh
air a' chruadal a bh' ann.

Nuair bha na peilearan 'nam frasan
a' builgeadh anns a' ghainmhich luim,   10
thàinig cuimhn' air Inbhir Chèitein
is treuntas dìreach 'na dhruim.

45.
Come and see

Come and see, come and see,
you will get comfort and support,
you will see the ruling priests of the land
and ministers of the shire.
They will serve you bitter bread,
food without value for your soul;
your spirit and your flesh
will become thoroughly acquainted with such loving.
They will fill the steep cup
full of bitter, grey wine,   10
you will get comfort and peace
and they will destroy your essential humanity.
But if you should fall down,
Hell will rise up on you.
They will go to heaven's heights,
but you will get the company of poets.

45.
Thig is faic

Thig is faic, thig is faic,
gheibh thu cofhurtachd is taic,
chì thu àrd-shagart tìre
agus ministear na sgìre.
Bheir iad dhut an t-aran goirt,
biadh t' anama gun toirt;
gheibh do spiorad agus d' fheòil
air a' ghaol ud aithne 's eòl.
Lìonaidh iad an cupa cas
làn den fhìon shearbh, ghlas,   10
gheibh thu cofhurtachd is sìth
is sgrìosaidh iad an daonda-brìgh.
Ach ma thuiteas tusa sìos,
èiridh Iutharna ort a-nìos.
Thèid iad gu nèamh nan àrd,
ach gheibh thusa còmhlan bhàrd.

Notes on the unpublished, incomplete and fragmentary poems

This section contains all known unpublished items by MacLean to have come to light so far, drawn from three principal sources, in Aberdeen and Edinburgh. Items are presented in alphabetical order of the opening line. Where no title was available, the opening line, within inverted commas, has been taken as title. The notes on each poem give detailed information about the source, variants or cancelled readings, and difficulties of legibility or interpretation. No attempt has been made to offer a full commentary as with 'An Cuilithionn' – this being considered beyond the scope of the present volume. The aim was simply to make the unpublished poems generally available in the centennial year of the poet's birth. A selection is to be included in a forthcoming new edition of MacLean's collected poems.

Twelve items in all[1] are drawn from ms 2864 and 2864/1 at Special Collections, in King's College in the University of Aberdeen. A note by Derick Thomson indicates that these materials were deposited by Douglas Young. MacLean's letter to Young dated September 25th 1940, quoted in the introduction to 'An Cuilithionn', provides a "terminus ante quem" for composition. Practically all of them would appear to have been considered for inclusion in what became *Dàin do Eimhir agus Dàin eile*.

A list in ms 2864 sketches one planned ordering of the 'Dàin eile', as follows: V 'An Dùn 'na theine', VI 'Air an adhbhar cheudna', VII 'Mi fhìn agus feannag fhireann air sràid am Port Rìgh', X 'Am Bàta Dubh', XIII 'Conchobhar', XV 'An Soitheach', XVIII 'Thig is faic'. Another list, in ms 2864/1, headed 'Eisgeachd is Mì-mhodh' (something like 'satire and impertinence'), gives a plan for what would become the 'Eisgeachd' section in the 1943 volume, as follows: I 'An Dùn 'na theine', II 'Air an adhbhar cheudna', III 'Mi fhìn agus an fheannag fhireann' [sic], V 'Soraidh le Nic Ualraig-Friseal', VI 'A Sheòrais MhicGhill-Eain fhiachail', VII 'Don Phàp a thug buidheachas do Dhia airson tuiteam Bhàrsalona'.

IV has been neatly snipped out with scissors from this list. Luckily a further copy has been preserved at f31 in ms 29557 in the National Library of Scotland, Edinburgh, so that 'Donnchadh is Goering, coinneamh an àigh'[2] could be restored from this source. Copies of six further Aberdeen poems[3] are included in ms 29557, where 'Na Cumhachdan a Tha' is marked in pen 'Eisgeachd' and 'Cumadh Tàilleir' 'omit', indicating that both items were at least considered for publication. This is also the source for MacLean's English versions of items 5 and 34.

MacLean writes, in a letter to Young dated May 27th 1943:

> I told you of certain bitter poems I had written in the desert. Well, I have added to them and now they are about 25 in number but I am very doubtful if they can ever be published, or if I want ever to publish, or even preserve them. They hint pretty clearly at the real truth behind others, but I should have appreciated that truth much earlier than I did. Even now I am not altogether sure of it. So don't mention them, at present, at any rate...

The notebook he presented to the National Library in 1964, now ms 14966, would appear to contain some of these poems. They constitute a subset of, or epilogue to, the 'Dàin do Eimhir' proper,[4] and it is possible, thanks to them, to construct a fuller picture of the somewhat sordid background to his involvement with the Scottish Eimhir, not clear to the poet until he was on active service. Some items preserved in ms 29567 (for which see below) also belong with this 'bitter' 'subset',[5] though their dating must be less certain than that of the items in the notebook.[6]

There would appear to have been two 'other' men connected with the Scottish woman: one of comfortable means, married and possibly bisexual, so that the poet more than once defines her relationship with him as adulterous, while the other, presumably the 'òigear Goill' or 'young Lowlander' of 'Dàin do Eimhir' XLVII, died on active service defending his country. There can be no certainty as to the actual facts of the matter. This is the version, however, delineated in these unpublished poems. MacLean overcame his reluctance to see them in print sufficiently to publish four.

The first stanza only of 'Knightsbridge, Libia' came out in *Poetry Scotland* in 1945, the starkly denunciatory 'Do Bhoireannach Briagach Coirbte' ('To a depraved, lying woman') in the same publication the following year, 'Mhag mo reusan'[7] around the same time in *An Gàidheal*, and 'An Dà Ghehenna' ('The Two Gehennas') in *Gairm* in 1961.

Fragmentary, incomplete and unpublished items from among the poet's surviving papers are included in National Library ms 29567, from which all the remaining poems are drawn. As might be expected, these are miscellaneous in nature. 'Am putan airgid' (like '1939. Fuil' in Aberdeen, of which a copy also exists in ms 29557) is closely related to the subject matter of 'An Cuilithionn', though it could well have been written some time afterwards. There are several poems of personal tribute to admired or celebrated contemporaries,[8] which take up the hallowed Gaelic tradition of public praise of notable figures. At least two items are experimental in nature, the evocative if not easily decipherable address to an artillery piece 'Air mullach làraidh, air an oidhche, ri taobh gunna-mhòir' and a dramatised fragment, 'Am fear bàthte', which reminds one of certain poems by Campbell Hay.[9] 'Thug an t-àrdan ort fuireach' belongs with MacLean's war poems proper, while 'Ruisia. As t-fhoghar 1941' is a tantalising fragment of a longer and evidently ambitious piece, giving expression to the depths of MacLean's concern for Soviet Russia after German troops had infringed the pact between Molotov and Ribbentrop and invaded that country.[10] Elsewhere it is clear that the poet's political radicalism did not ebb, or else revived notably, in the 1960s and 1970s. There are two versions of a praise poem to the most celebrated of the French Revolutionary armies, containing mentions of Mao Tse Tung and the Viet Cong, while 'Stàilin' shows that, in MacLean's estimation at least, the Soviet tyrant underwent a posthumous political rehabilitation.[11]

The publication of these items brings several poems of value finally into the public domain, while others can usefully serve to round out our understanding and perception of more successful and finished items which already form part of the poet's known work. Translations by MacLean have survived of nos. 5, 18, 25 (first stanza only), 34 and 40. See the note to no. 38 for a prose translation of stanzas not preserved in Gaelic. All remaining English versions are editorial.

1.
Donnchadh

Source: Abdn Univ ms 2864/1. A further copy in Edinb NLS ms 29557 f32 has the annotation, in pen and in the poet's hand: 'you had better not show this to the object as I don't think he would like it.' It is possible that the biting two-liner 22 concerns the same person, whose musical abilities would appear to have been severely limited.

2.
Don Phàp a thug buidheachas do Dhia airson tuiteam Bharsalòna

Source: Abdn Univ ms 2864, with these cancelled variants:
4 naoidhean] nan saoi agus] 's

original reading (not cancelled):
1 shlìom dhiadhaidh] an diabhail

The item is numbered VII under 'Eisgeachd is mì-mhodh'. A further copy is in Edinb NLS ms 29557 f31. A third copy, transcribed by George Campbell Hay, exists in Edinb NLS ms 26722 61r (indication from Dr Michel Byrne). In ms, city is given as 'Barcelona'; version here taken from the Edinburgh copy.

3.
'A Dhòmhnallaich urramaich'

Source: Edinb NLS ms 29567 f20

The opening line is a reference to a well-known 'port-a-beul' tune. An alternative version of the final line is added in pencil: 'ro aognaidheachd ar suidheachaidh', with 'chaochlaideachd' as an alternative to 'aognaidheachd'.

4.
Do Mhaighstir Alasdair MacCoinnich aig Dinneir Comann Gàidhlig Inbhir Nis 17.III.67

Source: Edinb NLS ms 29567 ff25–27: text is based on a fair copy f27 not in MacLean's hand. There are two drafts. Variants include:

1 a sheòid na fèile] Mhic Coinnich
4] earlier reading is preferred to what replaced it in the draft:
'cha d'fhàg thu bheag dhed leithid fhèin ann'
5 dhìrich] gasda
8] earlier reading 'cùm do shùil air urrachan slìoma'
9 tèid do shaobhadh] iad do thaobh-sa

5.
Na Cumhachdan a Tha

Source: Abdn Univ 2864/1, where it is marked 'V' in red
ink. Another copy in Edinb NLS ms 29557 f34, also marked
'V' in pen, has 'teangannan' in last line. MacLean's English
version is reproduced from f73 of the same ms.

1, 4 mort] the standard form today would be 'murt'

6.
'A Sheòrais Mhic Ghill-Eathain fhiachail'

Source: Abdn Univ 2864/1, where it is numbered VI under
'Eisgeachd is mì-mhodh'. A further copy is in Edinb NLS ms
29557 f31.

According to John MacInnes, George MacLean was the
"orraman" at Portree High School hostel, where MacLean
taught from 1934 to 1937.

7.
Snòtachadh

Source: Edinb NLS ms 29567 f21, typescript.

8.
Seamus Ó Conghaile

Source: Edinb NLS ms 29567 f22
3 tràighte] conjectural reading: ms has 'tnaithte'
4 seach] conjectural reading: ms has '[...]eadh'

9.
Cumadh Tàilleir

Source: Abdn Univ 2864/1, with following marginal variant in pencil:

6 aigne] gleus

Published in Whyte 2006: 195

10.
'Am bi dùsgadh anns an t-saoghal'

Source: Edinb NLS ms 29567 ff40r, 40v and 41r

The poem survives as a draft and, at certain points, editorial reconstruction must be conjectural. It is related in mood and theme to 21 '1793–94' and should possibly bear the same title. The two may be looked on as twin attempts at a single project. The 'Armée de Sambre-et-Meuse' was formed on June 29th 1794 by combining three previously existing forces. It played a key role in the conquest of the Austrian Netherlands and the Dutch Republic, and in the French invasion of Germany. On September 29th 1797 it became part of the Army of Germany.

Further readings:

1–2 Am bi dùsgadh anns an t-saoghal/mura tig e às an Fhraing?] A bheil dùsgadh anns an Fhraing?
13 iarainn] na daorsa
16 mathaichte] 'beairteach' also ''s i gorm'
31 uiread] uibhir
32 's a bha] original has ''s bha'
34 *alternative version*] is am fear aitreabh an tràigh
36 chreutairean bochda 'n t-saoghail] dhaoine bhochda taobh Loch Shubhairn
48 aice] editorial correction from 'aige'
49 mun Mheuse] mun t-Sambre is 'n Mheuse

The word 'dùsgadh' (ll. 1 & 3) in religious terminology means 'revival', implying that MacLean reinterprets hopes of a Calvinist reawakening in terms of those for a generalised political transformation. The reference at l. 21 to Paul's Epistle to the Hebrews 13: 14 'Oir an seo chan eil againn baile a mhaireas' ('For here we have no continuing city') also occurs at 36 l. 3. For the quotation from Mac Mhaighstir Alasdair in l. 27, see note to 'An Cuilithionn' II: 157.

11.
Dithis

Source: Abdn Univ ms 2864/1. The ms copy in Abdn 2864 has the following variants:

2 tè] aon
3 agus] 's
4 fear] fear eile

The poem may refer to Ian Murray, rector of Portree High School, and his wife.

12.
Mo ghaol san lios chreachte

Source: Edinb NLS ms 29567 f30

3] pencil annotation 'millte màbte am fonn' may represent a later version

13.
Don Urramach Tòmas MacCalmain
aig Dinneir Comann Gaidhlig Inbhir Nis 14.IV.61

Source: Edinb NLS ms 29567 f33, carbon copy of typescript
The poem is addressed to the Rev. Thomas M. Murchison, who spent much of his early life in Kylerhea (information from Ian MacDonald).

10 Chinn t-Sàile] original has 'Chinn an t-Sàile'

The capitalisation in ll. 7 & 11 makes it clear that Skye is intended. Line 17 presumably refers to the Donald Murchison memorial stone outside Kyle of Lochalsh. At l. 21 MacLean indirectly quotes a song which formed the basis for 'Dàin do Eimhir' XL.

14.
Air mullach làraidh, air an oidhche, ri taobh gunna-mhòir

Source: Edinb NLS ms 29567 f24, rough draft on f23r

Certain lines in the draft are of difficult interpretation. The close does not indicate whether or not a continuation was intended. In l. 11 'lasrachail' is a conjectural reading, and the word remains unidentified.

Cancelled variants on f23 include:

1 suaimhneach] sèimh
2 Cha leig mi mo thaic ort, a chanain, ach] 'chan urrainn dhomh mo chuideam a leigeil ort, a chanain, 's' cancelled, also 'cha leig mi cuideam ort, a chanain, is cha mhoth' phutas tu bhuat mi'
4 gu] dha smìor] 'sìol-?' second word illegible
6 bhuille chridhe] dòrtadh
8 nuair a tha] mar gu robh
11 (before 'brataich') 'na (deleted)

15a.
'Cha b' e 'n t-adhaltranas bu mhiosa' (version 1)

15b.
'Cha b' e 'n t-adhaltranas bu mhiosa' (version 2)

Source: Edinb NLS ms 29567 f33

These two realisations are designed to present the reader with as many as possible of the variants contained on this sheet. No definitive form of the quatrain exists, which is written twice, in process of elaboration and development. Further variants include:

3 [or 4?] mar do thogadh
4 fir eile sa bhatal] an òigeir Ghallda

16.
'Chì mi na coin a' tighinn'

Source: Edinb NLS ms 14966 ff10–11

The imagery of this item is strongly linked to that of 'Dàin do Eimhir' XXIX, 'Coin is madaidhean-allaidh'. If, as seems probable, 'teanntachd' is an internal rhyme echoing 'beanntan' at the end of the previous line, then the poem is clearly unfinished.

14 mur] conjectural reading: could also be either 'mus' or 'mun'.

17.
Shelley 8.VII.34

Source: Abdn Univ ms 2864, where 10 dheachd] deachd

13] comma in ms deleted after 'èibhle'

18.
Do Shir Lachlainn Mac Gill-Eain Dhubhaird
air ochdadhach ceann-bliadhna ath-thogail a' chaisteil

Source: Edinb NLS ms 29567 ff35–36 (Gaelic), 37–38 (English), fountain pen

A note on f38a indicates that MacLean recited this poem, specially composed for the occasion, in the Aros Hall in Tobermory in 1992. His translation.

41 dh'fhàgar] original has 'dh'fhàgas'

19.
'Cùis-bhùrta dhèanamh de mo bhuadhan'

Source: Edinb NLS ms 14966 f28

Punctuation in l. 3 is editorial.
4 gànrachadh] ms has 'gàrachadh', so that both reading and translation are here conjectural.

20.
'Dè a fhuair thusa, 'chridhe'

Source: Edinb NLS ms 14966 f16

21.
1793–94

Source: Edinb NLS ms 29567 f42 r & v

The poem survives as a draft and, at certain points, editorial reconstruction must be conjectural. It is related in mood and theme to 10 'Am bi dùsgadh anns an t-saoghal', which see for information about the army MacLean is celebrating. The two items may be considered alternative drafts of a single project.

A cancelled version of l. 18 reads ' 's iad ga dhearbhadh lem fuil'. A shorter draft survives on f39r, bearing the title given here. It contains an alternative version of l. 5 plus an extra line 5a, as follows: 'san robh an treuntas craobh-sgaoilte / mar fhalasgair mhòr air aonach', with 'a' sgaoileadh' as variant for 'craobh-sgaoilte'.

22.
'Donnchadh is Goering, coinneamh an àigh'

Source: Edinb NLS ms 29557 f31. In Abdn ms 2864/1, this item has been neatly snipped out with scissors from its place between 'Mi fhìn is feannag fhireann' and 'A Sheòrais Mhic Ghill-Eathain fhiachail'.

23.
Am fear bàthte

Source: Edinb NLS ms 29567 f23v

Tentative summary of a sketched dialogue, dramatic in nature, unique in MacLean's work. Variants are:

  3 barrachd] an còrr
  4 an coir] barrachd
    a' gluasad] *a' lontadh* [?]
  10 Cha dhùisgear gu bràth e] Cha dhùisg dad e

24.
1939. Fuil

Source: ms in Abdn Univ 2864

A copy typed by 'Miss Copeland's agency', marked 'not to be published', in Edinb NLS ms 29557 f37a, contains the following variants:

15 breugan] briagan
16 fheuch] fhiach
23 Morgan] Morgan,
27–28] commas preceding and following 'a Lunnainnich' and 'a Fhrangaich'

The text raises particular problems in the use of possessive adjectives, first- and second-person plural. The ms has 'bhur' in ll. 26 & 34, otherwise 'ar' throughout. In the typescript, ll. 27 & 28 have 'ur'. In this edition, 'ar' has been changed to 'ur' in ll. 8 (twice), 12, 13, 14, 24, 25, 30, 34, 36, 41, 42, 51 and 52, in accordance with the interpretation of the item offered in the English translation. This solution is only hypothetical and is offered as a provisional reading.

cancelled variants from ms:

17 slighe na corach] cùis nan sàr-fhear,
18 Blake, Liebknecht, MacGill-Eain, am Mùireach] Liebknecht, Lenin, MacGhill-Eathain, Stàilinn
48 air an aon t-seòl ud] leis na h-aon dòighean

25.
Knightsbridge, Libia June 1942

Source: Edinb NLS ms 14966 f14, written in pencil

The first quatrain was published in 1945 in *Poetry Scotland* 2 (with a colon at the end of l. 1). The second is published here for the first time. MacLean's English translation comes on the same page. The published version has 'not here my burden and extremity'. In the ms 'burden' has been added underneath 'load'.

26.
Mi fhìn agus feannag fhireann air sràid am Port Rìgh

Source: Abdn Univ ms 2864/1 typed copy, with 'boganachd' added for 'bogadaich' in l. 4. A further copy is in Edinb NLS ms 29557 f31, with earlier variants of ll. 2 and 3 as follows: 'le bhaothalachd brèige 's bosd;/gun tug e clisgeadh air a' Chuilithionn'.

The number VII appears to refer to an earlier arrangement of the 'Dàin eile' (see MacLean 1943). Elsewhere in 2864/1, this item carries the number III in a list of 'Eisgeachd is Mì-mhodh'.

27.
'Mhill thu h-uile nì a bh' ann'

Source: Edinb NLS ms 14966 f15

Punctuation in l. 3 is editorial.

28.
'Mo chasan brist' aig Alamein'

Source: Edinb NLS ms 14966 f3

The opening line indicates that MacLean continued to add items to the notebook after his most serious injury, so that certain of its contents should perhaps be ascribed to his period of convalescence in Raigmore Hospital, Inverness.

2 gonte le bior] brist' a nis

29.
Nighean Nochd

Source: Abdn Univ ms 2864/1, with following deleted variant:

3 cneas-bhàn] cneas-gheal

An annotation in Douglas Young's hand to a list sent by MacLean in his letter of April 27th 1941 indicates that this item was at one time to appear as XIV in the 'Dàin eile'.

A further copy is in Edinb NLS ms 29557 f28. Published in Whyte 2006: 194

30.
Do mo luaidh breugach

Source: Edinb NLS ms 14966 f18

cancelled variant
2 chlaon] bhaoth

31.
Mo Dhùthaich

Source: Edinburgh NLS ms 29567 f49 typed with rough
version biro pen on f48, where a further four lines are to be
found, as follows:

Tha tràigh Chalgaraidh a' sìneadh
'na gainmhich ghil bhuain
's a h-aghaidh air Treisinnis [?]
nach aidich g [sic]

The Treshnish Isles lie W of Mull.

32.
' 'S e bhith briste leis an dà bhristeadh'

Source: Edinb NLS ms 29567 f1 fountain pen

cancelled variants:
3 chuideachd] dhaoine
7 an spiorad daor] am meanmna l... (word illegible: reading
'daor' here is conjectural)

33.
'Shaoil mi i bhith fo èislean'

Source: Edinb NLS ms 14966 f1, with cancelled variant:

3 staid] chor

The reference in ll. 3–4 to the story of Abelard, who was
attacked and castrated as punishment for his sexual
relationship with the nun Heloise, indicates the nature of the
mutilation MacLean initially believed to render any physical
union between himself and the Scottish Eimhir impossible.
See also 'Dàin do Eimhir' XLVI and XLVII.

34.
Soraidh le NicUalraig-Fhriseal

Source: Abdn Univ ms 2864/1, where it is numbered V under 'Eisgeachd is mì-mhodh'. A further copy is in NLS ms 29557 f31, where it is again numbered V, while a copy on f33 is numbered VIII and marked 'omit'. A copy transcribed by George Campbell Hay is in Edinb NLS ms 26722 51r (indication from Dr Michel Byrne). MacLean's English version reproduced from NLS ms 29557 f72v.

Published in Whyte 2002: 160.

35.
Aig muir-tràigh

Source: Edinb NLS ms 29567 f34, typed

The reference in l. 2 is to John 6: 63: 'Is e an Spiorad a bheothaicheas; chan eil tairbhe air bith anns an fheòil...' ('It is the Spirit that quickeneth; there is no substance in the flesh...') For the following line, see note to 10: 21.

36.
' 'S tusa, Shomhairle, 'chùis-bhùrta'

Source: Edinb NLS ms 14966 f2

This final stanza, present in the ms version, was omitted (possibly because of strong language in line 3) when the first ten lines of 'Mhag mo reusan' were published in *An Gàidheal* 41 (1945–46): 74.

37.
'Tè lem bu mhiann an gille-mirein'

Source: Edinb NLS ms 14966 ff28–29

added variant, subsequently cancelled:
    1 bu mhiann] b' fheàrr

rejected variants:
    2 agus airgead spothte slìom] 's na bh' aige dh'airgead
    3 's thug an car às mo choibhneas] 'na na thug mise dhi de chaoibhneas' for 'às' ms has 'air'
    4 a dhìth] air dhìth

 9 briag na h-òinsich] a' bhriag gòrach
11 saighdearan] an armailt aig
12 san] le
13 shuarach] an uamhais
14 bha san spàirn] gun chiont

A cancelled version of line 8 runs 'breòite leis a' ghiamh'.
Line 7 originally read 'nuair a shaoil mi gu robh colann'. Ian
MacDonald proposes emending l. 10 to 'mum dheidhinn fhìn'.

38.
Ruisia. As t-fhoghar 1941

Source: Edinb NLS ms 29567 ff77–78, fountain pen. Only
two Gaelic stanzas of this item survive, written on a page
which bears the number 5 (f78). Pages 2 to 4 are missing.
Page 1 (f77) contains several prose paragraphs in English,
presumably a version of the opening stanzas from the Gaelic
original, now lost:

> There surely is restlessness tonight in the congregation
> of the corpses and all the million wounds and sores
> quiver with the greatness of their grief, the sickness of
> the poor dead whose lot was black labour.
>   It is not the blast of the high trumpet nor the
> lamentation of the crucified that is in the cry, but the
> shrill sore shriek, which has surpassed knowledge of evil,
> the fulfilment of all bitterness, if the Red Army is to
> [be] utterly broken.
>   A thousand years losing their esteem, the blossom of
> a generation dying and the growth of the hundreds of ages
> withering to a bare wilderness, the colour of death on
> every hope, if the head of their devotion is to be laid
> low.

The reference to the plight of the Red Army encourages a
dating between 22nd June 1941, when Hitler's troops crossed
into Soviet-held territory, and the Battle of Stalingrad
(November 1942 to February 1943), which marked the
turning of the tide in the Nazi invasion of Russia. The Gaelic
version of the title is supplied by the editor.

39.
'Tha 'ghort air cùl na fàire'

Source: Edinb NLS ms 29567 f55, with the following earlier variants:

2 aghaidh] cùl
3 liath] ghlas a'] gar
6 a'] gar a'] gar
11 mhaodal] bhrù leis an] air
18 càis] dàin

40.
Am Putan Airgid

Source: Edinb NLS ms 29567 ff56r & v (Gaelic), 57 r & v (English)

One of very few unpublished poems for which we have a full English version from the poet's own hand. The records indicate that MacLean's praise of the last MacLeod proprietor of Raasay is mistaken, given that evictions took place before his departure. Thematically the poem is closely linked to 'An Cuilithionn', though this need not necessarily indicate that it was composed at the same time.

41.
Stàilin

Source: Edinb NLS ms 29567 f74r & v, written in pencil on headed notepaper from the English Literature Department in the University of Edinburgh, where MacLean was Writer in Residence from 1973 to 1975. Pencil draft on f75 r & v.

42.
'Tha na beanntan gun bhruidhinn'

Source: Edinb NLS ms 29567, quatrains written on pages from a small format loose-leaf notebook, ff58–62. The readings 'ma' (l. 12), 'ghlug' (l. 22) and 'Chuil-fhodair' (l. 33) are conjectural. Originally 'tàrr' (l. 19) was 'tig', and an alternative version of the final line reads ' 's coma leinne a tuar.' On Ian MacDonald's recognition l. 42 'urchair' has been emended to 'iuchair'.

43.
'Thairg mi mo ghaol 's mo dhàin dhut'

Source: Edinb NLS ms 29567, f51v, the back of one sheet of a two-page draft of 'Còig Bliadhna Fichead o Richmond', bearing the title 'Ceann-rathaid gu Richmond, 1965'. This would suggest a dating to the mid–1960s. A draft which would appear to be at a very early stage. In l. 11 ms has 'eachdraidh' for 'eachraidh', which is emended at Ian MacDonald's suggestion. He offers this conjectural reading of a further ten lines in the ms (where [...] indicates an undecipherable word):

> is [...] iad anns a' bhristeadh/bhreisleach
> a' teicheadh ron bhalla-dìon
> 's gan [...] dheth air an tèile.
> Chuir gach fear aghaidh ris a' bhàs
> 's a chùl ri solas grèine,
> stad gach fear bu trèine.
> Mar bu trèine, 's ann bu luaithe   20
> a' teicheadh anns an ruaig
> a' teicheadh on tèarainteachd
> chan e gealtairean a [...]

44.
'Thug an t-àrdan ort fuireach'

Source: Edinb NLS ms 29567 f76.

The original title 'An Fhìrinn Leòmach' has been cancelled. An earlier version of the second stanza reads as follows:

> Smaoinich e air Ratharsair
> 's air a' Bhràighe Shìos is Shuas,
> agus thàinig seòrs' bristidh
> air a mhisneachd 's air uaill.

Giving the sense of 'heroism' to 'cruadal', one could interpret ll. 7–8 as 'and the heroism suffered a kind of weakening'. This would align the sense of the second stanza with the earlier version given above.

45.
Thig is faic

Source: Abdn Univ ms 2864/1, typescript.

Variants from ms in 2864:
  4 Agus] Eadhon
  5 iad] e
  8 is] 's
  9 iad] e
  12 iad] e
  14 Iutharna] Iutharn

The number XVIII presumably refers to a planned insertion in the 'Dàin eile' of MacLean's 1943 volume.

Endnotes

1. Nos. 1, 2, 5, 6, 9, 11, 17, 24, 26, 29, 34 and 45.
2. No. 22.
3. Nos. 5, 9, 11, 24, 29, 34.
4. See nos. 19, 20, 25, 27, 28, 30, 33, 36 and 37. 28 'Mo chasan brist' aig Alamein' was obviously written subsequent to MacLean's injury there. 16 'Chì mi na coin a' tighinn' does not belong among the 'bitter' poems, and may best be considered a preparation for, or offshoot of, 'Dàin do Eimhir' XXIX.
5. See nos. 7, 12, 15a & 15b.
6. For example, no. 43 was very likely written as late as the mid 1960s.
7. For whose final stanza see no. 36.
8. See nos. 3, 13, and 18.
9. Nos. 14 and 23.
10. See nos. 44 and 38.
11. See nos. 10, 21 and 41.

BIBLIOGRAPHY

Unpublished sources

National Library of Scotland

ms 14966 Mss and typescripts of unpublished poetry. Comprising pages excised from a largely unpublished notebook of poetry etc. [Sorley MacLean] 1943–1996
ms 29501 Letters to Sorley MacLean
ms 29540 Letters of Douglas Young to Sorley MacLean 1940–1968
ms 29557 Mss and typescript carbon copies of poems published as *Dàin do Eimhir agus Dàin eile* etc. 1932–1996
ms 29558 Typescripts and typescript carbon copies of 'An Cuilithionn' with annotations and corrections by MacLean and Douglas Young 1939
ms 29559 Mss, typescripts and typescript carbon copies of MacLean's translation of 'An Cuilithionn'; including incomplete typescript with annotations by Robin Lorimer etc. 1939
ms 29560 Mss, typescripts and typescript carbon copies of 'An Cuilithionn' and translations
ms 29561 Typescript of Douglas Young's 'projection' of 'An Cuilithionn' 1943
ms 29567 Mss and typescripts of unpublished poetry [Sorley MacLean] 1943–1996

accession 6419 box 38b Letters from Sorley MacLean to Douglas Young

Aberdeen University Library

ms 2864 & 2864/1 Mss and typescript copies of poems by MacLean, including full ms copy of 'An Cuilithionn', deposited by Douglas Young on June 11th 1941

Edinburgh University Library

Dymock, Emma *The Quest for Identity in Sorley MacLean's 'An Cuilithionn': journeying into politics and beyond* (Ph.D. thesis, 2008) x, 300 pp

Krause, Corinna *Eadar Dà Chànan: Self-Translation, the Bilingual Edition and Modern Gaelic Poetry* (Ph.D. thesis, 2008) vii, 317 pp

St Andrews University Library

ms38372 bound copy of Gaelic text with facing English translation by MacLean of 'An Cuilithionn' in typescript, dating from 1940 and deposited by Douglas Young

Published sources

Black, Ronald 1986 *Mac Mhaighstir Alasdair: the Ardnamurchan Years* (Isle of Coll)

Bewsher, F. W. 1921 *The History of the 51st (Highland) Division 1914–1918* (Edinburgh and London, Blackwood)

Bold, Alan 1988 *MacDiarmid: Christopher Murray Grieve, a critical biography* (London, John Murray)

Brown, Hamish ed. 2005 *Seton Gordon's Scotland: an anthology* (Dunbeath, Whittles)

Brown, Thomas 1893 *Annals of the Disruption with extracts from the narratives of ministers who left the Scottish Establishment in 1843* new edition (Edinbugh, Niven & Wallace)

Cameron, Hector 1932 *The Tiree Bards* (Stirling, Eneas Mackay for the Tiree Association)

Cameron, J. 1912 *The Old and the New Highlands and Hebrides: from the Days of the Great Clearances to the Pentland Act of 1912* (Kirkcaldy, James Cameron)

Campsie, Alistair Keith 1980 *The MacCrimmon Legend: the madness of Angus MacKay* (Edinburgh, Canongate)

Carpenter, Humphrey 1988 *A Serious Character: the Life of Ezra Pound* (London & Boston, Faber & Faber)

Cheape, Hugh 2009 'Traditional Origins of the Piping

Dynasties' in Joshua Dickson ed. *The Highland Bagpipe: Music, History, Tradition* (Farnham, Ashgate Publishing: 97–126

Dwelly, Edward 1988 *The Illustrated Gaelic-English Dictionary* (Glasgow, Gairm) (first published 1901–1911)

Eagle, Raymond 1991 *Seton Gordon: the Life and Times of a Highland Gentleman* (Moffat, Lochar)

Forbes, Alexander Robert 1923 *Place-Names of Skye and adjacent islands* (Paisley, Alexander Gardner)

Gill, Roma ed. 1989 *Christopher Marlowe: Dr Faustus* (London, A. & C. Black)

Groom, Francis 1894 *Ordnance Gazetteer of Scotland* (London, William Mackenzie) (new edition)

B. H. Humble 1986 *The Cuillin of Skye* foreword by W. H. Murray (Glasgow, Ernest Press, facsimile of 1952 first edition)

Hunter, James 2000 *The Making of the Crofter Community* (Edinburgh, John Donald)

Kenefick, William & McIvor, Arthur eds 1996 *The Roots of Red Clydeside* (Edinburgh, John Donald)

Likhachev, Dmitry S. 2000 *Reflections on the Russian Soul: a Memoir* translated by Bernard Adams, translation edited by A. R. Tulloch (Central European University Press, Budapest)

MacDiarmid, Hugh 1978 *Complete Poems 1920–1976* 2 vols ed. Michael Grieve and W. R. Aitken (London, Martin Brian & O'Keeffe)

MacDiarmid, Hugh 1987 *A Drunk Man Looks at the Thistle* an annotated edition by Kenneth Buthlay (Edinburgh, Scottish Academic Press)

Macdonald, A. & Macdonald, A. 1924 *The Poems of Alexander MacDonald (Mac Mhaighstir Alasdair)* ed. with translations, glossary and notes (Inverness, Northern Counties)

MacFarlane, Malcolm 1925 'Half a century of Gaelic vocal music' *Transactions of the Gaelic Society of Inverness* XXXII 1924–25: 251–272

MacGill-Eain, Somhairle see MacLean, Sorley

Mackay, Peter 2010 *Sorley MacLean* (Aberdeen, AHRC Centre for Irish and Scottish Culture)

Mackenzie, Alexander 1881 *History of the Macdonalds and Lords of the Isles* (Inverness, A. & W. MacKenzie)

Mackenzie, Annie M. 1964 *Òrain Iain Luim: Songs of John MacDonald, Bard of Keppoch* (Edinburgh, Scottish Academic Press)

Mackenzie, John 1907 *The Beauties of Gaelic Poetry and Lives of the Highland Bards* (Edinburgh, John Grant) (first edition 1841)

MacKillop, James 1998 *Oxford Dictionary of Celtic Mythology* (Oxford, Oxford University Press)

MacLean, Iain 1983 *The Legend of Red Clydeside* (Edinburgh, John Donald)

MacLean, Sorley and Garioch, Robert 1940 *17 Poems for 6d* (Edinburgh, Chalmers Press)

MacLean, Sorley [as MacGill Eathain, Somhairle] 1943 *Dàin do Eimhir agus Dàin eile* (Glasgow, William MacLellan)

MacLean, Sorley 1970 'Crìoch dàin fhada a stadadh gu h-obann anns an Dùbhlachd 1939' *Gairm* 72 (am foghar): 319–321

MacLean, Sorley, George Campbell Hay, William Neill & Stuart MacGregor 1970 *Four Points of a Saltire* (Edinburgh, Reprographia)

MacLean, Sorley 1976 'Some Raasay Traditions', *Transactions of the Gaelic Society of Inverness*, XLIX (1974–76): 377–97

MacLean, Sorley 1977 *Spring tide and Neap tide: Selected Poems/Reothairt is Conntraigh: Taghadh de Dhàin 1932–72* (Edinburgh, Canongate)

MacLean, Sorley 1985 *Ris a' Bhruthaich: the Criticism and Prose Writings of Sorley MacLean* ed. William Gillies (Stornoway, Acair)

MacLean, Sorley 1999 *O Choille gu Bearradh/From Wood to Ridge* Collected Poems in Gaelic and in English translation (Manchester & Edinburgh, Carcanet & Birlinn)

MacLean, Sorley 2002 *Dàin do Eimhir* edited by Christopher Whyte (Glasgow, Association for Scottish Literary Studies)

MacLeod, Frederick T. *The MacCrimmons of Skye* (Edinburgh, Henderson & Hamilton)

MacLeod, Neil 1902 *Clarsach an Doire: Gaelic poems, songs, and tales* third edition – revised and enlarged (Edinburgh, Norman MacLeod)

MacLeod, Norma 2002 *Raasay: the island and its people* (Edinburgh, Birlinn)

MacPhail, I. M. M. 1989 *The Crofters' War* (Stornoway, Acair)

Matheson, William ed. 1938 *The Songs of John MacCodrum, bard to Sir James Macdonald of Sleat* (Edinburgh, Oliver & Boyd for the Scottish Gaelic Texts Society)

Matheson, William ed. 1970 *The Blind Harper: the Songs of Roderick Morison and his Music* (Edinburgh, Scottish Gaelic Texts Society)

Meek, Donald E. 1995 *Tuath is Tighearna (Tenants and Landlords): Gaelic poetry of social and political protest from the Clearances to the Land Agitation* (Edinbugh, Scottish Academic Press)

Meek, Donald E. 1998 *Màiri Mhòr nan Òran: Taghadh de a h-òrain le eachdraidh a beatha is notaichean* (Edinburgh, Scottish Academic Press)

Nicolson, Alexander 1930 *History of Skye: a Record of the Families, the Social Conditions, and the Literature of the Island* Glasgow, Alex. MacLaren & Sons)

Nicolson, Angus 1979 'An Interview with Sorley MacLean' *Studies in Scottish Literature* XIV: 23–36

Orr, Willie 1982 *Deer Forests, Landlords and Crofters* (Edinburgh, John Donald)

Pyman, Avril 1980 *The Life of Aleksandr Blok* Vol.II The Release of Harmony 1908–1921 (Oxford, Oxford University Press)

Reed, Laurance [198?] *The Soay of our Forefathers* (no publisher, no date: consulted in Glasgow University Library, shelfmark History DX906.S6 REE)

Reiman, Donald H. & Freistat Neil *The Complete Poetry of Percy Bysshe Shelley* (Baltimore & London, John Hopkins University Press)

Riach, Alan [2010] *What is Scottish Literature?* (Glasgow, Association for Scottish Literary Studies)

Richards, Eric 2008 *The Highland Clearances: People, Landlords and Rural Turmoil* (Edinburgh, Birlinn)

Robinson, Mairi ed. 1985 *The Concise Scots Dictionary* (Aberdeen, Aberdeen University Press)

Ross, Raymond & Hendry, Joy eds 1986 *Sorley MacLean: Critical Essays* (Edinburgh, Scottish Academic Press)

Sharpe, Richard 1977 *Raasay: a study in island history* (London, Grant & Cutler)

Sillar, F. C. & Meyler, Ruth 1973 *Skye* (Newton Abbott, David & Charles)

Sinclair, Archibald 1879 *The Gaelic Songster/An t-Òranaiche* (Glasgow, Archibald Sinclair)

Smith, G. S. 2000 *D. S. Mirsky: a Russian-English life* (Oxford, Oxford University Press)

Smith, Sydney Goodsir 1975 *Collected Poems 1941–1975* (London, John Calder)

Stier, Hans-Erich et al. ed. 1973 *Völker, Staaten und Kulturen: ein Kartenwerk zur Geschichte* Erweiterte Ausgabe (Braunschweig, Georg Westermann)

Thomson, Derick 1974 *An Introduction to Gaelic Poetry* (London, Gollancz)

Thomson, Derick ed. 1983 *The Companion to Gaelic Scotland* (Oxford, Basil Blackwell)

Thomson, Derick ed. 1996 *Alasdair Mac Mhaighstir Alasdair: Selected Poems* (Edinburgh, Scottish Gaelic Texts Society)

Watson, Frederick 1925 *The Story of the Highland Regiments (1725–1925)* (London, A. & C. Black)

Watson, J. Carmichael ed. 1965 *Gaelic Songs of Mary MacLeod* (Edinburgh, Scottish Gaelic Texts Society)

Whyte, Christopher 2005 'MacLean and Modernism: "Remembered Harmonies"'' in John M. Kirk & Dónall P. Ó. Baoill eds *Legislation, Literature and Sociolinguistics: Northern Ireland, the Republic of Ireland, and Scotland (Belfast Studies in Language, Culture and Politics 13)* (Belfast, Cló Ollscoil na Banríona) pp. 86–102

Whyte, Christopher 2006 'Sorley MacLean's *Dàin do Eimhir*: New Light from the Aberdeen Holdings' in Michel Byrne, Thomas Owen Clancy & Sheila Kidd eds *Litreachas & Eachdraidh: Rannsachadh na Gàidhlig 2 Glaschu 2002/ Literature & History: Papers from the Second Conference of Scottish Gaelic Studies Glasgow 2002* (Glaschu/Glasgow, Roinn na Ceiltis) pp. 183–199

Wilson, Susan ed. 2010 *The Correspondence between Hugh MacDiarmid and Sorley MacLean* (Edinburgh University Press)

INDEX

Note: This index covers the 'Introduction' (pp. 1–28), the 'Commentary' (pp. 120–216) and the first part of the 'Notes on the unpublished, incomplete and fragmentary poems' (pp. 290–292). A 'Glossary of placenames, persons, historical events and abstract concepts mentioned in "An Cuilithionn"' can be found on pp. 228–239. No such glossary is provided for the unpublished poems. In what follows, SM refers to Sorley MacLean, except for his own main entry where he is MacLean, Sorley.